Morning

Morning

Gene Amole

DENVER PUBLISHING COMPANY   1983

International Standard Book Number: 0-914807-00-5
Library of Congress Catalog Card Number: 83-72934
Copyright © 1983 by Gene Amole.
All rights reserved.
Printed in the United States of America.

Cover photograph by Frank Murray
Cover design by Melanie Moyer
Book design by Brad Thompson
Second Printing November 1983

To Trish

Contents

3. Lifestyle, life-style

4. Derelict dialect: Inner dialogue

5. Paternity suits: Family matters

6. Who gives a beep?: New technology

7. Good memories: Personalities

8. Super Bowl soup & other recipes

9. Yule spiel: Holidays

Foreword

For the past six years Gene Amole has been captivating readers of Denver's Rocky Mountain News three times a week with his column.

The column has been a success since he kicked it off on Dec. 18, 1977. The subject matter of his essays is as diverse as the interests of the man himself.

The variety is one of the charms of Amole's column, partly because his readers never have the faintest idea of what he's going to write about next — a condition, by the way, that also frequently afflicts the writer himself — but one that he never fails to correct in time for his edition deadline.

One thing that makes a writer great is an ability to make readers see, hear and feel — not only the world about them but life and emotion as well. It is a comparatively rare ability. Those who have it have learned the basic secret of good communication, simplicity.

Gene Amole is that kind of writer. He communicates. He sends a message to the reader that the reader understands. Amole talks his language. He doesn't clutter up the thoughts he wants to communicate with fuzzy syntax and weirdly complex sentence structure. The voice is active. The verbs are strong. The sentences are short and simple. The message is eloquent.

Gene, like a poet, also understands that language is like music. It has a beauty of sound and rhythm that, properly used, enhances communication.

But beyond his ability to communicate, there are many other facets to Amole. He knows Denver and Colorado better than most. He was born here, and grew up here. He has watched Denver soar to greatness. He loves the city and the country but most of all the people. And he understands them.

That understanding has been broadened in a Denver radio career that has spanned some 42 years, plus military service with Gen. George Patton in World War II, and a couple of stints as a foreign correspondent.

As we began preparing this collection of some of Amole's columns we were impressed with the timelessness of many. They are as readable today as the first morning they were published, which says a lot for their quality. Winston Churchill said that newspapermen "write in water," but Amole proves that's not always true.

The range of his work is extraordinary. Some, like the columns that begin, "Morning," and "Leaves," approach poetry in their beauty, as do some of his phrases, such as "Happiness is in bits and pieces . . ." or "The sunrises ease the pain of life's darker moments . . ."

Amole presents us with a bit of everything — from humor (Gene doesn't take himself very seriously) to nostalgia to history to sadness to politics to cooking (he's a great chef) to puncturing the phony.

The Rocky Mountain News is proud to have Gene Amole appear regularly in our pages and equally pleased to be able to present this splendid collection for your enduring enjoyment.

RALPH LOONEY
EDITOR, ROCKY MOUNTAIN NEWS

Preface

FREEDOM.

When I first met Michael Balfe Howard he was editor of the Rocky Mountain News. I had known him only casually when he called late one afternoon in the autumn of 1977 and asked me to write a column. The offer was a complete surprise. Since I was involved full-time in the operation KVOD, a radio station I owned with Ed Koepke, and was still doing occasional television programs on a free-lance basis, I couldn't see how I would have the time.

But Michael persisted. We discussed it further at lunch a couple of days later. Michael is very persuasive, and I suspect he instinctively knew I really wanted to take a shot at it. I agreed to try it for six months. "You'll do it for a year," he said.

Michael assured me I would be free to write on any subject I wished, and my copy would not be changed, except for corrections in style. It was his view that to be credible, a columnist must have that freedom, even though his or her views may be sharply different from the official editorial policy of the newspaper, as mine sometimes are.

I had that freedom then, as I have now. In recent years, though, I have come to think of it not so much as a freedom as I do a responsibility. It is a burden I must enjoy carrying, otherwise I wouldn't still be hacking away at it every day.

A newspaper column is like a nymphomaniac. Every man wants one until he gets one. Before long, desire gives way to demand, and then it's simply a matter of living by performance alone. The late New York Times sports columnist Walter "Red" Smith put it better when he said: "Writing a newspaper column is easy. All you do is roll a sheet of blank paper into a typewriter, and then you stare at it until small drops of blood form on your forehead."

I had no illusions about the demands of the trade. I had written nightly television commentary for five or six years and knew all about blank sheets of paper and drops of blood. Even so, the idea of writing for the newspaper appealed to me because I naively believed ideas expressed in print are more enduring.

I know now that there is no such thing as immortality in this business. Think of it as a three-times-a-week opportunity to display one's ignorance.

None of the columns in this book was written at leisure. They are not thoughtful little essays. All were produced under the pressure of a deadline. Even the first column was written that way. The title of this book comes from the first word in that column.

Michael is no longer the editor of the News. He remains a good and trusted friend. Ralph Looney is the editor now. It has been under his quiet and steady leadership that the Rocky Mountain News has become the dominant newspaper in the Rocky Mountain West. He was kind enough to write the foreword to this volume. He has been wonderfully supportive during the years I have worked for him.

I suppose these reprinted columns are little bits and pieces of me. They are what I thought about things at the time I wrote them. In some cases I may have since changed my opinions, but the columns remain much as they were first published. In most cases, I have not used columns written about the daily flow of hard news.

My most controversial column is included on page 112. It was my idea of what would happen if Jesus returned to Earth and came to Denver. Many thought the satirical approach was blasphemous. Others wrote to me and expressed the view that the column was a profound commentary on materialism in today's secular world.

The column introducing the Idea Fairy is on page 110. So are all the recipes. I must confess that I get more mail about my meat-and-potatoes recipes than anything else I write.

While I wrote all the columns, I certainly didn't put together the book by myself. Without the help of three people, there would have been no book. They are Brad Thompson, Diane Martinez and Carol Samson.

Brad was special projects editor at the News when he approached me with the idea of a book of my columns. He has been in overall charge of editing and production. Brad also assisted in selecting the columns we would use. The final editing was done by Zoe Lappin and the nice people on the News copy desk.

Carol, an excellent short-story writer, teacher and Ph.D. candidate at the University of Denver, also participated in the selection process. She arranged the columns into thematic chapter categories. Carol has been encouraging me to assemble this book for a number of years.

I am grateful to Diane for the many long hours and days she devoted to the project. She is an editorial clerk in the newsroom. From the News library, she duplicated every column I had ever written. Once the final selection of columns was made, she typed them into the computer system from which the type was set. I have the satisfaction of knowing that if no one else ever looks at this book, Diane has read every word.

In closing, I want to express the real affection I have for this newspaper. Everyone must be somewhere, and I know I must be here. The newsroom is my natural environment. Newspaper people are among the most stimulating, the funniest and the most entertaining I know. They are my good companions and cherished friends.

I have dedicated this book to my wife, Trish. Her understanding surpasses all logic. My mother, my children and my pets have helped. They have not only supplied much of the material for what is between these covers, but they have given me something more important — their love.

1

AUTUMN PLEASURES: HUMAN CONDITION

First column

MORNING.

It is the innocent time of day. The air is clean. A small black dog frisks through a familiar backyard routine. The light is bright from the window of an East Colfax all-night coffee shop. Great flights of Canada geese rise swiftly from suburban reservoirs.

Downtown, the first trash and delivery trucks clank through half-empty streets. Street lights and neon signs go out as the new day's light begins to fill the sky.

There is the aroma of fresh coffee. It makes its secret way out of the kitchen and up the stairs. Soapy water swirls into the drain, and the clean, white terry cloth towel brings life to a body not quite ready for the day.

There is cartoon music on the television and Mozart on the radio. There is lunch money on the kitchen table and a limp mound of pajamas on the bedroom floor.

The first sunlight touches the top of the buildings downtown and then shimmers down the panels of glass and steel. In the sky, there are layers of night clouds that turn copper, then fuchsia, and then a pale gold. And all at once, the northern sky is filled with grays and blues.

The traffic is just a whisper at first. And then a growl. Finally, a snarl. The freeways seem to coil and uncoil like a mindless serpent.

And then, morning is over. The day has lost its innocence and we are at work.

I love the morning. It is my reason to be. I would like it to last all day. Morning tingles. It is exciting. I even like those empty, old cottonwood branches against the Western sky, I like to hear dishes clatter and cats scratch at the door.

I want to watch little girls comb snarled hair. It feels so good to stretch in the morning. Waitresses are scrubbed clean and are starched. People on elevators smile and there are little sniffs of cologne in the air.

I was born in Denver and since I can remember, the Rocky Mountain News has been a part of my morning. I have as much affection for the News as I do for all the sights, sounds and smells of each new day. Honestly, I am so pleased to be here. To be a writer for the News has been my longtime, not-so-secret ambition.

Even though I have been in broadcasting for a long time, I have always had great respect for the written word. It has an enduring quality lacking in electronic communication.

I hope what you read here will add some texture to your morning. I'll be rattling some cages. You might as well know I am an implacable foe of malignant bureaucracy. The proliferation of governmental subdivisions in metropolitan Denver is an insanity. Duplication, waste and artificial boundaries are killing us. The pollution of our air is obscene.

By integrating only one of 14 metropolitan Denver school districts, the United States Supreme Court has done violence to public education here. Rather than integrating our schools, the high court has resegregated them.

I shall want to deal with the human condition in some of these columns. Perhaps we can laugh at ourselves on this page. Sometimes I suppose we'll cry. There's nothing wrong with that. It's OK to cry. Take it from me. I have been known to cry at supermarket grand openings and eighth-grade continuation ceremonies.

Expect also to read here about this city's cultural awareness. The Denver Symphony Orchestra and its management remain deeply divided. I am worried about who is going to pay for the Denver Center for the Performing Arts. I suspect it will be the taxpayers.

I am interested in city planning. Architectural integrity long has been neglected in Denver. When an ugly building goes up, someone ought to say it's ugly.

I'll try to make the writing as spare and understandable as I can. That way, if you read the first couple of paragraphs and don't like the column, you can turn the page to Charlie Brown, Broncomania or whatever is more to your liking.

Thank you for making me a part of your morning. I'll try to deserve your time.

December 18, 1977

O pain, O boredom

COPING.

As I grow older, I find myself coping less successfully with such annoyances as arthritis, shortness of breath and hearing loss.

Memory sometimes can be a problem. My choice as the worst of all vexations, however, is attending meetings. I just can't manage them anymore. Attendance at a meeting has become as impossible for me as the 75 push-ups I used to be able to do.

There is no way I can sit there and listen to even one more report. It is bad enough to endure the meeting you are in, but it is cruel and unusual punishment to make you sit there and listen to the minutes of the last meeting. Agony layered upon agony.

Meetings are physically harmful. My left leg begins to twitch uncontrollably the very minute the chair/man/woman/person taps his/her/its teaspoon against a half-filled water glass at the head of the table and calls for order.

The purpose of the meeting used to be to develop some kind of program. That is no longer true. Experience has taught us that nothing ever happens to programs that are developed in meetings.

A change had to be made, so we modified the language. Instead of developing a "program," the well-run meeting of today formulates what is now called an "action program."

As with the program, nothing ever comes of the action program, either. But by calling it an action program, participants have the feeling that something is actually being accomplished. The word "action" connotes movement of some kind.

Maintaining concentration is a major problem. The minute someone stands up and says, "I think it is important for us to establish meaningful guidelines," the mind begins to slip away.

My thoughts sometimes wander to fresh baked apple pie. I can just see the brown, syrupy Jonathan apple juice bubble up through the slits on the top crust. I silently wonder if there is any Swiss cheese in the refrigerator.

Another kind of reaction is triggered when the speaker says,

"There is general agreement that our approach should be goal-oriented."

I want to jump up and scream, "They won the toss. We'll defend the north goal so the sun will be in their eyes. Now let's get in there and win this one for the Gipper!"

I have tried several methods of concentrating on what is happening at meetings. The self-inflicted wound sometimes works. Take the sharpest of your car keys and auger it into the palm of your hand. Mind not to get blood on your trousers or shirt.

Try disrobing all those in attendance. Mentally, of course. There is probably some Freudian implication here. No matter. Whatever works.

Passive resistance may be the best long-term defense against the meeting. Arrive early and select a seat in a shadowy corner. Try to find a location where your chair is against a wall.

After the meeting begins, wedge your elbow between the wall and your thigh. Rest your chin in your cupped hand. That way, your head won't bob when you fall asleep, and you will appear to be listening thoughtfully. Wear spectacles with tinted lenses so that your closed eyes will remain undetected.

Try to keep the head tilted forward to avoid snoring. There is nothing so disruptive as someone who snorts, wheezes and rattles during a report from the nominations committee.

When my life finally ebbs away, and I am dispatched below, I know what to expect. There will be no fire and brimstone. No cauldrons of boiling oil. The infernal powers of evil and darkness will be visited upon me by someone who uses words like "ergo" and who ignores my motion to adjourn.

That's hell.

September 28, 1980

Touch of spring

AWARENESS.

Too early to think of spring? There are all those little spots of dirty snow in the shady places. The ground isn't exactly brown. The color is more of a tan.

It's still winter, all right. The frost line is so deep this year. It will be awhile before we see the grape locusts, crocuses and first tulips.

Spring has a great advantage over the other seasons. People enjoy it three ways. There's the pleasant yearning for it. We are feeling that now. When it finally comes we enjoy every warm breeze of it. And after it has gone, how nice it is to recall spring's loveliness.

Trees without leaves have a special beauty. The branches are like random lace patterns against the sky. That's the way they look at a distance.

Look closer, feel the slender endings of twigs. They are becoming limber. Carefully touch the tiny bumps that are spaced along each one. Give this simple act total concentration.

It is important that the hand is soft against the surface. That's the best way to touch springtime. The changes now are so subtle. The senses are rewarded. Life's warmth passes from one being to another.

It is sad that some will never have this communion. It takes a little extra time. It means letting go of stress and anxiety for a moment. It can be difficult to put worry and apprehension aside.

That's the way it is, though. There doesn't seem to be time enough to look up at the sunrise. Does it matter to the sunrise? Probably not. It will just go on and be stunningly beautiful anyhow.

It is so nice to carry a sunrise through the day. It is a sort of guarantee that some good will come out of it all. It doesn't matter what else happens. The memory is filled with the colors of copper, bronze, pale blue, zinc and gold.

We have somehow come to believe that we are all entitled to a great happiness along the way. Where did we get this notion that there is a remarkable climax in life? It can be painful to gradually realize that there is no single ecstasy out there in the tomorrow of things.

One of life's early lessons ought to be that there is a happiness for everyone. It is important to believe that. But there should be more attention given on how to find it.

It isn't a matter of waiting for it to happen. The secret is recognizing it when it comes along. Happiness is in bits and pieces. That's true, isn't it?

Much better that way. The sunrises ease the pain of life's darker moments. There is some coarseness in all of our lives and touching the tip of a twig in late winter is a pleasant contrast.

Our time here is so short. It is so wasteful to spend it waiting for what could be. And a life shouldn't be squandered by regretting what might have been.

Someone once said that there is a whole universe in a single drop of dew. That's true. But it can't be seen or experienced without stopping to take time to examine it.

Looking outward and inward into the infinity of things is one of life's great excitements. Happiness is certainly there. It is also in the face of a child.

Watch a tiny house finch roller-coaster across the sky at dawn. Feel the cool breeze of night just before sleep. Happiness is in the warmth of having someone close. It is even in a single grass blade that has somehow pushed through a crack in the concrete.

Happiness is awareness.

February 19, 1979

Fallen leaves

LEAVES.

We have been up to you-know-where in leaves at our house. I managed to get the front yard pretty well cleaned up before the snow on Sunday.

Anyone who has big trees knows all about justice. He who sits in the shade during the summer has to rake leaves in the fall.

A fairly good case can be made for not raking them. Leaves are supposed to be good fertilizer. Cycle of life.

Those who prefer not to disturb the natural order of things can take comfort in what someone told me a long time ago. He said, "The Lord grew these leaves. Let the Lord pick them up."

There's only one problem with that. Instead of picking up the leaves, the Lord sometimes blows them over into the neighbor's yard. The neighbor gets angry at you, not the Lord.

Poets have always found dead leaves to be attractive symbols. So have composers. Claude Debussy wrote a quiet little piano prelude entitled "Feuilles Mortes."

Fort Collins pianist Wendel Diebel, a Debussy scholar, dug around to find out exactly what he had in mind. About the prelude, Debussy wrote, "From the fall of the golden leaves that invest the splendid obsequies of the trees . . ."

It is easy enough to talk about dead leaves that way if you don't have to rake them. I know. I used to have romantic notions about leaves.

Years ago, I wrote a song lyric. You won't remember it because it was never published. Part of it said, "The swirling leaves of autumn/the moonlight on your face/A moment once remembered/your soft and warm embrace."

Now you can understand why it was never published. I had a tendency to write material of that sort when I was young. I am sure that I am now protected by the statute of limitations.

Leaves aren't so bad when someone else is doing the raking. That view is shared by most kids. I can remember diving into great piles of leaves when I was a little boy and lived on West Maple Avenue. We lived around the corner from the old Webber Theater.

If you have ever been down Maple, between Broadway and Acoma Street, you will remember it for its magnificent maple trees. They must be almost 100 years old.

I have a picture of my father on the street when he was about 10. He is shown sitting on a little donkey. Those maples in the background must have been 10 or 15 years old at the time.

Years later, when I was a boy, Grandpa used to rake the leaves in big piles on that same street. The other kids and I liked to jump into them. Along about dusk, he'd pile up the leaves again and set fire to them.

That was my favorite time. We'd gather around and warm our hands. A thin wisp of smoke would climb up through the cold November air to the naked branches above.

The smoke had a pleasant, pungent odor. When the last embers died down, there would be a soft blue haze over everything. Then we would go inside. Grandma had spareribs and kraut on the table.

It is too bad we can't burn leaves anymore. Pollution. Too many people burning too many leaves. I have been tempted to take just a small bag of maple leaves outside of town and burn them. You know, some quiet little place where I could watch the flames and smell the smoke.

I didn't get around to the cottonwood leaves in the back yard last Sunday. Too many of them. And besides, the Bronco game was about to start. I'll try to get to them next week.

Or next spring.

November 6, 1979

Go fly a kite

SIMPLE PLEASURES.

You could always tell it was March because little boys brought their marble bags to school. It was as though they had all simultaneously received some sort of mysterious, silent signal.

Hopscotch, mumbletypeg, jack stones, string tops and rope skipping were other springtime rituals. That's the way it used to be. Some kids still enjoy these simple pleasures, but their popularity is on the wane.

It's partly the fault of television. It takes so much of their leisure time. And then there is the compulsion some parents have to enlist their young into uniformed regiments of soccer and baseball teams.

Kids aren't left on their own long enough to learn to shoot a marble or memorize all the verses to "Down by the ocean, down by the sea. Johnny broke a bottle and blamed it on me."

There probably were lessons to be learned in playing marbles "for keeps." It may have bordered on gambling, but it was really more a game of skill than of chance.

One kid always seemed to be better at marbles than the rest. He held his shooter between the tip of his forefinger and the knuckle of his thumb. If he could lag well enough to get the first shot, he could usually blast four or five of your marbles out of the bull ring before you ever got your first shot.

Some little girls were particularly gifted at playing jacks. They always had an air of nonchalance about them. They would whip through their twos, threes, fours, fives and even sixes with such annoying ease. This sort of thing is called "hand-eye coordination" now.

There probably are a lot of middle-aged people who still feel these childhood stirrings. It really wouldn't take much to get them down on their knees agan. That is if it weren't for dignity and arthritis.

There is one simple pleasure from childhood that ought to be carried into later life. It's one that leaves dignity fairly well intact and isn't too stressful on a couple of gimpy knees.

Kite flying. There is just no human experience quite like it. It treats the senses in a very special way and it is just as much fun for the Geritol set as it is the little squirts.

Socio-cultural theorist Marshall McLuhan popularized the notion that technology is the extension of man. Television is the extension of the eye. Wheels are an extension of feet. The gun is an extension of the fist and the computer an extension of the mind.

The kite technology is an extension of the human spirit.

The Greeks were the first kite fliers. It is believed that Archytas of the city of Tarentum invented the kite sometime between 400 and 300 B.C.

The exhilaration he must have felt then is easily recaptured today. That there are jet planes, helicopters and space satellites in the same sky now makes no difference.

It must be that the kite flier imagines himself to be the kite. It is sort of like sending oneself up there to look down on the world.

There is great joy to watch the kite catch the right breeze and climb steadily higher as the string whirrs from around the stick. The insistent pull feels good against the hand. The kite seems to be a living thing.

Then there is panic. There is a very real feeling of danger when the wind suddenly stops, or the kite begins to spin rapidly toward a tree.

If the string breaks and the kite falls, the kite flier rushes to see if it somehow survived. There is a deeper concern than just for paper, sticks and string. It is almost as though a life were at stake.

Behaviorists try to tell us how to cope with the complexities of our lives. Maybe they should take a look at kites and the people who fly them.

If there is a trim little kite climbing up above the park, chances are there is a happy person at the other end of the string. A human spirit is soaring.

Go fly a kite.

March 14, 1979

Id's all id your dose

RITE OF SPRING.

The Idea Fairy was looking at the big newsroom clock when I walked up to my desk. She was sitting on the telephone book and winding her tiny wristwatch.

FAIRY — Buster! You look terrible. Your eyes are all puffy and your nose is red. Hay fever?

ME — Djes.

FAIRY — What did you say?

ME — I said "djes." You are absolutely ride. I do hab hay feber. Bmy siduses are all clogged ub. I can hardly breed.

FAIRY — Taking anything?

ME — Tried everythig. Nothig worgs. Id's the polled id the air.

FAIRY — What about the capsule with the tiny time-release pills?

ME — They dry ub by dose, alride, bud . . .

FAIRY — . . . but you feel like you are swimming in molasses. Everything is in slow motion. You can't think straight. Is that it?

ME — Djes.

FAIRY — Do you wheeze, cough, sneeze, rattle, cry and wake up in the night because your tongue is like a board, and the inside of your mouth feels like it is filled with cotton?

ME — Djes. All of dose thigs.

FAIRY — Buster, I hate to tell you this, but maybe the whole thing is in your head.

ME — Dno. Id is also id bmy chesd.

FAIRY — I don't mean that. What I am trying to tell you is that maybe it is more of a psychological problem than a physical one. Everyone knows there is an emotional overlay in some asthma cases. You want to talk about it?

ME — Thad's cradzy.

FAIRY — No it isn't. I've been watching you. You are always stuffing one of those plastic squeeze bottles in your nose. Did you know those things are addictive? It says in the fine print that you shouldn't use them all the time. Besides destroying the lining of your nose, I suspect you are unconsciously seeking some kind of nasal gratification.

ME — Ridigulous.

FAIRY — Don't be so sure. A physician right here in Denver conducted a test on a group of patients suffering a variety of respiratory allergies. Do you want to hear about it?

ME — Do I hab a choice?

FAIRY — Half the patients were given their regular allergy immunization shots. The other half were given a placebo.

ME — Placebo?

FAIRY — Djes. I mean yes. Now you have me doing it. A placebo is an innocuous substance used more for the mental relief of the patient than for its actual effect on the disorder. It is inert. A placebo is used in a controlled experiment to test the efficacy of another substance.

ME — Stob id!

FAIRY — Anyhow, many of the patients who were getting shot with distilled water instead of their medication did just as well as the patients who were getting the real stuff. This would seem to suggest that a lot of people have runny noses because their heads aren't on straight.

ME — Shud ub.

FAIRY — I know you are irritable, Buster, but you really ought to throw away those pills and quit squirting that stuff up your nose. All those things can have dangerous side effects. Think about your liver.

ME — I cand't stob thigig aboud mby dose.

FAIRY — Tell yourself you *don't* have hay fever. Say: "I *can* breathe deeply. My nasal passages are clear. My nose *isn't* red. My lips *aren't* chapped. My ears *aren't* ringing. I am not swallowing a lot of goop. I don't need to cough." Mind over matter.

ME — Leave bme alode.

FAIRY — One more thing.

ME — Djes?

FAIRY — Wipe your nose.

April 12, 1981

Man's best relative

NATURAL SELECTION.

I hadn't meant to get involved in the dispute between the evolutionists and the creationists. My hands have been full with income taxes and spring hay fever. Don't need a bunch of Bible thumpers and scientists coming down on me.

Not much chance they'll ever compromise. Polarization has set in. The scientists won't buy the Adam's rib story. The creationists can't accept the idea that they are related to baboons. It's an image problem.

Doing outside research, I have come up with my own theory of how we got here. It still has some rough edges, and I'm not quite ready to ask the Legislature to pass a law giving it equal teaching time in the schools. Still though, it does have merit. After looking around at other life forms, I have come around to the view that man is descended from the poodle.

Charles Darwin was on the right track with his "Origin of Species," but he made a wrong turn when he selected the ape as man's forebear. It is true that people do bear a physical resemblance to monkeys — some more than others. But from a standpoint of disposition, we have much more in common with the poodle.

They have the same bad habits and fall victim to the same temptations we do. When I look into the face of my poodle, Yastrzemski, I see myself looking back. It's not the ears. It's more in the eyes.

I didn't think I would ever like poodles. I had always believed them to be snippity little things, usually carried about by snippity people.

Yazzie, as we call him, has never been told he is a poodle. We didn't want him stereotyped. You know, let him find his own way. Now, he has turned out to be about as laid back as the rest of us.

Joyce Brothers, NBC's psychologist, had a radio program not long ago about how Americans regard their pets. Turns out that more than 80 percent of those surveyed think of their dogs and cats as family members, not animals.

Brothers also reported that pets have a tendency to take on the physical characteristics of the people who own them. If a person overeats, the dog is probably a fatty. This probably explains why it is sometimes difficult to tell the difference between people and animals at dog shows.

You can imagine how I felt the other day when Yazzie's veterinarian told him he had to lose 10 pounds by October. No more salami. No more Monterey Jack cheese. No more eclairs. No more red wine. No more (sob) hot corned beef sandwiches on pumpernickel with horseradish.

"His liver probably weighs 5 pounds," the doctor said. "Put him on one-half cup of diet dog food twice a day. Not another morsel."

We started the regimen the next morning. Yazzie looked at that pitiful helping of Fit and Trim as though he had been betrayed. He turned to face me, sat up, crossed his paws over his round tummy and began to make noises in his throat that sounded for all the world like: "Don't do this to me, Geno. At my age, the quality of life is more important to me than its length. Let's you and I have a little snack."

I feel so sorry for him. Yazzie whimpers softly when I don't give him the end of my breakfast bacon. When we get back from our walk along Bear Creek, he parks himself under the cupboard where we keep the jar with the sugar cookies. I can hear his stomach growl and rattle at night in his sleep.

In the world of the older dog, there are few things as important as eating. Take that away, and there's not much left except arthritis and cloudy vision. Come to think of it, much the same thing is true with some of the rest of us. I have tried to talk to him about nutrition, wellness and moderation. He just sits up and crosses his paws and makes those pitiful noises.

It's tough.

April 9, 1981

Wiser, you're not

FIFTY-SIX.

Yesterday was my birthday. More accurately, it was the 56th anniversary of my birth. I have had just the one birthday and that was May 24, 1923.

It has become increasingly apparent that not much good comes from getting older. Unless, of course, one is fond of ringing in the ears and not having so much hair to worry about.

Why do we make such a fuss over birthdays? Being born is an involuntary act. It requires no special talent or skill. You are not even asked if you want to be born.

People should be like racehorses and have their birthdays all on the same day. Some Oriental cultures do this and it works out fine. Everybody wishes everyone else a happy birthday and people can get on with the business of getting old.

People are supposed to become wiser as they grow older. Horse feathers. The older you get, the more opinionated and set in your ways you become. Wiser, you're not.

Most of life's decisions are made early in the game. After that, it is more a matter of dealing with mistakes made during youth.

After you pass into the middle years, you decide such things as where you are going to wear your stomach. Do you let the paunch hang out over the belt? Maybe it would look better to pull up your pants over the top, so that the belly is covered.

Or do you stop drinking beer?

Society does seem to tolerate eccentricity more in old people than in young. Might just as well take advantage of it and be a little goofy.

I once knew a lawyer here in Denver who felt that some privilege went with age. His name was Warwick Downing and he was as sharp as a tack until the day he died.

Downing's office was in the Equitable Building. Sometime in the late twilight of his life, he decided he would no longer walk down to the corner when he wanted to cross Stout Street to get a cup of coffee at Keable's Sandwich Shop.

He jaywalked. It didn't matter how heavy the traffic, Downing would hold up his hand and walk straight across the street. It was quite a sight to see that fragile old man, looking neither to the left nor the right, triumphantly crossing Stout Street.

Cars would screech to a stop. People would honk their horns and shake their fists. They would glare at him and shout all kinds of things. It didn't matter to Downing. He crossed the street where and when he wished.

I liked that.

I also enjoyed something Sheldon Peterson once told me. Peterson is a broadcasting executive, and a good one. I used to work for him when he was news director at Channel 7.

He drew me aside one day and said, quite gravely, "After man reaches the age of 40, he is no longer required to open third-class mail."

Isn't that marvelous? That's the sort of information you expect to get on top of a mountain from an old man with a gray beard.

Now that I am 56, I have made a decision like that. I will no longer appear as a speaker or master of ceremonies before any organization whatsoever.

I used to do that sort of thing a great deal. Not any more. I have come to the painful realization that I don't really have anything to say. Actually, I never did.

I knew I had had enough when I began to memorize the songs they sing at Lions clubs. It was time to quit when the potted Swiss steak and cold mashed potatoes began to taste good. No more Kiwanis or Rotary luncheons. Ever.

No more fund-raising roasts. I have run out of jokes about politicians, the RTD, air pollution and Rocky Flats. Years of public speaking have convinced me that Alben Barkley was right when he said, "The best audience is one that is intelligent, well-educated — and a little drunk."

Another quote: *"Geno, you are not getting better. You are getting older."* — Lawrence A. Winograd, M.D.

May 25, 1979

Hurry up and wait

QUEUEPHOBIA.

Psychiatrists ought to give it more of their attention, and quit spending so much of their time on guilt, denial and schizophrenia.

Queuephobia means fear of standing in line. It is as common to the urban condition as hydro onus probandi (mistrust of the Water Board) or Bronco-apotheosis (jock worship).

Dealing with supermarket checkout lines is particularly frustrating. The short line isn't necessarily the fast line. Beware of the little twerp with only a half-dozen items in his buggy.

Chances are he is only holding a place in line for his wife. She is a powerfully built woman and her hair is up in pink plastic rollers.

Not only does she have two completely filled shopping carts in tow, but she also is waving a fistful of discount coupons. The kids are right behind, and they have armloads of soft drink bottles to be redeemed.

By the time you get up to the checker, your ice cream has melted, there are little green spots on the bread and the frozen pizza has gone limp on you.

Same thing with drive-up banking. It's always good advice to avoid lines where there are commercial vehicles. Their business can be complicated and time-consuming.

Watch out for the scroungy kid in the old sports car. He may appear to be the sort who will just whiz through to cash his unemployment check. That's a dangerous assumption.

All too late, you discover there has been a computer error in his bank statement and he is there to get it corrected. He also wants to deposit his lifetime penny collection and make the final payment on his parents' FHA home improvement loan.

Waiting in line for restroom facilities is particularly annoying. It is difficult to make small talk with others in line while regretting that third cup of coffee you had at dinner.

Competition for plumbing facilities is particularly intense at concert intermissions and after long convention meetings. As people crowd into the limited space in the restroom, some unfortunate queuephobes have been known to suffer from acute bashful bladder.

Simply put, bashful bladder is inability to perform while in the company of others. While waiting for nature to take its course, you become aware of the restlessness of those in line behind you. There is much clearing of throats and some angry whispering.

It may help to imagine trickling waterfalls, spring rainstorms and whistling teakettles. That failing, the best thing to do is leave the building immediately and proceed directly to the nearest Conoco service station. Or clump of bushes. Whichever comes first.

Carwash lines are the worst. Beware of the young man with time on his hands, quarters in his pocket and a slightly dusty Datsun.

Most people could wash that little car spotlessly clean with just one quarter. Two at the most. Not this kid. Washing his car is a ritual.

He raises the hood, cleans the engine and then devotes himself to the grill. He's not happy to just wash the outsides of the wheels. He does the insides, too. Under the fenders he goes. He cleans front and rear axles and crawls under the car to squirt the drive shaft.

This is his recreation. Like the long-distance runner, he is trying for euphoria. He smiles to himself as he caresses the hood with gentle strokes of the spray. Finally he leaves. He takes his fantasies with him and drives that immaculate Datsun into another line — a line of traffic.

Quote: *". . . will the line stretch out to the crack of doom?"* — Shakespeare.

March 21, 1979

For love of a pickup

KEEP ON TRUCKIN'.

I have decided to keep my 1965 Ford F-100 Twin-I-Beam pickup truck. Can't bear to part with it, even though there are dents in the fenders, doors and hood. The bumpers are rusted, the radio is shot and there is a rag sticking out of the gas tank where the cap should be.

When I bought it four years ago, there were 93,000 miles on the odometer. I have no idea how many miles she has on her now. The speedometer cable busted a couple of years ago.

I really didn't need the truck. It was just something I always wanted. Now that I have it, I wonder how I got along all those years without it. My neighbor, Dick Stevens, was right when he told me, "Every man ought to have an old pickup truck at least once in his life."

The value of the truck extends beyond its utilitarian worth. Somewhere around the house is an article I once clipped from a 1978 issue of The Washington Post. Author Jack McClintock wrote of his 1953 Ford F-100, "There is no love more innocent and pure than a man's love for his pickup truck."

In my own case, a lot of it has to do with the rich fantasy life I lead. People in the communications game have little to show for their work at the end of a day. Today's newspaper column winds up tomorrow on the floor of a bird cage.

But when I drive my truck, I imagine myself doing honest work. I rattle around in the industrial part of the city and make believe I am delivering a machine tool part for Mac. Mac, as you have already guessed, is the mythical foreman I work for.

I find the truck helps me to be more assertive when I buy something at the lumberyard. People who work in lumberyards intimidate me. When I get some fence posts or plywood, I sense a certain disdain when the man helps me load the stuff into my station wagon.

But when I pull up in the truck, I am treated with more respect. The guy at the loading dock doesn't talk down to me. A sort of camaraderie grows between us.

It is always a good idea to have one of those yellow caps with "CAT" printed on the front. Wear an old checkered shirt. A pair of work gloves stuffed in the hip pocket of the jeans is also a nice touch. Tune the radio to a station that is playing Willie Nelson records and crank 'er up high.

I almost went overboard when I got my pickup. I thought about putting a row of small amber lights across the top of the cab. You see them on trucks all the time. I'll have to admit, though, that I have no idea what the lights are for. I may eventually put a couple of fog lamps on the front bumper. Can't tell when you'll hit a patch of fog out on the job.

I have also considered getting a camper shell. I could doll it up with decals of pheasants, ducks and trout. I'll put my CB radio call letters on the back. Would it be too corny to get some of those paste-on letters at the dime store and print out "My Little Camping Buddy" on the side? If I put a gun rack in the back window and "Strickland for Governor" sticker on the bumper, I'd have what is known as an "American Original."

Actually, I'm not going to do any of those things. I am going to get my truck fixed up, though. My son, Jon, says we can get it "cherried out" for about $1,400. I may have Kenz and Leslie take a look at the motor and see if it's worth souping up a little.

I figger we'll go with a candy apple red. Mebbe get some of them big tires with white letters. Wonder what you have to give for one of them roll bars. Probably slap on a pair of cherry bomb mufflers. We'll slip down to Limon. I dunno about you, but I could sure use some of them good biscuits and gravy at the truck stop down there.

Keep the shiny side up and the greasy side down, good buddy!

May 28, 1981

Fishin' wishin'

2₀3891.

That's the number of my 1980 Colorado resident fishing license. I bought it the other day at Dave Cook's. I had only meant to pick up a canteen for my daugher to take on a camping trip.

I knew when I got it that I couldn't take the time this summer to actually go fishing. The $7.50 fee was well-spent, however, because it will trigger pleasant fantasies. I am also getting a column out of it.

Knowing that there is a fishing license in my billfold permits me to close my eyes and imagine myself in a quiet and secluded mountain valley. The smell of ponderosa is in the air.

If you look at that shady spot at the edge of the stream, you will find a six-pack of beer in the cold water. That shoebox over there is filled with cold fried chicken and bread and butter sandwiches.

Until 1962, the Colorado fishing season extended from the third Saturday in May until Oct. 1. The hours of fishing were from sunrise to sunset. That's all changed. It is now legal to fish 24 hours a day, 365 days a year.

I remember when the law was changed. It prompted poet Thomas Hornsby Ferril to complain that unlimited fishing had taken away half the fun. He wrote that much of the pleasure of fishing came before the season started. There was time to anticipate, and time to oil your reel and repair tackle.

One of the most skilled persons at fishing I ever knew was my Aunt Gladys. She and my Uncle Frank lived in the little mountain town of Telluride.

Aunt Gladys picked up my mother and me one summer in Montrose to drive us up to Telluride. The road runs along Leopard Creek. Just before we started up that long hill that leads to town, Aunt Gladys pulled the car off the road.

She got out, went around to the trunk of the car and took out an old metal fishing rod. She explained matter-of-factly that she was going to catch some fish for dinner that night.

My aunt came back in about 20 minutes with the nicest mess of trout you have ever seen. Even though I was just a little boy at the time, I can recall being impressed with how easily she did it.

No fooling around with complicated gear. No waders. She was wearing an ordinary housedress and apron. Aunt Gladys caught those fish as effortlessly as today's women shop for groceries at the supermarket.

It is at this point that I should make a confession. I am the world's worst fisherman. Put me at the edge of a lake that has just been stocked, and this kid can't even catch cold.

I have tried fly-fishing, spin-fishing and trolling. Nothing. Not a nibble. I don't even catch the little ones the other guys throw back.

If I bring along worms, the fish are hitting black gnats. Let old Geno come to the pond with salmon eggs, the fish develop a sudden hunger for cheese balls.

OK, so my technique isn't the greatest. That's an understatement. It is terrible. I can drop a line into a bathtub and somehow get it snagged.

I fall in the water. My knots come untied. I lose hooks. The leader snarls. My reel gets fouled. Worst of all, I forget where I stashed the beer and the cold fried chicken.

So you see why I'm not going fishing this summer. It is better for all of us if I just stay here in town and think about fishing. It goes so much better in my mind.

There I am, alone at the bend of the stream. I skillfully work my line across the clear water. My little gray fly dances seductively.

Suddenly, there is a rainbow of blurred light out of the water. The big fish strikes hard. The line whirrs out of the reel. The pole bows.

Slowly, patiently, I work the big fellow close enough to land him with my net.

Yeah.

June 12, 1980

Sights and sounds
of summers past

SUMMER SOUNDS.

The voice of the meadowlark is lost in morning's angry traffic snarl. A portable stereo destroys the soft laughter of a child. And the whisper of cottonwood leaves isn't heard because of an ambulance siren.

Urban noise dominates our ears. And without realizing it, pleasant sounds of summers past have fallen silent.

I want to believe they are still out there, waiting by some magic to be heard again. Somewhere in the middle of a lazy day, it would be nice to hear the sound of a horse slowly clopping down the alley.

"Veg-ta-BULES. Veg-ta-BULES," the old Italian man would shout. The wagon's wheels crunched through gravel. The horse had been there so many times, he knew where and when to stop.

Backdoor screens slammed when women came out to see what the old man had that day. He'd roll back the canvas cover, and there were rows of yellow corn, fresh beets, small dills ready for pickling, plump tomatoes, bunches of sweet green onions, clusters of bright red radishes.

The women would touch and smell for freshness. Everything was from those tidy little truck farms out in Adams County. The women exchanged small talk while the horse swished away the flies with his tail, and the old man weighed each order on a small scale at the rear of the wagon.

Remember the taste and smell of fresh green beans? They had simmered with bacon a good part of the afternoon, and at dinner they were usually served with chopped white onion on top.

And the blue Maddox Ice Co. truck came through the alley during the morning. Kids hid behind hollyhocks until they heard the iceman clank his tongs on a cake of ice and walk through the back gate. Then they'd scramble on the back of the truck to grab little chips of ice to suck.

When evening came in Denver, children would go to a friend's house and call, "Joey, Joey, can you come out?" I don't know why we never went to the door. My wife, Trish, remembers in Park Ridge, Ill., it was the custom to shout, "Yo ho! Yo ho! Janet!"

Then you could hear children playing in the twilight. There would be a game of hide-and-seek and a small voice would count to 100 by fives. There was the sound of a scramble, and then, "Ready or not, here I come!"

The game was over when a voice called, "Ollie, Ollie, oxen free!" We would lie down on the moist grass and look up at the Milky Way, a great splash of light across the black sky. We didn't know it then, but city kids 50 years later would never see it that way.

We'd stay outside in the warm evening until we could hear "The Perfect Song" through the open living room window. It was the theme for "Amos and Andy" on the radio and time for bed.

Sleep came quickly on a daybed in the screened back porch. Night birds called to each other in the distance, and crickets began to saw away at the night.

June 15, 1982

Autumn pleasures

ANTICIPATION.

Better than realization? Not when it comes to autumn. It always seems to be brighter than we had remembered. Fresher and crisper, too.

I am not one to lament the passing of summer. It has become like the guest who has stayed too long — welcome at first, but now somewhat trying.

That's probably not fair. It has been a nice summer. It has been quiet in the city, and there has been enough rain to keep the lawns green, even through the hottest days.

It is just that yardwork has become drudgery. The hollyhocks are leaning over, and the vine geraniums are getting stringy. The kids have worn out their summer clothing, and people are tired of getting into hot automobiles.

One of the nicer advantages of living here is that we have clearly defined seasons. I have never understood the attraction of Southern California. I don't know how people who live there are able to endure the monotony of what is almost a one-season climate.

Is it possible that one's sense of awareness is dulled by living in such places? There is great drama when seasons change in Colorado. When it is autumn, it looks like autumn.

If all you could see here was a single sunset, you would know the season. It won't be long before the clouds out over the Plains will turn to bronze at dusk. The colors will deepen as we get close to November.

Of course, the turning of the aspen is lovely. But there are beauties on the prairie, too. Subtle beauties. Walk through a stubble field with a good dog sometime.

Watch him sniff by fence rows that have snagged frostly tumbleweeds. He'll frisk along until he smells something. And then a great rooster pheasant will explode out of the brush. He'll scare the daylights out of you as he whistles up into the air. And then he will glide easily over to the next field.

There are autumn pleasures in the city, too. Bear Creek Park is almost deserted in the evening. The leaves on the big cottonwoods are a bright yellow. They are dry, and you can hear them clatter against each other in the evening breeze.

It is nice to watch the great flights of Canada geese begin to move along the evening horizon. In the neighborhoods, there are also autumn birds. Watch for the Bohemian waxwings.

They don't come every year. But when they do, they are a sight to behold. They are handsome little birds, dressed in grays and browns. Their tails are yellow banded and their wing feathers are sometimes tipped with bright red. There are crests on their heads. Watch for them in crabapple trees. They love dried fruit left on the twigs.

People turn inward during autumn. Families seem to come closer together. So do friends. On a chilly day, watch how people walk closer together as they scurry along 17th Street.

Watching the weather change is exciting. Sometimes the wind will pick up suddenly. You can almost smell the pines as it blows down from the hills. It is that fresh.

The clouds seem to be moving wildly up above when the wind blows that way. And then there are quieter times when they move in a stately procession across a darkening afternoon sky.

It is autumn. It is a time to feel, to listen, to see. The year has become mature and beautiful and exciting. Don't miss an instant of it.

The apples are red and crisp. There is nothing that smells better than pork loin roasting in the oven. It is time to squeeze the hand of a child and to embrace a friend.

Celebrate!

September 20, 1979

School days

FRESH VARNISH.

I still smell it when I think about going back to school. Those old three-story brownstone schools we used to have in Denver had a lot of woodwork. The custodians varnished it during the summer months.

When vacation was over, and the first day of school came around, the smell of varnish was still in the halls. The wooden banister on the steel-stepped staircases sometimes were a little tacky.

It wasn't long before the newness of the varnish had worn away and the halls were filled with the usual school smells — chalk dust, library paste, little kid sweat, orange peel and the oil from the wide mops the custodians pushed down the halls.

Sometimes the desks in the classrooms were varnished. They never were sanded down first. The custodians just slapped another coat of Valspar over ink stains, scratches and carved initials.

The desks were bolted to the floor. The tops were hinged and there was space underneath for a Big Chief tablet, some penny pencils and a couple of books.

The seats folded up so students could stand in place to recite. The side supports usually were black, filigreed cast iron. There was an inkwell at the upper right hand corner of the desk and a groove that served as a pencil holder.

There were other nice things about the old schools. The blackboards were really black, not green. The ceilings were high. The teacher used a long pole to open the top windows for ventilation. And on cold days, there was the reassuring clank and hiss of the steam radiators.

Whatever their faults, there was a lot to be said for those old buildings. They looked like schools, inside and out. There was no doubt what went on there.

That's not always the case with newer school buildings. Some of them look like penitentiaries, others like chick hatcheries. Some of the suburban schools resemble shopping centers.

Nothing is bolted down anymore. The desks move and so do the walls. The kids don't stay put either. They are platooned around from room to room and teacher to teacher.

There's probably not much encouragement these days for students to develop loyalty and affection for their schools. The rooms probably won't be the same next year, or even next week.

There is no criticism intended in this observation. Today's way of educating probably is only a reflection of a society that has become more mobile and less rooted to tradition.

Still, as some of these stately old buildings are bulldozed into memory, I have the uneasy feeling that we are losing something that we shall never be able to replace.

There was something so secure about old schools. There is no way of proving it, but I believe that those solid structures directly influenced generations of children to positively structure their own lives.

At my age, I would be expected to hold these views. But it was a pleasant surprise for me that my own children shared at least some of them.

Three of the four were fortunate to have attended the old Bromwell Elementary School on Josephine Street. It has since been torn down and replaced with a very attractive new school.

All three regretted that "their" school wasn't there now. They spoke of it in affectionate terms — terms I have never heard them use in describing newer and more modern schools they have since attended.

Sometimes we forget that schools are not just for right now and the future. They are places to go back to. They are buildings to re-explore, maybe just to find initials carved on an old desk.

Or just to smell the varnish.

August 22, 1979

Well, I never . . .

AGE OF INNOCENCE.

I have come around to the view that it occurs in life somewhere between middle and old age. This is somewhat contrary to the traditional notion that innocence is lost at puberty.

The old geezers are the guiltless ones. Well, relatively so. In my own case, there are a lot of things taken for granted these days that I have never done.

For example, I have never smoked marijuana. Not even once. There, it's out. Don't be embarrassed for me. Try to think of the first century Publilius Syrus maxim that said, "Confession of our faults is the next thing to innocence."

There probably are several reasons why I haven't tried the stuff. I grew up at a time when it was widely believed that just one puff of "devil weed" would send you out to kill, rape and pillage.

I suppose that down deep inside I am afraid that I might like it too well. I'm that way with jelly beans. Can't get enough.

Not long ago, I was talking to a friend of mine about marijuana. He was about my age and had never tried it either. His reasons were about the same as mine.

He conceded that it was sometimes important to remove some of the sharper edges from reality. "But dammit," he said, "gin was good enough for my daddy. It was good enough for me. Why isn't it good enough for the younger generation?"

Incidently, it was Max Morath who said, "The dry martini is just a socially acceptable way of drinking raw gin."

That reminds me of a war correspondent from the London Times I used to know in Korea. When we played poker, he would hold his bottle of Gordon's gin between his legs. From time to time, he would reach down, take the bottle and drink directly from it.

I asked him why he didn't just put the bottle on the table. "For two reasons," he said. "I don't want you bloody fools to drink my gin, and besides, I want to keep it warm."

Something else I have never done is to see an X-rated movie. About the raciest thing I have observed on the screen was in "Gone With the Wind." It was where Clark Cable said to Vivian Leigh, "Frankly, Scarlett, I don't give a damn."

And then there was that part where he carried her upstairs and the camera dissolved into the next scene. I always just assumed that he went to his room and she went to hers.

Back when I was a kid, it was a big deal to sneak away and look through the underwear section of the Monkey-Ward catalog. It certainly isn't that way now.

About the closest thing to an X-rated movie I have ever seen were those Army venereal disease training films we were required to see during World War II.

There never was any real danger of VD outbreak in our outfit. We always were stationed in areas where there were absolutely no women.

Actually, our closest contact with members of the opposite sex was in those VD movies, and we used to look forward to seeing them.

To be honest, I probably never have gone to those sleazy X-rated theaters because I am afraid I might be seen going in. Come to think of it, though, you hardly ever see anybody going into those places. There must be a back entrance.

I knew a radio and TV sportscaster who never missed any of those movies. It didn't seem to bother him that he might be recognized.

I asked him what those movies were like. He said it was just the same thing, over and over. Pretty soon, it even gets to be dull.

Oddly enough, he said, while all the pornography was taking place on the screen, the sound was music by Bach or Mozart. He wondered if I might go with him some time. Knowing of my love for classical music, he said if I objected to what was on the screen, I could always close my eyes and just listen to the music.

September 13, 1979

Autumn memories

JONATHAN APPLES.

The Idea Fairy was perched on a stack of old clippings on my desk when I came into the newsroom. She was looking down at her new shoes.

ME — Those heels are pretty high, Fairy.

FAIRY — Listen, when you are only 8 inches tall, you need all the help you can get.

ME — I like you better in your Hush Puppies.

FAIRY — You can be so square, Buster.

ME — You worry too much about your height. Be what you are.

FAIRY — Listen to who is talking. You're the guy who wears those bulky sweaters to camouflage your pot. And what about the way you comb the side of your hair over the top of your head?

ME — It is too nice a day for talk like this.

FAIRY — You're right. The first day of autumn is very special.

ME — The cooler nights mean sounder sleep. You wake up feeling better about things. Air smells sweet in the morning. Nice, tart Jonathan apples are in the stores.

FAIRY — Some of the honey locust and wild plum leaves are tinged with yellow. I like it when the cottonwoods start to turn. You can hear them clatter in the wind.

ME — A lot of people think they have to go to the mountains to enjoy autumn. There's a lot of beauty all around us . . .

FAIRY — Right here in town!

ME — Yes. I like to see the evening sky reflected in the south lake at Warshington Park.

FAIRY — Warshington Park?

ME — Not always. When we were kids, sometimes we just called it Warsh Park.

FAIRY — There's no "r" in Washington.

ME — There was when we were kids. Houses were heated by coal then. When autumn came, you could see gray smoke coming out of chimleys.

FAIRY — The word is chim-ney. Chimney. I don't see how a man your age, who has been in this business as long as you have, could talk that way. Does autumn make you regress?

ME — Makes me feel like a kid again. I can still smell the chicken and dumplings simmering in the pot at Grandma Fiedler's house. And then there was the feeling of going back to Alameda School the first day. New varnish on the stairway banisters. I can hear the high voices of the kids: "My countrytisofthee, sweet landofliberty, ofthee Ising."

FAIRY — Hey, slow down. You are getting carried away, and you are not putting spaces between some of your words.

ME — But that's the way it sounded. Mom and Pop would take me to see the stage shows at the old Orpheum Theater. I can remember getting all dressed up to go for a Sunday drive. We would go up Turkey Crick Canyon . . . .

FAIRY — Creek, not crick.

ME — The road was twisty then. I would get carsick, and we

would have to come home before we saw the aspen. It was more fun to jump in the big stacks of maple leaves in front of Grandpa's house.

FAIRY — Buster, stop it! This is 1981 and you are babbling about how it was 50 years ago. You go a little heavy on nostalgia sometimes. Most people weren't even alive then.

ME — Autumn is timeless. It has different meanings for all of us. For me, it is a time of pleasant memory. I like Pocky Marranzino's advice about writing a column.

FAIRY — What is that?

ME — If you can't make the readers laugh or cry, try to make them remember. By the way, Fairy, I do like your new shoes. They make your legs look nice.

FAIRY — Cool it, Buster. Better you should regress and get back to the chicken and dumplings.

September 22, 1981

Nutrition nonsense

HELP!

I'm being held captive by the nutritionists. It has been a week now, and there is no relief in sight. I may try to tunnel out tonight.

You know how it is with me. There is nothing more important in life than meat and potatoes. My father was that way. I can still hear him tell the waitress at the old Oxford Hotel: "Bring me steak smothered with pork chops."

During times of stress, I can find blessed relief by sitting down to a platter of stewing hen and dumplings. Drizzle them with light gravy made from a little bit of fat, some stock, flour and milk. Lordy!

I like pig knuckles and sauerkraut. Slather my meat loaf with chili sauce. There aren't enough noodles for me. I make a slumgullion beef stew that is absolutely heroic.

Give me honest food. Everyone should have grilled ham steak and fried hominy at least once a week. A cold, blustery Sunday afternoon screams out for roast pork loin and oven-browned spuds.

I have always stood four-square for these things. I am one who doesn't eat just to keep the old bod' going. I eat for pleasure. Food is recreation. Right?

Wrong.

I woke up the other Sunday morning with a special yearning for corned beef hash mixed with chopped pickled herring and kosher dill pickles. I wanted it browned in a skillet and a poached egg nested on top.

I was all set to rassle it up, maybe with some French toast on the side, when I noticed my wife, Trish, standing in the corner of the kitchen. She was quietly stirring a little cup of yogurt.

Fearing the worst, I ran to the medicine chest. Sure enough, standing alongside the Alka-Seltzer and Pepto-Bismol was a bottle of brewer's yeast tablets. There were also d-alpha tocopherols, 100-milligram pills of pantothenic acid and other dietary supplements I can neither spell nor pronounce.

Returning to the kitchen, I found Trish still standing in the corner. I have a theory that people stand in the corner when they eat yogurt because they are not supposed to enjoy it. I hate yogurt.

"We are going to start eating more nutritious foods," she announced quietly. "Gayelord Hauser is very big on adding 16 ounces of raw vegetable juice to the diet every day."

"You know what Gayelord Hauser can do with his raw vegetable juice!" I shot back. "And besides, I have never liked the way he spells his first name."

It was no use. I know we'll be on this health food kick for awhile. It will be one culinary delight after another. Nothing like a mess of wheat soy varnishkas after a tough day in the newsroom. For a little morning eye-opener, a lip-smacking cup of sweet acidophilus milk is hard to beat.

Some years ago, when we were going through a similar period of nutritional uplift, Trish served a casserole made of bulgar, garbanzos, parsley flakes and half-cooked carrots. "There now, doesn't that look delicious?" she said.

One of my sons — Jonathan, as I recall — wept openly and left the table. I helped myself to a small portion, pretending to relish every bite. Those left at the table seemed to be watching every move I made.

It doesn't do any good to argue. I have been told again and again about my rising cholesterol level and my protein imbalance. I know I should drink 10 glasses of water a day. Avoid salt, sugar and anything that tastes good. Don't tell me about the benefits of low-fat cheese.

I suppose I can make it for awhile on granola munchies, tofu and dried apricots. But one of these days, Baby, I'm gonna break out of here and get me a steak smothered with pork chops.

February 10, 1981

Goose bumps

I thought of them the other evening when a flock of locals flew right over Depew Street. They couldn't have been higher than 100 feet from the ground. They were gone almost as quickly as they came. I am always excited at the sight and sound of those big birds.

The geese I saw were probably on their way over to Marston Lake. Bill Logan, our outdoor editor, told me it will be late next month before we see big flocks of migratory Canada geese.

Logan said there are about 5,000 resident geese scattered between Denver and Fort Collins. He calls them "common" geese. The flocks get larger each year. Some of the migratories like it so well here they just decide to stay.

I get a kick out of the geese that waddle around Sloans Lake. They seem to thrive on urban living. I have noticed they sometimes get in the way of bikers and joggers. They just refuse to be hurried out of the way.

There was a time some years ago when I didn't have those friendly feelings about geese. It was at that time in life when autumn had a different meaning for me. Autumn was hunting time.

Henry Swan, a Denver surgeon, used to take me out to his lease on the South Platte. He had somehow managed to tow an old refrigerator railroad car out there in the middle of a stubble field. He had fixed up the inside with a small kitchen and sleeping space for a half-dozen people.

We were on one of our annual excursions when I came face-to-face with three of the biggest, most beautiful geese I had ever seen. But, I am getting ahead of my story.

Henry and I drove out to the river on a Saturday afternoon. It was the last day of the pheasant hunting season. As we were driving through one of the countless farm gates, Henry spotted a big rooster pheasant.

We jumped out of the car. His dog started working along the tumbleweed-filled ditch. Up popped the bird. Henry nailed him with one shot.

We had pheasant for dinner that night. Henry, a superb cook, made a white wine and mushroom sauce. We ate the bird, laughed, told a lot of lies and sacked out early.

The next thing I remember was Henry hollering that it was 4 a.m. The temperature had dropped to 14 below zero. Everything was frozen solid, including my feet.

Henry and I stumbled out of that old refrigerator car and into one of the coldest mornings I could remember. The full moon was bright. It glistened on the frosted corn shocks.

We made our way toward the blinds on foot. We must have walked several miles. It was so cold. The dog didn't want to come. It was that cold.

When we finally got there, we noticed that a part of the river hadn't frozen over. We found some cover and settled in, figuring that when it became light, a few ducks might come in.

Just as the eastern sky began to glow, we started to load our shotguns. We had spotted some geese moving along the horizon and decided to use No. 2 shot.

I snapped three shells in my old J.C. Higgins pump. Henry's more expensive Browning automatic was frozen solid. The geese began to move closer. Henry tried to melt the ice on his gun with a Zippo lighter. No go.

All of a sudden, three big and beautiful Canadas began to fly up the river, right toward us. Henry banged his fist against the Browning. Still no go. "All right, Geno, it's up to you," Henry whispered. "I'll tell you when to shoot. Not yet. OK, now lead them a little more. Not yet."

The geese were then so close we could almost touch them. "Get ready. Now, Geno," Henry said urgently. "Now! Pull the trigger, you sonofabitch!" I couldn't do it. It was mesmerized by those magnificent birds. There was no way I could shoot them. They were too beautiful. Too alive.

Henry forgave me. I think.

October 9, 1980

On the air

COMING DOWN.

That's the hard part for the disc jockey. He has a love-hate relationship with his job. It's a groove when it all comes together. It's a bummer when it doesn't.

The toughest part is when the red light goes off and it's reality time. He has to be himself. That's not easy when everyone likes the sharp, clever announcer who has been on the air for the last four hours. People may not like the real guy underneath.

Playwright Moss Hart believed successful actors often had unhappy childhoods. They carried a need for fantasies into the adult world and worked them out on stage.

Maybe.

It might be the same for the DJ. His stage is the radio station control room. He blends phonograph records, commercial and chutzpa into "his sound."

He can make more than $100,000 a year. He can also work for minimum wage. It depends on a lot of things. Luck. He has to be at the right place at the right time. He must be a compulsive worker. That's important. He must know his audience.

Running studio equipment is easy. A chimpanzee could do it. A jock's communication abilities are much more important.

Certain to be a success in the fall TV season is the CBS situation comedy "WKRP in Cincinnati." It's an amusing program about a rundown MOR (middle of the road) station. A new program director changes the musical format and WKRP finds success in the highly competitive world of top-40 rock 'n' roll stations.

There are a couple of spacey disc jockeys and other small station stereotypes broadcasters will recognize instantly. The station manager is a fuddy-duddy. The sales manager is typically overdressed and opportunistic. The old-school news director is a mousy little guy. He is wedded to the notion that his mission in life is to read hog futures over the radio.

And then there is the busty receptionist. She spends much of her time before a mirror. Her charms aren't lost on other members of the staff.

The series is just getting started. There are endless situations and there'll be a lot of dubbed-in laughs.

The real world of the DJ isn't all that funny. He lives in a schizophrenic environment where he is never quite sure who he really is. He's certainly not the same person to his wife as he is to his listeners. That might have been her expectation when they married, but that's not the way it really is.

Unwinding when the red light goes off is the tough part. One of the problems is the expectation of others that the DJ is "up" and "on" all the time. He is expected to be funny, clever and sharp off the air as well as on.

He knows his frozen smile is phony. In many ways, he is like the politicians. He has cultivated the art of speaking briefly to admirers. He establishes quick eye contact, and then moves to someone else.

The DJ has mixed feelings about being alone. He has a longing for it. He's also afraid of being by himself. It gives him too much time to contemplate the cosmetic way he has to live.

He has booze and drugs to contend with. They seem to offer an escape from his two worlds. They don't. They are more likely to deepen his occasional bouts with depression.

It's not all bad. A DJ gets the good tables at restaurants. Headliners come to his table at a nightclub. He is invited to a lot of cocktail parties. But this part of his life gets to be a drag. Parties and appearances only lengthen the time he has to wear the frozen smile.

There are the times when he just wants to stop everything and just stare at an empty wall. That can be bad. It gives him time to think about just where this life of his can possibly take him.

But then there's tomorrow. It will be better then. He'll be in the studio with his records. The red hand sweeps to the top of the clock. He'll hit the button of his theme cartridge. The music is loud. Hold it and fade. Mike switch.

The red light is on.

September 14, 1978

Sob

FOR CRYING OUT LOUD.

Why is it that women are permitted to cry and men are not? Jesus was the only male in history who was allowed to weep in public.

William Billings, a popular composer during America's war for independence, wrote a song that said, "When Jesus wept, the falling tear in mercy flow'd beyond all bound. When Jesus groan'd, a trembling fear seiz'd all the guilty world around."

That's not the way it is with the rest of us. I know this to be true because I am a male crier. That's right, one of your real tear shedders. Great big wet ones. Without fail, I will bubble up at the slightest expression of tenderness or poignancy.

I cry in the morning when the sun comes up. Isn't that silly? Why would anybody want to cry during a beautiful sunrise? It must be that I am saddened to see the day lose its innocence.

There is a radio commercial that makes me cry. It's the one where a father has put a second mortgage on the house to pay his son's college tuition.

In the background you can hear the sounds of graduation. The school orchestra is wheezing through Brahms' "Academic Festival Overture." A finance company has loaned the money. The kid gets his diploma and says, "Thanks, Dad." That's when I choke up.

I cried when Floyd Little played his last game for the Denver Broncos. It was just too much when coach John Ralston put his arm around Little and the two walked off the field together.

There is a conventional psychological wisdom about crying. It is supposed to indicate that the crier has been rejected somewhere along the line.

It also works the other way around. Male political figures who cry in the open are certain to be rejected. It is believed that Maine Sen. Edmund Muskie lost the Democratic nomination for the presidency because he cried during a New Hampshire appearance.

A conservative newspaper in that state had printed some unflattering information about Muskie's wife. He called a press conference to refute what he considered to be unfair and dishonest allegations.

He was in control when he began to make his statement. But then as he continued, it became more difficult for him to speak. Muskie started to cry. It probably was more out of anger and frustration than it was out of sadness.

But when the scene was shown on national television, he lost his chance to win the nomination. The public apparently felt that a man who cried because his wife had been unjustly attacked was not qualified to be president.

Hubert Humphrey often cried during his many years of public service. It is revealing, however, that when he was dying of cancer, Humphrey didn't cry. Everyone else did, though.

Adlai Stevenson probably spoke for all losing politicians back in 1952 when he was defeated for the presidency by Dwight Eisenhower. During his concession statement, Stevenson explained how he felt.

He said he was reminded of what Abraham Lincoln had told friends under similar circumstances. "He said he felt like a little boy who had stubbed his toe in the dark. He was too old to cry, but it hurt too much to laugh," Stevenson said.

There probably is little hope for men whose feelings are so close to the surface that they sometimes lose control and have to cry in the open. The best bet is to wear dark glasses and carry plenty of handkerchiefs.

Quote:

"Oh! would I were dead now,
Or up in the bed now,
To cover my head now
And have a good cry!" — Thomas Hood.

August 3, 1979

Kilroy was there

GOOD RIDDANCE.

News reporter Al Gordon asked me the other day if I planned to write some kind of retrospective about the decade. Probably should.

If it's OK with you, instead of writing about the '70s, I think I'll put down a few lines about the '40s. That was the last of the really great decades.

Besides, I have been writing about the '70s for the past 10 years and I am sick of it. Honestly, I don't have any more insights now than I did on Jan. 1, 1970.

I've had it with Watergate, Vietnam, Nixon, abortion, marijuana, the energy crisis — the whole scene. No point in spading it up again.

The '60s were no better, just crazier. As I remember it, it was a major milestone when television showed us the riots in color instead of black and white.

Hardly anybody remembers what the 1950s were like because they were so dull. Those years had something to do with malt shops and sha-na-na.

That's not the way it was in the 1940s. Anybody who was around then will tell you that we had ourselves some kind of decade.

It began with Glenn Miller and the orchestra playing "Moonlight Serenade" over the radio. The popular fashion among high school girls was a little number called the "torso dress." It was tight, short and looked groovy with saddle shoes and bobby socks.

Rex Stout ground out all those wonderful Nero Wolfe detective novels. Remember Fritz and Archie Goodwin? Archie was Nero's leg man. While waiting for two hours in a doctor's office, it was Archie who said, "I was so bored that I was trying to figure out a third way of crossing my legs."

Greer Garson won the Academy Award in 1942 for her performance in "Mrs. Miniver," the story of home front heroism in England during World War II.

Garson (we used to say Miss Garson in those days) got a plaster Oscar instead of a gold-plated one because of wartime austerity. Her acceptance speech was an hour long. She couldn't stop. Just rambled on and on. Longest Academy Award acceptance speech in history.

It's about the war. It was the last time most people can remember when Americans had a common purpose and were all pulling together.

The passage of time has dimmed the memories of how cruelly cold it was in Bastogne and how sickening the stench was at Buchenwald.

It is better to remember going AWOL in Paris, sleeping under the bridges that cross the Seine and drinking wine with a crazy Polish priest and an irreverent Irish cavalry sergeant.

If you liked that kind of action, you would have loved the '40s. You would have laughed at the "Kilroy was here" signs that were scrawled on the Siegfried Line pill boxes.

And then when your troop ship sailed into New York harbor, and you saw the Statue of Liberty, you would have cried. The Andrews Sisters were on a little tug boat. You could hear them singing over the public address system, "Boogie Woogie Bugle Boy of Company B."

Peace was wonderful. It was getting a "ruptured duck" sewn on your uniform. It was coming home on a troop train and being discharged at Fort Logan.

Peace was going to work, eating lobster at Lande's on East Colfax, watching Harry Truman beat the system, listening to Charlie Parker records and stopping every now and then just to listen to the quiet.

The '40s.

December 20, 1979

2

CITY LIGHTS: DENVER

City lights

I have been poking around West Maple Avenue, the block where I lived as a child. It is between South Broadway and South Bannock Street.

It all started when I was trying to find an alternate route from southwest Denver to the Rocky Mountain News. I always seem to get trapped by a stalled coal train at Santa Fe Drive.

I have learned I can use the Alameda underpass and then turn north on Cherokee. That puts me only a block away from Bannock and a straight shot downtown. Keep it under your hat. We don't want everyone to know.

Anyhow, my shortcut takes me through the old neighborhood. Both my father and I spent our childhood years on West Maple. Grandpa Amole first owned the house at 48 and then the one at 64 W. Maple Ave.

I suppose my first memories of anything were of Broadway. I loved the lights. My parents claimed I would scream bloody murder when they turned the baby buggy off Broadway onto Maple.

Everything north of Maple was "up Broadway." South was "down." When Grandpa would take me for a walk, I always wanted to go "up." That's where the action was. We'd get smoked herring at Werner's Delicatessen, strawberry ice cream cones at the Broadway Creamery and pickled pigs feet at the Boy's Market.

All those places are gone now. So is the old Irvington Hotel, Berg's candy store, Lantz Laundry and the Eat-A-Pig. Urit Jory's Drug Store is now a paint company. Urit made a great cherry phosphate, and he also kept some hard stuff under the counter for his pals during Prohibition.

My mother taught school and Pop traveled for Hendrie and Bolthoff, so I spent a lot of time with Grandma and Grandpa. He worked all night at the railroad yards and was free to be with me afternoons.

We used to watch semipro baseball at Merchant's Park, or the "old brickyard," as it was called. We'd sit on the narrow, green bleacher boards along the third base line. Grandpa filled me with peanuts, strawberry pop and information on squeeze-play strategy.

When I was old enough to go to school, I went to Alameda. The best part was stopping in at the little school supply and notions store at West Byers and South Bannock. Bill McClelland and I would get penny candy. Remember those little metal pie pans filled with chocolate candy? They came with tiny spoons.

Opal Gordon was my first grade teacher. It was Mrs. Gordon who discovered I needed glasses. I was the only kid in the room who couldn't cut out a paper gingerbread boy. I couldn't see her demonstrate how to do it. I thought everything was supposed to be blurry.

Sure enough, I had very poor vision. I don't suppose I'll ever forget the day I put on my first pair of glasses. I just couldn't get enough of seeing. Everything was so sharp and clear. I had never really seen a flower or a tree as it really was.

The old neighborhood is run-down now. The alleys are cluttered and trashy. Even so, I enjoyed nosing around the alley behind our old house the other day. It was like stepping 50 years into the past.

I thought I could hear Grandpa calling for Jim, his pet squirrel. He would stand on the back porch and shout, "Jim! Come on, Jim!" Jim would frisk out of the tree and up to Grandpa and would eat right out of his hand.

I've noticed a lot of young families are buying old Victorian homes north of West Ellsworth Avenue. That part of the old neighborhood is coming back. Maybe the same thing will happen to Maple.

When spring comes, I am going to start for work a little early one day. I'll stop off at Archer Park and sit in the sun for awhile. I'll remember the chili at Murphy's restaurant and seeing Charlie Chaplin in "Modern Times" at the old Webber.

And then I'll remember the lights on Broadway.

January 29, 1981

Hopping bells, the Cosmo style

FRONT BOY!

Magic words if you were a bellhop at the old Cosmopolitan Hotel. I was, and a little bit of me will die when the old place closes Jan. 1.

The Cosmo has fallen on hard times since the new Fairmont and Marriott hotels have opened.

I was still in high school when I badgered bell captain Cliff Graves into hiring me as a lobby porter at $2.34 a day.

It was my job to clean the spit and cigar butts out of the sand in the lobby trash receptacles. I also swept the floor, cleaned the ashtrays, straightened the chairs.

By the time four years had passed, I had advanced to service elevator operator, front elevator operator, bellhop and finally captain of my own shift.

I learned a great deal of life, death and love — much more than from the public education system. I also mastered guile, hustle, con, great hall speed and other survival skills upon which I still rely in my sunset years.

Even though the bellhop salary was only $15 a month, I turned $100 a week in tips. That wasn't too shabby back in prewar Denver.

We did it by peddling club soda, ginger ale, illegal booze and a wide variety of interesting drug store sundries from our lockers in the basement. You could triple the cost of stuff like that after 10 p.m.

I remember running out at night after the kitchen has closed and buying a 20-cent hamburger from Opal over at the Red Wing Cafe. I'd bring it back, put it on hotel china, throw on a few potato chips and a pickle, and take it up on a room service order and charge $8.

The term "front boy" comes from being the next — or front bellhop — in rotation. That meant a room-service order or checking in a guest. Each was a chance to make a tip or "rap," as we called it. Failure to get a tip was to be "stiffed."

The key to success was to remain high on the front rotation. Run the halls without being caught. Beat the other guys back to the lobby to sign in after each front. That's where the hall speed came in.

It has been years since I have been up in the old Cosmo, but I'll bet I still know it as well as the back of my hand. Can't run that fast anymore, though.

Neither can Bill Reed. After years as Denver's best radio sportscaster, he's now an account executive at Channel 9. The late impresario Bob Lotito was a busboy under *maitre de* Max Hummel. Bob Stapp, now an auto dealer, was superintendent of service.

Bob Ewing was the all-night guy. Ray Baker was a room clerk. Virgil Kidwell and Guy Van Portfliet were in the Valet Shop. Jimmy Battaglino was my best pal. Brad Morse was manager. Henri Petitjean was chef. There was good old George Sandoval.

And you know something? Kenny Bolsinger is still there. Still answering "front boy!" He's 70 now, but he can still sprint down those halls. Kenny doesn't know what he'll do when the Cosmo closes down.

I know he'll find something. He was the best of all of us. He knew how to make people feel welcome — to give real service. In these times, Kenny's kind of service is almost a lost art.

October 12, 1982

Diamond in the rough

CELEBRATION.

The Denver Press Club will mark its Diamond Jubilee this fall. In these days of planned obsolescence, hardly anything endures for 75 years.

Survival of the Press Club has not been because of its membership, but rather in spite of it. Newspeople are notoriously poor managers of their own affairs. In any event, plans are in the works for a series of parties and events the last week in October.

There was a time when the Press Club was known formally as the Denver Press Benevolent Association. The idea of the name was to suggest that the purpose of the club was to donate money to widows, orphans and other unfortunates.

There was very little of that. The tax people finally cracked down. They forced the club to be what it always was — a place reporters could go for cheap food and drink.

There are various categories of membership. The club's modern clientele includes public relations types, judges and other rascals who contribute to what is loosely defined as the "editorial content" of newspapers and broadcast stations.

Before the Press Club was remodeled in the 1950s, it had a stand-up bar. Subway straps dangled from a ceiling beam. The idea was to hold on to the strap with one hand, leaving the other hand free to drink.

The club's main source of income in those days was a row of illegal slot machines. The manager was a salty, old ex-boxing writer by the name of Abe Pollock. At his death, it was determined that there was some confusion over the proceeds from the one-armed bandits and Abe's personal estate.

That was when Jimmy Fillas became the club's steward. He had

been a bartender at Wade's Keg, a tavern next to the old Denham
Theater on 18th Street.

Fillas endeared himself to reporters by feeding them cheese and
crackers when they were broke. When he shifted his operations from
the Keg to the Press Club, the hungry reporters followed.

His impudent style of management delighted some, offended others. Fortunately, there were more of the former than the latter.
People would come from some distance for the dubious distinction of
being insulted by Fillas.

If Fillas had ever heard the maxim, "familiarity breeds con-
tempt," he must not have believed it. Arnold Toynbee, the distinguished British historian, once found his way into the Press Club. He
hadn't even finished his first drink before Fillas was calling him
"Arnie."

Fillas retired some years ago. He moved to California because of
his emphysema and because his wife got a better job there. He will
no doubt take a deep breath and return for the October festivities.

The Press Club has been in its present building at 1330 Glenarm
Place since 1925. It is right across the street from the much larger,
more affluent and prestigious Denver Athletic Club.

The club's board of directors redecorates the place every decade
or so, but the atmosphere has remained about the same. The poker
room in the basement still has Herndon Davis' oil wall mural of a
composite Rocky Mountain News and Denver Post newsroom.

There are caricatures of past and present active members in the
dining room. The walls of the second floor banquet room are covered
with old photographs. Newsmen from the past look out at the future
from under slouched hats.

The club is now managed by Ernie Azlein, a retired Associated
Press staffer. He said he took the job because he loves the place.

I guess we all do.

August 14, 1980

Theatrics

KISS OF DEATH.

I hesitate to speak on behalf of the historic Paramount Theater. Based on my track record, support here may be just the thing to doom the old joint.

Recall my plucky defense of the legendary Denver Press Club building? I wrote warmly of its past, its colorful members, its ink-stained ambiance. And what happened? The membership voted 400 to 14 to tear it down and move into the basement of a skyscraper.

And then there was that touching yarn about my Grandpa Amole's elms. As a pioneer lad, he planted those stately trees around what was then Courthouse Square on 16th Street. Hotshot New York developer William Zeckendorf ignored my protests. The elms were cut down in 1956 while I stood alone and watched with tear-rimmed eyes.

On the other side of the coin, I conducted a militant campaign to have the old D&F Tower torn down. It became valueless, I thought, when the surrounding buildings were razed. It was a genuine imitation of an ersatz campanile.

Did anyone listen? Nope. They made a diagonal patch from mismatched brick, slapped it across the scar on the 17th Street side, and the old dump still stands like some kind of sore thumb on the hand of fate. But it is perhaps well placed, anchoring our lovely 16th Street Mall.

That is why I'm not so certain the Paramount needs my help during the legal battle over its future. Landlord Joseph Gould is trying to wrest control of the theater from Historic Paramount Foundation Inc., which is controlled by Historic Denver Inc. It has been said around this town that with preservationist friends like Gene Amole, who needs enemies?

But I do have warm fuzzies about the Paramount, and it isn't because of its "Early Depression" style. I thought its art deco was cornball when it was built by Temple Buell in 1930, and the passage of time hasn't altered that opinion.

My association with the Paramount goes back to Jan. 2, 1946. That was the day wartime government restrictions on man-on-the-street radio broadcasts ended. I was fresh put of the Army, and adman Max Goldberg hired me to originate a daily program on KMYR, "Meet Me at 12:30," from in front of the Paramount.

In the seven years that followed, I bantered with about 10,000 passers-by in weather conditions ranging from bitter cold to blazing hot. My shtick was to ask quiz questions and give theater tickets as prizes.

Lots of laughs. The Paramount manager, Ralph Batchelet, came up with celebrity interviews now and then. But it was the everyday stuff I liked the best.

There were surprises, such as the day the well-dressed man put his hand on my shoulder and began pushing me down to the sidewalk just as I started to interview him. "On your knees!" he shouted. "Get down on your knees and confess your sins to the Lord Jesus Christ, just as I did in a Chicago hotel room in 1936."

And then there was the lady wrestler who took a shine to me. "After the show, Baby," she said, "we'll go somewhere and we'll see if you can break my favorite hold. I call it 'the cobra clutch.' "

Hello, Juanita, wherever you are.

April 1, 1982

Restoration fails to exorcise Oxford

GHOSTS.

I toured Denver's old Oxford Hotel with some friendly old ghosts the other day. My pop was there. So was Harry Inglee, Luther Turner and a bunch of the salesmen, or "agents," as they called themselves, from Hendrie and Bolthoff, a company that used to be across 17th Street from the Oxford.

Walt Miller came along. His barber shop was in the basement for years. So did Eddie, the combination bootblack, janitor and hotel valet. I don't believe I ever heard his last name. All wanted to see what the 92-year-old hotel at 1600 17th St. looked like now that it had been restored in 1983.

Actually, it won't have its grand reopening until Saturday, June 18. But Sherry Pahler, director of sales and marketing agreed to give us an advance tour. She had heard how we all loved the old place.

Walt Miller probably gave me my first haircut. Pop took me there Saturday mornings for years. In addition to giving shaves and haircuts, Walt also removed warts and performed other minor surgery. He prided himself on being a distant relative of the famous soprano Gladys Swarthout.

The white tile in Walt's shop was spotless. The humor was not quite so clean. Blue cigar smoke always tinged the air. Eddie softly whistled the blues as he popped the shine cloth over the perforated wing tips of your oxford shoes.

The ghosts said they would miss the old coffee shop with red and white checked tablecloths, but when Sherry showed us the new Sage Restaurant, they were impressed. Light fixtures were original, as were the colonnades and the floral detailing on the ceiling.

We were all surprised at the Cruise Room, the art deco bar added when prohibition was repealed. "Why, it is just like it used to be," someone whispered. And it is. Every detail. There was some quiet laughter and horse play as the ghosts shared private memories.

When Sherry took us into the Oxford Club, no one said anything. She explained that it is a private club now that already has 200 members. None of us had ever seen the stained glass skylight over the dining room. The club's two rooms have the original wood wainscotting and sterling silver chandeliers. Someone — I think it was Eddie — said, "Elegant. Just elegant."

Sherry explained that the Oxford will be catering to the top 1 percent of the hotel trade. When she took us through some of the Victorian and art deco rooms, we could see why. Only original antiques are used for furnishings. Cotton sheets and 100 percent wool blankets are on the beds. White terry cloth robes are in the bathrooms.

We all approved of the restoration. Walt was somewhat put off, though, because there was no barber shop. But he and Eddie felt better when Sherry showed us the original black and gold barber shop sign on the wall in the Sage Room.

"At least we weren't forgotten," Walt said.

June 14, 1983

Goodbye, Byers

It is sad that Byers is one of the Denver junior high schools scheduled to close next year. It is one of 16 schools on a citizens' committee hit list.

The committee was appointed by the Denver Board of Education to determine which schools must be closed in the first major overhaul of court-ordered busing since 1976. Under court supervision, the district has suffered a 40 percent enrollment drop since the Denver schools were ordered desegregated.

Student enrollment has declined from 96,000 to 60,000. The number of Anglo students has dropped from 65 percent to less than 50 percent. The Board of Education has no other choice but to close the schools, nine of which are elementary and seven junior high.

As reporter Bob Weiss pointed out in his Saturday Rocky Mountain News story, the hit list is bound to touch off considerable controversy. Parents will fight, probably unsuccessfully, to preserve what little is left of a neighborhood school system.

They have a point. It is difficult to restore and repopulate older neighborhoods with young families if neighborhood schools are closed. It has become redundant to keep belaboring some of the unfortunate consequences of school busing, however.

My sadness at the expected closure of Byers is for personal reasons. I went to school there almost 50 years ago. It is difficult for me to think of that particular part of old south Denver without Byers.

I can close my eyes and still hear the reedy voices of the kids in the auditorium singing, "Byers, Byers, First in Everything." That was the official school song back in the '30s.

The melody, as I learned in later years, was not original. It was rather the Neapolitan love song, "Funiculi Funicula." Instead of, "Byers, Byers, first in everything," the Italian lyrics are, "Jammo, jammo, coppa, jammo ja."

The English translation comes out, "Come on, come on, to the top we'll go." It was a song composed in 1880 in celebration of the opening of the funicular, or cable, railroad on Mount Vesuvius.

Getting back to Byers, I can still remember how apprehensive I was the first day in the seventh grade. Byers was the big time. No more elementary school kid stuff. There were classes in wood and metal working. There was a printing class, and every boy who went through Byers in those days was required to learn bricklaying.

Another big change was our first encounter with men teachers. For many years, elementary schools were dominated by women. At long last, boys were able to relate to men teachers. That was important to us.

Junior high gym classes were much different from elementary school. The Byers boys' gym teacher was Roy "Dolly" McGlone, a tough squarish disciplinarian. I can still remember how scared I was as I sat with the other "scrubs" and listened to Dolly McGlone tell us on the first day what was expected of us.

He told us we would have to buy gym suits and athletic supporters. There was confusion in the locker room that first day we put on the gym suits. We were somewhat lacking in sophistication about intimate athletic equipment.

We must have been hilarious as we fumbled around with the supporters, or "jock straps," as we would later call them. A lot of kids didn't know how to put them on, or what went where and how, so to speak. The trick was to coolly watch somebody else out of the corner of the eye, taking care not to betray nervousness.

Dolly McGlone — we always used both names — then lined us up in the gym and told us how to "pinch in and tuck under." That meant pulling the buns together and standing up straight. To this day, everytime I see someone with poor posture, I have a deeply rooted urge to tell him to "pinch in and tuck under."

Goodbye, Byers.

December 2, 1980

The 'real Denver' is gone forever

COWTOWN.

The headline on William Gallo's Sunday News' story about downtown architecture asked, "Where is the real Denver?"

He talked to architects and critics about our downtown. They agreed that our skyscrapers ignore Denver's individuality. Almost identical structures can be found in Houston, San Francisco, New York, Chicago.

Absolutely true. We have traded our soul to the devil for the big time. Denver has been lusting after the big time since I can remember.

We apologized for being an "overgrown cowtown" by proclaiming, "We are a mile closer to the sun," or, "We have the largest whatever between Kansas City and the West Coast."

But we were just kidding ourselves. We really wanted those cookie-cutter tall buildings, freeways, suburbs and all the other superficial accouterments of the big time. We wanted to look like New York, San Francisco and Chicago. Well, we got our big time, and the devil claimed our soul. Perhaps the more important question is, "What was the real Denver?"

We have always had imitative architecture. Our cherished D&F Tower is a copy of St. Mark's campanile in Venice. The old Windsor Hotel was supposed to look like Windsor Castle. And our post office is a poor replica of a Roman bath house.

If there is anything traditional about us, it is that we have coveted other architectural styles. In our pursuit of the big time, we never really made the effort to create an appropriate style for our climate, our terrain, our people.

Our lost "real Denver" had less to do with structures than it did with the consequences of making the big time. We had to give up our small time, our overgrown cowtown.

The Loop at 15th and Arapahoe is gone. It was the Denver Tramway Co. Terminal where the old trolleys turned around, and where, as Elwood and Max Brooks advertised, "working people can bank on a transfer at the Central Bank & Trust Co."

We lost an important part of downtown when the Home Public Market closed. Remember the rich smells of warm bread, pickled herring, fresh ground coffee? The butchers walked on sawdust behind the counters. Produce gleamed like rows of jewels. There was clatter, loud talk, cash registers jingling. It closed when The Denver Post moved there from its "bucket of blood" plant on Champa Street.

We were ashamed of gaudy old Curtis Street with its Empress, Isis and Rialto theaters. But didn't those coney islands and fried onions smell great in Sam's No. 3? Hardly anyone remembers Hop Alley. And not many will admit remembering the old Ace High bawdy house.

We gave up Keables' sandwich shops, the Tabor Grand, the Oxford

Hotel coffee shop, Harry Bramer's, the Mozart Bar, Pell's Oyster House, McVittie's, the Blue Parrot Inn, the Golden Eagle, Boggio's, the Navarre, the Shirley Savoy, the Albany and the Mizpah Arch.

That Denver is gone. Forever.

February 22, 1983

Naming names

STREET TALK.

The intersection of Broadway and Ellsworth Avenue is where it all begins. It isn't the precise geographical center of metropolitan Denver, but it is the point where Denver's street and avenue grid system begins.

Broadway separates east from west Denver. Ellsworth Avenue divides the north from the south. Avenues to the north are numerical. Those to the south are a jumble of states, colleges and universities, geographic locations and people.

The streets in the center of the city are confusing, even though some are alphabetized. West of Broadway, Indian tribes come first. They are followed by famous men.

East from Broadway are more famous men, mixed with some flowers, geographic locations and women's first names. The grid system begins to make sense with the double alphabet east of Colorado Boulevard. The first street is a place or person. The second is a plant, tree or shurb.

The man who has been in charge of naming Denver streets is Frank King, a city engineer. "I've been at this since 1949," King said, "and I'm naming new streets every day."

Actually, King names streets for the entire metropolitan area. He named all the streets in Broomfield and Montbello. "I'm particularly proud of Montbello," King said. "Since it is not far from Stapleton International Airport, I decided to name the streets after air bases around the world. People liked that. Some men said they wanted to buy a house on a street with the same name as an air base where they had served."

The bible of Denver street-naming is Origin of Denver Street Names by Anna G. Trimble. She did her research project for the Denver Public Library back in 1932.

She wasn't able to track down the origin of all Denver street names, but she did establish the history of most of them. She learned that Annie Place was named after the wife of Dr. Hugo Brinkhaus, a prominent landowner at the turn of the century.

Baldwin Court was named after Ivy Baldwin, a daredevil balloonist and tightrope walker of the 1890s.

Batavia Place was named after the capital of Java by Baron Walter B. von Richthofen, the uncle of World War I's famous "Red Baron," Manfred von Richthofen.

Elizabeth Street got its name from Elizabeth Byers, wife of the founder of the Rocky Mountain News. The record isn't clear on Fillmore Street. Researchers believe it was named after either a pioneer, Maj. John S. Fillmore or President Millard Fillmore.

Hooker Street is interesting. It was named after Joseph Hooker, a Union general in the Civil War. Hooker's name lives in yet another context today. Prostitutes are called "hookers." It was the same Gen. Hooker who supplied men with paid sexual companionship during the Civil War. Since then, "hooker" has been a common name for a whore.

King says Denver put a stop to letting real estate developers name streets at the end of World War II. "It got too confusing," he said. "At one point we had 17 different Elm Streets."

King spends most of his time naming those little streets that turn up between established thoroughfares. "Courts run north and south and places run east and west," he said.

He always has been interested in Denver streets. King was born in Denver 61 years ago. "My father was in the U.S. Postal Service and used to have to sort mail by streets. I guess that's where it comes from," he said.

King admits it is difficult to trace the origin of some street names. Pearl is a good example. It appears to have been someone's first name. The last name has been forgotten.

As for Thrill Place, "I have no idea about that one," King said.

November 16, 1978

Wow chow

When Woody Paige told me the other day the last Rockybilt hamburger stand had been hauled away, I got to wondering how many other delights were slipping into history. There ought to be a way to keep track.

Remember the dollar-size cinnamon rolls at the Golden Lantern restaurant on Broadway? That's the kind of thing I mean. Those rolls came in little wicker baskets. They were mixed in with plump parkerhouse rolls and bran muffins, which weren't so bad either.

Before the fast-food franchises automated chocolate milkshakes, there were two places in town that made the best malts and shakes. One was the Pencol Drug on East Colfax, and the other was at Clark's Drug Store in the old Albany Hotel on 17th Street.

When Clark's finally closed down, some of the ladies who worked behind the fountain went to work at University Park Drug, across East Evans from the DU campus. Joe Morgan's drug store on Downing Street and East Evans Avenue also made a dandy malt.

The infinite variety of pasta dishes at Natale Boggio's 18th and Broadway Rotisserie also ought to be mentioned. And wasn't that a nice little bar on the first floor of the Navarre? There was no better steak in town then the one Joe "Awful" Coffee served at his Ringside Lounge on lower 17th Street.

Remember Opal? She was a waitress at the Edelweiss on Glenarm Place. Opal took great pride in the intricate way she folded her floral print handerchief, pinned at the shoulder of her white uniform. She took personal charge of Leonard Cahn's "Dawn Patrol," a loose confederation of sports writers, broadcasters, gamblers and other misfits.

I always thought the best downtown sandwich shops were run by the Keables family. I went to the one on Stout Street. Harold Keables worked behind the counter in the summer. He taught at South High School the rest of the year. Keables was the best creative writing teacher anywhere.

I miss the old Sky Chef restaurant at the airport. It was fun to take the kids there on their birthdays and hear Tony Muro play "Happy

Birthday" on the Steinway grand as the waitress brought the cake with the sparkler on top to the table.

Getting back to Stout Street, who can forget Rosen's Delicatessen? I loved the beet horseradish and the salami and eggs. Great pastrami sandwiches and chicken soup with matzo balls.

My favorite downtown watering hole was Wade's Keg on 18th Street. It was a hangout for reporters. Herndon Davis had painted portraits of early day Denver journalists on the booths in the back. When the place was sold, the booths were torn out and burned. Tragic. Fortunately, some of Davis' other Fourth Estate portraiture remains at this writing on the walls of the basement poker room at the Denver Press Club.

Can't forget Shaner's. It was better before it expanded. Small, intimate, thick corned beef sandwiches. Neat place to split a martini with one of the Van Schaack secretaries. And what about the bar in Lad Felix's Mayflower Hotel on 17th Avenue? No, I didn't forget the Albany Bar.

The Beacon Supper Club? Willie Hartzell and Jerry Bakke tore up the joint every night with "When the Saints Go Marching In." There was a lot of the same kind of action at the Taylor Supper Club on the west side of town. Buddy Greene, Frankie Burg, Al Fike, Kenny Smith and organist Clyde Rogers.

There were so many more. Pell's Oyster House, Pagliacci's, the coffee shop at the Oxford Hotel, the Pick-A-Rib, the Rossonian in Five Points, the old Manhattan on Larimer Street, the malt shop at 38th Avenue and Federal Boulevard, Murphy's on South Broadway, Benny's Basement, the Blue Parrot Inn, Lund's Swedish pancake house, Harry Bramer's Bar, the Mozart on California Street.

Remember?

June 28, 1981

Let bygones be . . .

DUST TO DUST.

I said goodbye to the old 16th Street years ago. It must have been about the time those lovely concave display windows were torn out of the Gano-Downs store at 16th and Stout streets.

As I picked my way around construction barriers and excavation rubble Friday, I tried to remember 16th Street the way it was. I would stop now and then, close my eyes and attempt to conjure up an image of the Golden Eagle department store.

You could almost tell where you were by the smell. If it was perfume, it was the front entrance to Neusteters. There was always the pleasing aroma of freshly polished mahogany inside the dark and cool showrooms of the old American Furniture Co.

Do you remember how Woolworth's smelled like popcorn? There was the strong scent of medicine at the entrance to the Republic Building. Fontius, Florsheim and Thom McAn stores smelled of saddle soap and leather.

Sixteenth Street had its sounds, too. A stately procession of street cars clanged at every intersection. There were the soft chimes that signaled floor walkers at the Denver Dry and May Co. department stores. Traffic cops Mike Carroll and Dominic Crow whistled the signal changes on Stout and Champa streets.

The ornate Denver Theater marquee is just a memory now. So are the French beveled glass mirrors, the marble paneling and the crystal chandeliers.

Wrecking balls are smashing the entire 500 block on 16th Street into a parking lot. It is just as well. The Denver Theater has become a sleazy haven for porn movie addicts.

It seems like yesterday that, when the house lights dimmed at the Denver, there was the dramatic roll of timpani, and the Fred Schmidt orchestra would rise out of the pit for a 40-minute program of light classical music.

There were others. Donnelly James and his band, with Willie Hartzel and Janet Bible. Lee Forbstein left the Denver to be a highly successful motion picture composer and arranger. Ted Mack succeeded Major Edward Bowes as the bell-ringer on the "Amateur Hour." Remember Mary and Edna Dodd at the mighty Wurlitzer?

The Denver Theater opened Nov. 19, 1927, the year Charles Lindbergh made the first solo flight across the Atlantic. The Great Depression descended on America two years later.

The Denver played an important role during those years. It gave us a way to escape the hard times, even for just a couple of hours. We were able to walk away from the grimness of our lives and step into an ivory and rose world of make-believe.

We could forget the soup kitchens and hobo jungles as we walked by oil paintings into that magnificent, domed auditorium. The carpets were thick and the curtains were a heavy brocade.

The movies we saw were made of the same fantasy stuff. We saw Dick Powell and Ruby Keeler, Jeanette MacDonald and Nelson Eddy and Myrna Loy and William Powell. After just a little bit of time in the old Denver Theater, we were ready to go back out and take some more of the real world again.

I am not one of those who mourns the razing of the Denver Theater. There was no way it would ever be restored to what it was, or to what it once meant to our lives. That's also true of so much of the old 16th Street.

It had deteriorated so much in recent years. Some of the quality stores are still there, but so much of the street has gone over to tacky little places that seem to specialize in the shoddy.

The new 16th Street Mall won't solve any traffic or pollution problems, but it may give downtown a new lease on life. Maybe 16th Street can again become the place to be seen, to have fun and to make you feel you are close to Denver's heart.

June 15, 1981

Corina's carnival

NOSTALGIA.

The Trocadero Ballroom at Elitch Gardens in the 1950s. Errol Garner's record of "Misty" was a great favorite at Lande's on East Colfax. Remember those thick chocolate shakes at the Pencol Drug. And what a view from the Top of the Park at the Park Lane Hotel.

Lad Felix fixed up the bar at the old Mayflower Hotel and it was the place to be at 5 p.m. Shaner's? Of course, kosher dill sticks and the best pastrami sandwich in town.

That's the way it was for most of us. Those were the warm times. They were easy and comfortable and middle class. Ray Perkins was on KFEL. Malt shops and memories.

It wasn't that way for Corina Trujillo.

It was at the same time and in the same city, but she recalls another Denver. Her world was not 17th Street or Washington Park. It wasn't Capitol Hill or University Hills. It was Curtis Street.

"I arrived in Denver in November of 1950 from Trinidad. I was just 16 and really very innocent," she writes. When you haven't seen much of the world but Trinidad, Curtis Street in Denver can seem almost like a dream.

"The carnival only came to Trinidad, Colo., once a year. But Curtis Street was like that every day." It was exciting for Corina. There were arcades, theaters and neon signs. The clear, sharp sound of Raphael Mendez's trumpet could be heard from almost every juke box.

"The movies and lights made a square, little 16-year-old girl feel like she was in the most exciting place in the world. I don't like living in the past. But I do really miss those times."

People seemed different then. They felt better about themselves. There wasn't as much fear. That's the way it seemed to Corina. "I was not afraid to walk anywhere then. In those days a young hick was safe on the streets.

"Everybody seemed happy. I know I was. There were so many interesting people and I met a lot of them. I was a waitress in all the different 'Coney Island' places along Curtis Street. I even worked for old 'George the Chinaman.' He owned a cafe across the street from the old Post Office garage at 19th and Champa. Remember?"

Sure they were happy days. The truckers used to hang out at the Milwaukee Tavern at 19th and Curtis. There was the Paris Inn at 19th and Lawrence and Dikeou's candy store.

There were the winos, too. Corina and her friends shared Curtis and Larimer streets with them. You'd see them around the Gin Mill and the Fun House.

They'd shamble up and down Larimer and would gather at the Reverend Baber's Citizen's Mission at dusk. There was no tomorrow for them. Today was the bottom of a bottle of 69 cent "muscatoo."

The cops would try to get them off the streets by dark. Big Mike Carroll, the patrolman on Larimer Street, would sometimes buy a soup bone for them and send them under the Cherry Creek bridge to build a fire and make a pot of Mulligan stew.

Corina has some bitter memories too. "Believe me, I was used and misused. I was only 18 when I got married the first time. I thought I knew everything. I had a head full of knowledge, but it was all about the hep people.

"I am just sorry I was a dropout at school. I wanted so much to be a writer. I was young. Those were happy days for me, though. But I sure was a worry to my mom."

Life has become steadier over the years. Corina met her present husband in 1956. Curtis Street means a great deal to him, too. "He is a real Denverite. My husband was born at home and his own father delivered him. It was at 2442 Curtis."

They both remember how good the Mexican food was at the old La Bonita on Larimer Street. They haven't forgotten the laughter and the fun.

Corina's Curtis Street is no more. It has been bulldozed away. The neon lights are gone. So are the juke boxes, the old Rialto Theater and the El Paso del Norte.

Her memories are common to many. They are a warm and poignant part of this city's heritage.

January 24, 1979

How could I forget?

Nostalgia II.

The vegetable wagons had awnings on top and canvas side curtains that rolled up. They traveled up and down Denver alleys back in the '30s. You always knew they were near when the old Italian vendor would sing out across the neighborhood, "Veg-a-ta-bules!"

Displayed in the back of the wagons were neat rows of sweet corn ears, green beans, fresh picked tomatoes, chard, unshelled peas and bunches of green onions. The old horse at the front of the wagon would whip his tail at the flies while the man at the back would weigh what had been purchased.

That beautiful produce came from truck farms in Adams County. They aren't there any more. Denver just sprawled out and those neat, little farms got themselves all covered up by asphalt, warehouses and progress.

A yearning for the past probably afflicts those of us who aren't all that happy with the present and who are apprehensive about the future.

That's what nostalgia is about, although the definition of the word has changed over the years. But then, what hasn't?

Judging from the number of calls and letters about Wednesday's column, there's no small amount of interest in Denver when it was smaller and cleaner.

I keep forgetting this because I have been around here so long. The past somehow gets all squished into the present and I have difficulty keeping the two apart.

For example, I thought everybody knew about Joe "Awful" Coffee. But then I guess there is a whole generation of people who have come along since he closed his Ringside Lounge on lower 17th Street.

Joe had been a professional fighter and his smashed-in face showed it. He was small and muscular and he never stopped talking. When you went into his restaurant, Joe would sometimes meet you at the door and would spar with you all the way to your table.

The booths had boxing ring ropes at the tops of them. The wall was covered with autographed glossy pictures of the likes of Jack Dempsey, Gene Tunney and Primo Carnera.

Visiting celebrities ate there. Impresario Arthur Oberfelder used to bring in ballet dancers, opera stars and actresses. Joe would jump on their tables and sing his own curious and off-key version of "O sole mio."

Metropolitan Opera bass-baritone Jerome Hines was a great friend of Coffee's. Early one morning he called Joe from Stapleton Airport. Joe was asleep. Hines insisted he get dressed and come immediately to the terminal building.

Sure enough, Hines was waiting at the main entrance. There was no missing him. He was a mountain of a man. Without a word, Hines scooped up little Joe, cradled him in his arms like a baby and sang in his thunderous voice, "La donna e mobile."

That's class.

As you might have guessed. Joe called and wondered why he wasn't mentioned in that column about the lower downtown Denver that isn't anymore.

He says those old pictures from his restaurant are packed away in his garage. "I don't know what I'll ever do with them," he said somewhat wistfully.

Joe is philosophical about change. "It's different down there now. A lot of new people. Young people. I like 'em. New ideas. But it is different," he said.

No question about that. There's a lot more concrete. More parking lots. More tall buildings. That's for sure. But there's no Ringside Lounge now.

It would be nice to walk into a restaurant on 17th Street and have some little banty rooster of a man in a double-breasted suit run up to you and start shadow boxing. Maybe dance with a waitress in the aisle.

Forgive me, Joe. How could I forget?

January 26, 1979

Red-letter day

MEET ME AT KIDDYLAND.

If we're going to Elitch Gardens Amusement Park, I'll be hanging out with the little tykes. They're more fun. And the Kiddyland rides aren't so scary.

In raising four children, ages 9 to 25, I have been a fairly steady customer at Elitch's over the years. There is no accounting of the number of times I have gasped and lurched my way over Elitch's two roller coaster rides. One is called the Wildcat. The other is known as the Twister. Or is it the Whiplash? No matter.

It doesn't matter because I will never have to ride on them again. You see, this last week we had a real red-letter day. It was Thursday, July 27, to be precise. That was the day that Susan, the youngest of the Amole offspring, learned that she was old enough and tall enough to go on any of the Elitch rides without Daddy.

Whoop-dee-doo!

Do you have any idea what this means? No more Tilt-O-Whirl or Calypso. I have been slammed into for the last time by those careening bumper cars. Goodbye to Round-Up and Sky-Ride. Farewell to Spider and the Haunted House.

July 27, 1978.

I have given it its own paragraph. Deservedly so. It is a date of great importance. It belongs up there with those very special times. It is certainly the equal of a first kiss. It ranks with either a simple confirmation or a very expensive bar mitzvah. It may even be as important as that historic moment when the principal finally exceeds the interest on one's house payment. It's that significant.

A confession. Actually, I never liked the rides at Elitch's. Even as a kid, I hated them. No offense intended. Elitch Gardens is a marvelous place. It is clean, well run, attractive. It is a fine summer theater, or "theatre," as they spell it. As amusement parks go, Elitch's is one of the very best.

I am the one who is wrong. People come from all over to go to Elitch's. They wait in line to go on those rides. They profess great pleasure at being tumbled about in whirling, speeding contraptions. Not this kid.

When I was a little boy, I used to jump and dance around my parents and plead with them to let me go on the roller coaster. It was all a lie. I didn't want to go on the roller coaster then any more than I do now. If God had intended man to ride on a roller coaster, he would have been born with roller skates attached to his keester.

My very worst amusement park experience came during my senior year in high school. I was attracted to a charming brunette classmate by the name of Virginia Belle Whelan. She had enormous brown eyes and her lightly perfumed hair was the color of mahogany. When she smiled, two tiny dimples formed just under the soft curve of her cheeks. Nice legs, too.

Anyhow, I had taken her to Elitch's. My expectations and hopes were high. It was senior night for our class and Dick Jurgens' orchestra was playing in the old Trocadero Ballroom. Wow!

Somehow in all of this, it became important that I take Virginia Belle on the Loop-O-Plane. Perhaps I was goaded into it by others in our party. I can't remember. In any event, it seemed to come down to a matter of my manhood. It is uncomfortable to have one's manhood questioned, particularly when in the company of someone like Virginia Belle. So, we got in the Loop-O-Plane.

You know what those things do. The arc gets greater and greater until finally the passengers (victims) go all the way around. That's the way it was with us. Then they stopped the thing while we were upside-down at the top. She was hanging like a Raggedy Ann doll from the seat belt, limp as could be. All the change in my pockets fell out, as did my car keys. I lost my rimless glasses. Everything.

Finally, they brought us down. I was too sick to help Virginia Belle. When we finally got out, I staggered over behind the Loop-O-Plane and pitched my cookies into the Elitch petunias.

We rode home in stony silence. At her front door, she was already putting up her hair and had her mouth full of bobby pins. Memories.

Hooray for July 27th.

July 30, 1978

'58 — a vintage year

A VERY GOOD YEAR.

It would be difficult to match the City Hall Christmas light display of 20 years ago. If there is such a thing as a vintage year of outdoor yule decor, it would have to be 1958.

In October, Mayor Will Nicholson announced that for the first time since 1919, there would be no Civic Center Christmas lights. There were legal entanglements when the city had drawn up its budget a year earlier.

City Auditor Tom Currigan had ruled that it would be illegal to spend any city funds for the traditional lighting. He was upheld by the courts, and it appeared that there would be no lights for Christmas.

Prodded by Rocky Mountain News columnist Pocky Marranzino, a civic group was formed to collect $10,000 in contributions to put up the lights and keep the tradition alive.

We were involved in something called Rush to the Rockies at the time. No one was quite sure what we were celebrating. There was the vague notion that it had something to do with either the beginning of Denver or the gold rush.

While the lights were going up, a Pioneer Village was built in Civic Center, just across Bannock Street from City Hall. It was supposed to look like the Denver of a century earlier. There were saloons, a bank, a general store and a stable. Make-believe gunfights were staged to lure Christmas shoppers downtown and away from suburban shopping centers.

That's not all. The Martin Co. put one of its Titan intercontinental ballistic missiles up in the middle of Civic Center. It was 90 feet tall and lighted from thrusters to dummy warhead.

Across Broadway, a ramshackle log cabin stood on the Capitol lawn. The structure had an uncertain heritage. Some claimed it was Colorado's first territorial legislative building. Others held to the view that it was a Chinese hand-laundry trucked up from Colorado Springs.

Now you have the picture. The Baby Jesus next to the City Hall steps. Santa Claus, Rudolph and the other reindeer were on the other side. Pioneer Village, the Titan ICBM and a Chinese hand-laundry. They were all wrapped up in a single, glittering cultural package.

The sound was interesting. Christmas carols piped over the public address system were often punctuated by gunfire as the sheriff and the bad guys shot it out in Pioneer Village.

All of this was watched with great interest by members of the Cactus Club, a Denver eating and drinking society. There was something missing, they concluded. There was no privy behind the log cabin.

They waited until Feb. 21, 1959, to make their move. At midnight, they unloaded a privy they had purchased for $45 from Louisville coal miner Chick LeFebre.

The 40 Cactus Clubbers on hand for the dedication paid rapt attention to poet Thomas Hornsby Ferril. He had written a dedicatory ode honoring coal miners in general and LeFebre in particular. Part of it said —

"So, salute the fervid Chick,
The man who brings into each soul,
The feeling of the warmth of coal,
And brings us also for our need,
Some little isolation from the day,
And gently pass our cares away."

Denver police were called, but they declined jurisdiction. The Sanitation Department was closed on Saturday. William H. McNichols Jr., private secretary to and brother of Gov. Steve McNichols, said the privy was not an official part of the Rush to the Rockies celebration. He said he was unaware of its existence until he looked out of the executive office window Saturday morning.

The privy disappeared sometime Saturday. No one in official circles would admit to knowing where it went or that it ever existed.

In reflection, one is left with the conclusion that the privy was really the only practical aspect of the display. The missile seemed to negate the Christmas idea of peace on Earth. Pioneer Village looked like a movie set.

If the log cabin was a historic building, it certainly would have had a privy out back.

Historical accuracy, to say the least.

December 11, 1978

A Bear market

THE BEARS.

I am thinking of forming a committee-of-one to keep Triple-A professional baseball in Denver. I got the idea from Gov. Richard D. Lamm's 70-member Colorado Pro Sports Committee.

The initial goal of Lamm's group is to help the Denver Nuggets and the Colorado Rockies sell enough season tickets to keep the teams in Denver. My plan is to develop a strategy to keep the Bears in the minor leagues.

Lamm is convinced we are in danger of losing the Nuggets and the Rockies because of their shaky financial conditions. "Their owners are in deep trouble," he said. "It's important for the whole ambiance of the state to have these teams. We want to articulate to everyone just how important these teams are."

Being in the articulation game myself, I am interested in creating a baseball ambiance in which the spectators can still identify with the players and, at the same time, afford to go to the games. This can't be done in the major leagues of any sport.

Money is lavished on outsized jocks to stuff, slam, run, throw, hit and otherwise perform physical skills with monotonous efficiency. Anyone looking for a folk athlete hero these days can't find one for less than $1 million a year.

In the economic crunch of things, the fans are finding it tougher to support their high-living superjock heroes. It is open to serious question whether perpetuating the system is a proper matter for civic concern.

But I suppose the constantly escalating cost of pro sports should find its own ceiling. If a community is unwilling to pay outrageous ticket prices, let the franchise owners and players take their chances elsewhere.

In sports, as in all other career pursuits, there are trade-offs. There must be a little pleasure in the game itself. That should be worth something. Not many of us can slam-dunk a basket in the last second of play to win the game. As Gypsy Rose Lee once said, "The sound of applause is delicious."

Jocks certainly have a right to as much money as the traffic will bear, but the luster of franchise ownership is no longer shining so brightly for fat cat owners such as the disenchanted Peter Gilbert, owner of the Colorado Rockies.

As for Triple-A baseball, it is still possible in this town to watch the Bears play for as little as a $3 general admission ticket. Top price is $4.50 for a press-level box seat. That leaves enough money for peanuts, hot dogs and beer. Try that with any other pro sporting event in town.

And from my admittedly narrow perspective, baseball has more to do with the American character than all other sports combined. It is, in fact, the game of life. And in the Bears' 1982 schedule, Triple-A baseball is clearly a great sports bargain.

Dick Conway, a cab driver I once knew, put it so much more eloquently:

"And so it is that when men, now grown up, gather to discuss outfielders and team standings and RBIs, their conversation is not so boring, nor so inane, as their wives believe. For they speak a secret language. Like men who have all once been lovers of an ineffably beautiful woman, now faded with time, they speak, not to each other, but in order for each to recall truly the haunting mistress of his youth."

April 8, 1982

Opportunity to learn

GANDY DANCERS.

They were the section hands who laid railroad tracks across the West. The name came from their rhythmic movements as they worked with tools produced by the old Gandy Manufacturing Co. of Chicago.

The company is gone now, but gandy dancers are still out on the Plains. The need for them has sharply increased in recent years because of the energy crisis.

Ladell M. "Butch" Thomas, administrator of Emily Griffith Opportunity School, explained in an interview that 800 section hands have been trained in Denver just during the past 18 months. "Burlington Northern asked us to set up the program. Their tracks are wearing out rapidly because they are hauling so darn much coal."

Thomas said Opportunity School was able to train and have each class on the job in two days. "Most of these people were totally unemployed. A lot were drifters and wanderers. Some of them didn't even have an address. After two days here, they were out earning $7.50 an hour. And that was on top of their subsistence, if they were out on the road. That's not too bad, considering they had absolutely nothing at all when they came in our door."

It isn't just the down-and-outer who studies "Introduction to Gandy Dancing." Thomas said college students are taking the course as a way to get summer employment and save money for school. "It is also a good way for them to get in shape," he said.

Founded in 1916, Opportunity School has given vocational training to more than 1.25 million students. There are now more than 800 instructors in the program at the main building downtown and at the 130 satellite locations. Thomas estimated that there are about 35,000 students enrolled in one or more of the school's 350 courses each year.

"It's strange," Thomas said, "but we are better known around the world than right here in town. A week doesn't pass but what vocational educators from other parts of the nation and other countries come to study what we do. And yet there are people right here who don't know what a valuable educational resource is available to them, and at no charge, if they live in the city and county of Denver."

At a time when the quality of public education is being questioned, and public school enrollment in Denver and other major cities is declining, there are waiting lists for many of Opportunity School's courses. Free training programs are available for everything from licensed practical nursing and certified aircraft mechanics to basic interior design and computer programming.

"Our programs are constantly changing to meet the needs of the job market," Thomas said. "We pride ourselves in that, and also at how succcessful we are in placing our students either in new, higher paying jobs, or in helping them upgrade their skills to get promoted where they already work."

Opportunity School students, unlike community college students, can gain immediate entry into training programs. They don't have to wait for semester or quarter breaks. They also aren't required to take courses unrelated to their vocational education. The time spent in training averages nine months compared to the two-year associate degree programs in community colleges.

Opportunity School still maintains its adult high school and general education equivalent programs, as well as the many avocational courses that cover everything from Oriental cookery to landscape and indoor gardening.

The average age of Opportunity students is 27. Racially, they are about equally divided between Anglo, Chicano and black, although more and more Southeast Asian refugees are entering the programs.

Quote: *"Honey, there's all tomorrow that ain't been touched yet."* — An old black woman, quoted by Emily Griffith.

March 29, 1981

Mountain tribe stood up to Zeus

REUNION.

Leaders of the strangest political coalition in Colorado history gather Wednesday afternoon at the Governor's Mansion to remember the summer of '72. They will talk about how they kicked the establishment in the pants and helped kill ambitious plans to hold the 1976 Winter Olympics in Colorado.

Viewed a decade later, it seems almost impossible that a ragtag band of environmentalists, hippies, liberal Democrats, war protesters and conservative Republicans could take on the power structure and win. But win it they did, and the stage was set for profound political change.

It began innocently enough in 1968 when Denver business and civic leaders formed the Denver Olympics Committee. Its initial bulletin stated in fine chamber-of-commerce style, "Denver, Colorado, capital of 'Ski Country U.S.A.,' nestled near the snowy spine of North America's Rocky Mountains, is bidding for international greatness as the U.S. candidate for the XII Winter Olympic games in 1976."

The campaign was a success, and the International Olympics Committee designated Denver the host city. Whoop-dee-do! There is nothing this town likes better than recognition. We were tired of being the best whatever between Kansas City and the West Coast. We wanted the big time.

At first, you couldn't find anyone against the idea. Gov. John Love and Mayor William H. McNichols Jr. were for it. So were bankers, businessmen, labor leaders and politicians. A shoo-in.

But then projected costs began to escalate. Poor planning of events surfaced. State and local programs were threatened by diversion of funds to Olympics facilities. Environmental dangers were posed. The games were seen as triggering unnatural population growth.

For the record, the first organization formed to oppose Olympics planning was POME, an acronym for "Protect Our Mountain Environment." It was headed by Vance Dittman, a retired Indian Hills law professor. He didn't believe the Evergreen area would have enough snow to support cross-country ski competition. International Olympics Committee President Avery Brundage would later comment, "Now we know why they call it Evergreen."

The bubble burst in November 1972 when Coloradans vetoed state spending for the games by a whopping margin of 178,534 votes. It was the first time any place in the world had spurned an Olympics bid.

In the process of rejecting "international greatness," Colorado voters chose new political leadership. The anti-Olympics fallout ended the political career of Sen. Gordon Allott, R-Colo. Rep. Patricia Schroeder, D-Colo., won her first term with the help of anti-Olympics forces.

Two years later, Richard D. Lamm, a leader in the movement, was elected governor. In the same election, Gary Hart, another vocal games opponent, unseated veteran Sen. Peter Dominick, R-Colo.

The Winter Games were moved to Innsbruck, Austria, and when they finally opened in February 1976, we all watched on television.

August 8, 1982

I tell you what I'm gonna do

FOOLPROOF.

I'm working on a scam that is going to put me on Easy Street. If you want to shake down the public, there is no better place than Denver.

Oh sure, I'll probably get caught. It won't matter so long as I get plenty of pre-trial publicity. That way, they'll never be able to get an impartial jury. The trick is to con people in the open where everyone can watch.

Don't jump to conclusions. This column is not about William Riley, the real estate investment whiz accused of bilking 600 investors of some $6 million.

Not a bit of it. Wipe that out of your mind. Riley has pleaded not guilty to 10 counts of securities fraud and one of conspiracy. I prefer to think of him that way — as clean and pure as the driven snow.

Unfortunately, Riley's dealings have become such common knowledge that his trial will be moved from Denver to a community where he is not known. They might try St. Petersburg, Fla., where he was arrested June 25, practicing his skills under another name. In St. Petersburg, no one knows William Riley.

Denver has proved to be a profitable city for the creative, ah ... let us say, entrepreneur. Perhaps it is something about the water, lack of oxygen in the air, gullibility of our citizens. Or maybe there is an uncommon number of us just crooked enough to want to get in on the larceny.

The daddy of them all was Jefferson Randolph "Soapy" Smith. He practiced sleight-of-hand chicanery on Denver street corners before the turn of the century. Smith sold bars of soap for $5 by suggesting some of them were wrapped with $100 bills, a version of the old walnut shell game.

"Cleanliness is next to godliness," Soapy would shout, "but crisp greenbacks in the pocket is paradise itself!"

Henry M. Blackmer, Denver financier, slipped away to Europe in 1924 to avoid testifying in the Teapot Dome oil scandals. He returned in 1940 to plead guilty of tax evasion. Blackmer, by the way, was the founder of Cherry Hills Village.

Hudson dealer Fred Ward was my favorite swindler. When his multimillion-dollar auto empire went kaput in 1951, it was revealed Ward had not only snookered the little guy on the street, but bankers, entertainment figures and highly placed members of Gov. Dan Thornton's staff.

Who could forget Silas W. Newton, inventor of a "doodlebug" oil-divining machine? It never located any oil, but it did find $50,000 of industrialist Herman Flader's money. Newton was convicted in 1954 when two Colorado School of Mines professors opened the device and found it empty.

Allen J. Lefferdink's scam was insurance. He told his investors in the 1960s, "When you reach for the stars, you don't come up with a handful of mud." They reached for their wallets and came up with $6 million for his 14 bogus corporations.

Oilman John M. King, once worth more than $600 million, was packed off to prison in 1976 after being convicted of euchring a Swiss-based mutual fund out of megabucks.

Quote: *We cheat the other guy and pass the savings on to you* — Soapy Smith.

July 8, 1982

'Twas a humdinger
to humble a human

BALONEY.

It is reassuring to learn our lives are not completely controlled by technology. And as the city digs out from our award-winning Blizzard of '82, we have learned once again there is a higher authority than the computer.

At least I haven't heard of anyone's car being dug out of a snowdrift by computer. Software technology was of no use in clearing Denver streets or getting Aunt Minnie to the airport.

The airport itself is usually a model of computer efficiency. Passenger agents use their winking terminals to route passengers through complex airline schedules. But it was all over when someone tried to fool Mother Nature.

In my capacity as co-owner of that plucky little radio station on top of Ruby Hill, I was particularly humbled by the blizzard experience. We are talking snow, Baby, I mean major-league snow!

When it became obvious Friday our night shift people couldn't get to work, I prevailed upon my friend, Danny Stubbs, to take me to the station in his four-wheel-drive pickup. I had filled a knapsack with cans of soup and sandwiches and had borrowed a slumber-party sleeping bag from my daughter.

Since the road into the station was impassable, Danny dropped me off on West Jewell Avenue to walk the rest of the way. I didn't know it then, but it would be 18 hours before I would be able to leave.

The snow wasn't falling. It was flying horizontally into my face. And as I started to climb the hill, I realized the drifts were up to my armpits. I repeatedly stumbled and fell, taking note each time that the snow was getting deeper. It was difficult to get up because there was nothing to hold on to. The minute I fell, I would instantly be covered with snow and would lose my bearings.

I wasn't exactly panicked. What kind of story would be in the paper after they had discovered my frozen corpse?

"Searchers found the body of elderly disc jockey Gene Amole Sunday on the snow-swept slopes of Ruby Hill. He was in a fetal position and was clutching a can of Campbell's Chunky Bean soup and a slumber-party sleeping bag."

But it wasn't time for my obituary. I managed to wheeze into the station a short time later to join Jocko Samson for what would be a holiday broadcast marathon.

I tried several times to sleep on the floor, but it was no go.

Finally, I took a breakfast break at 6 a.m. Since I had overdosed on Santa cookies and other traditional yule sweets, I decided to eat one of the baloney sandwiches I had brought from home the day before. There wasn't anything to drink but a bottle of warm Chablis left over from an office party.

So there I sat with my stale sandwich and my warm wine. I snapped on a small black and white portable TV we keep at the station and watched "The Flintstones."

Ho! Ho!

December 28, 1982

Too late — too bad

PAPA'S PAPER.

That's the way Helen Bonfils always referred to The Denver Post. It was her father, Frederick G. Bonfils, who, along with Harry Tammen, founded the Post on Oct. 28, 1895.

The flamboyant Bonfils died Feb. 2, 1933. Miss Helen, as she was known to Post staffers, immediately assumed management of the newspaper. As she did, she said, "Papa's spirit directs the Denver Post today just as much as it did when he was sitting right here."

Papa's spirit no longer directs the Denver Post. Neither does Miss Helen's. It has been eight years since she died. The city wonders what kind of spirit guides the Post now.

The Post is being sold. Its financial affairs are hoplelessly entangled with taxpayer money. Publisher Donald Seawell has compromised the Post's integrity by involving it directly in the events it is supposed to be chronicling.

People who have lived in this town for a long time wonder what Miss Helen would think of recent events. Would she have wanted the Post sold to save the foundering Denver Center arts complex?

How would Miss Helen feel about that threat to evict the Denver

Symphony Orchestra from the concert hall that was built for it? And how would she react to the despair so many Post employees now feel about the newspaper they love?

"If she knew what was happening to the Denver Post now, she would turn over in her grave." That's the view of someone who was close to her until the day she died.

Choosing not to be identified, the friend also said, "The newspaper was her first love. The theater came next. Miss Helen often told me that she would never sell the paper."

She liked to remember "playing actress" during her childhood days at the Bonfils Mansion, 1500 E. 10th Ave. She made theatrical sets from boxes, cheesecloth and pieces of "Papa's paper."

In later life, Miss Helen became an actress and producer. Her friend remembered, "She was in her glory when she was around theater people. They seemed to stimulate her — make her laugh and be happy."

She married director George Somnes in 1934. He died in 1956. Three years later, Miss Helen married Edward "Tiger Mike" Davis, a flamboyant oil wildcatter. That marriage ended in divorce in 1971. Davis had been hired by Somnes years earlier as Miss Helen's chauffeur.

During those years, she became a successful Broadway producer. Among her successes were the highly acclaimed. "A Thurber Carnival," "The Affair," "Enter Laughing," "The Killing of Sister George," "The Hollow Crown," "The Pleasure of His Company" and "Slow Dance on the Burial Ground."

As she grew older, Miss Helen's health failed. She was a diabetic. "The only thing she really enjoyed was a piece of divinity fudge," her friend remembered, "but she couldn't have it."

It was during this period that Seawell, a producer she had met in New York, began to assume greater control over the Post.

The year before she died, she signed documents in her hospital room that made Seawell president and treasurer of the corporation. At her death, he assumed complete control, even though he was not a journalist.

Recalling that period, Miss Helen's friend said, "I think she knew before she died that when she made Seawell president, she had made a wrong move. But it was then too late."

Too late and too bad.

August 7, 1980

In this community, our roots are deep

LATE SNOW.

It was the spring of 1859, as stormy as our spring of 1983. Heavy wet snowflakes had fallen almost all of April 22 on tiny Auraria, Kansas Territory. "Not much of a town," historian Robert L. Perkin would write a century later in his "The First Hundred Years." "A raw little settlement far out in Indian country. An orphan huddle of cabins and nondescript shacks in the wilderness."

There was only one building in Auraria with glass windows — "Uncle Dick Wootton's Saloon," owned by Richens Lacy Wootton, frontiersman, gold seeker, trader. It was in his drinking establishment along Cherry Creek that Volume I, No. 1 of the Rocky Mountain News was printed on a Washington hand press.

The founding editor was William N. Byers, a young Omaha man who had written a guidebook for those who were heading for the gold diggings in Colorado. Although he was a temperate man, Byers told settlers to take along three gallons of brandy. "Intended for medicine," he explained.

Byers advised the pioneers: "Carry your principles with you; leave not your character at home, nor your Bible. You will need them both, and even grace from above, to protect you in a community whose god is Mammon, who are wild with excitement, and free from family restraints."

The community, of course, is what is now Denver. The frontier was exploding, and the trails, as Perkin wrote, "were black with men and animals and luminous with hope." The Rocky Mountain News was born in those times.

Like the rest, Byers came for gold and silver. He found neither. But he stayed because he sensed his newspaper was an important part of history and should chronicle the half-mad tumult of the times. The Rocky Mountain News has been doing just that since the wet April morning it was "baptized in snow water," just 124 years ago.

Our roots are deep in this town. And I suppose to some, the community's god is still Mammon, and the tumult is still half-mad.

But Denver today is not free from family restraints. All things considered, it remains one of the best places in the world to live and to raise a family.

Will the News be here for the next 124 years? Will there even be a Denver after the next century and a quarter? Will the Earth survive?

Around here we deal with immortality one day at a time, one edition at a time, one deadline at a time. There is one thing I am sure of, though. There will always be newspapers. And so long as there are, I can't imagine this city without the Rocky Mountain News.

It has its good days, its bad days, its in-between days. But let me tell you something, the old Rocky is the heart and soul of this town. If you want to know Denver, its story is written each day on these pages.

Byers would be pleased to know that the character and principles he cherished are intact.

Happy birthday to us.

April 24, 1983

3

LIFESTYLE, LIFE-STYLE

You bet your life

LIFESTYLE.

I have about had it with that word. No one just lives anymore. We all have a lifestyle. Livestyle? Lifestyles?

Doesn't matter. There are no hard and fast rules for made-up words. The best definition I have found comes from the Harper Dictionary of Contemporary Usage. Lifestyle means "the overall pattern of one's attitude and conduct."

There are three ways of writing the word. It can be written solid. Lifestyle. That's the way we do it at the Rocky Mountain News. Some, however, write it as two words. Life style. The New York Times, Harper's and Webster's New World hyphenate it. Life-style.

The Harper people explain, "When it is written solid, the meaning is not so readily recognizable. Writing it as two words somehow seems to destroy the 'oneness' of its meaning."

Harper's then smugly declares, "The New York Times prefers the hyphenated form and so do we." So there, too. Usually, no one argues with The New York Times in these matters. Its decisions are handed down on engraved stone tablets.

Well, we are not knuckling under to Harper's, Webster, or even The New York Times. We are going to continue to zip it out in the same guiltless fashion as we used to say, "YourmotherwearsGI-shoes."

But back to the original point. While the dictionary definition suggests the word describes a general way of getting through the day, most people understand it quite differently.

When I hear the word, I visualize a bunch of 28-year-old pretty people. They live in what they call "condos," and they rub suntan oil on each other's backs while around the swimming pool. They go cross-country skiing together, drink white wine, play footsy in a hot tub.

There are minor variations on this theme. If they happen to live near the ocean, you'll find them baking clams and watching the sunset. Out here in the wide and wonderful West, they are astride horses or climbing mountains.

Rarely do we ever see these people at work. Fleeting TV images show them just leaving the office for a night on the town. Whatever they do for a living, they must do pretty well at it.

You don't see that bunch huddled on a street corner waiting for the RTD. They don't push carts with flat wheels through supermarkets. They don't brown-bag it at lunch time.

They laugh, enjoy each other's company, drive Japanese "Z" cars, play tennis and drink a lot of Michelob on weekends.

It probably isn't fair to characterize a bunch of empty-headed pub-crawlers as the only ones who have a lifestyle. You can't keep something that good to yourself. Word gets around.

As expected, the sociologists have latched onto it. They know a good made-up word when they see one. Actually, behavioral scientists of all kinds take a back seat to no one when it comes to making up words. You will remember they were the ones who gave us "parenting."

They also taught us how to "prioritize" and to "conceptualize." This kind of language is very contagious. It quickly spreads and "impacts" on the bureaucracy. Then we have an epidemic on our hands.

Sociologists, being the creative "human relationists" they are, plunge ahead and give us new meaning. We now have "alternative lifestyles."

That apparently means we all don't have to hang around fern bars, happily talking of raquetball and the newest yogurt flavors. We have choices.

As seen from the sociological perspective, an alternative lifestyle might be engaging in a *menage a trois* relationship. It could be an experiment in communal living and doing work in the fiber crafts. Or it might be something as simple as packing off with the Gypsies.

Whatever a lifestyle is, it apparently isn't staying home and taking care of the kids.

December 30, 1980

That snobby bouquet

MIXING METAPHORS.

Tell the barkeep you want "a strong, bold trumpet call." If he has any sophistication at all, he'll uncork a bottle of Chateau Mission-Haut Brion.

It is more likely that he will say, "Look Buddy, the only music we got in here is on the juke box." He then might suggest that you are not playing with a full deck.

Better you should just ask for a glass of red wine and he'll probably pour you a shot of Gallo's Hearty Burgundy. Most people wouldn't know the difference anyhow.

It is true that wine is increasing in popularity, not only as a beverage to accompany meals, but also as a drink to round off the sharper edges of a particularly trying day.

It apparently isn't enough just to drink the stuff and get a nice little buzz. It also is important to learn how to talk about wine.

Mixing one's drinks may be poor judgment, but mixing metaphors is OK, so long as one is writing poetry or describing wine and cheese.

It just doesn't make it these days to say. "Gee, that tasted good. Lemme have another glass of that stuff."

It is much better to swirl the wine around in the glass for moment. Pause to experience the aroma. Take a small sip. Hold the wine in the mouth for a few seconds. Let it slide past the palate. Wait for the aftertaste.

Then it is proper to speak. Say, "I am amused at this little wine. It is really quite witty, almost impertinent. Hit me again."

The idea is to use words not normally associated with somethng that is liquid. Wine snobbery demands creative use of language.

It isn't necessary that descriptions of wine always are in agreement. Take Chateau Margaux, for example. Gourmet magazine decribed it as "tight-bound springs."

Depending upon how one relates to the term "tight-bound springs," the senses of sight, touch and sound can be involved. Boingg!

The same wine, Chateau Margaux, is described in the reference work, Wines of the World, as ". . . sweet to the end: ethereal, fascinating, perfect."

Oenologists (wine experts) really go bananas over Chateau Lafite-Rothschild. It is to wine what baseball slugger Reggie Jackson is to October.

Andre L. Simon, a noted French wine authority, took one sip of an 1864 Lafite and wrote, "It was incredibly good! Not merely alive but lively; ruby red, not pink; fairly sweet still; very smooth, gentle and charming, its bouquet discreet but intensely clean, without any trace of 'dead leaves' not objectionable in very old wines, but a warning that the end is at hand!"

Gourmet magazine didn't fool around with a bunch of semicolons when it reviewed Chateau Lafite-Rothschild. It simply described it as "a Mozart aria."

It is left to us to decide whether the reviewer had in mind *"Voi che sapete"* from "The Marriage of Figaro" or *"Batti, batti, o bel Masetto"* from "Don Giovanni."

People who like wine also like cheese. They go together. Sort of like beer and pretzels.

A wedge of properly aged Camembert can be described as having "an admirable stamina and just the proper balance." Brie cheese should neither be "frail" nor "robust." It ought to have a "cello" quality to it.

Cheeses, like wines, are changed by time. Liederkranz flavor varies according to age. It really changes from hour to hour. It takes an expert to know when the time is "right."

When Liederkranz is new the flavor is described as being "tenor." When the cheese if fully cured and the center is quite soft, the flavor is described as being more "baritone."

Quote: *"I have never tasted Liederkranz, although I have stepped into it from time to time."* — Grandpa John T. Wison.

June 20, 1979

A primal yawn

IN TOUCH.

People who are doing well in these times are not only the energy barons or the computer geniuses. They are also the ones who were on the ground floor of the self-improvement game. Teach people how to get in touch with their true feelings about anything, and the world is your oyster.

There are workshops, seminars and meetings. As Barbara Haddad Ryan reported in the News recently, it is now possible to major in meeting planning at Metropolitan State College. Her story conjured up images of students learning how to arrange pencils and yellow note pads on long tables, and how to put the proper number of ice cubes in Thermos decanters.

The well-known semanticist, S.I. Hayakawa, now a Republican senator from California, gained an international academic reputation for his treatise on meeting attendance. He emphasized the importance of how to listen instead of jumping up and spouting your own ideas.

Joe Weatherby, well-known art teacher at Wheat Ridge High School, has taken note of the increasing number of other self-improvement and "how to" books in print. There are some splendid mental health volumes on his reading list.

They include: "Whine Your Way to Alienation," "The Primal Shrug," "Guilt Without Sex," "Creative Suffering" and "Ego Gratification Through Violence." Weatherby's list also has such helpful parenting guides as "Molding Your Child's Behavior Through Guilt and Fear."

Taking the wholeness approach to well-being, Weatherby's library has a number of titles that relate to physical health and fitness. "Tap Dance Your Way to Social Ridicule" is an excellent example. Others include: "High Fiber Sex," "Bio-feedback and How to Stop It," "Creative Tooth Decay," "Understanding Nudity," "Optional Body Functions" and "Skate Your Way to Regularity."

English composer Benjamin Britten was fond of saying that the music he wrote was useful. Weatherby's reading list is not without volumes containing practical information as well. Under the heading of "Business/Career Opportunities" is a book entitled, "Tax Shelters for the Indigent." Others are: "How to Profit From Your Own Body," "I Made $100 in Real Estate," "Talking Good: How You Can Improve Speech and Get a Better Job" and "Looter's Guide to America's Cities."

"Home Economics: You Can Do It Yourself" is another category of books Weatherby claims is just jam-packed with functional data. There are plans for a dandy little weekend project in "How You Can Convert Your Family Room Into a Garage." "Sinus Drainage at Home," "What to Do With Your Conversation Pit," "How to Cultivate Viruses in Your Refrigerator" and "Christianity and the Art of RV Maintenance" are others.

These are high-technology times in which we live. It has become increasingly difficult to find gratification in work. The computer programmer rarely sees the fruits of his labor. The broadcaster's words are lost as soon as they are uttered. Today's newspaper becomes tomorrow's garbage wrap.

That is why arts and crafts have become so popular. Those whose work is in the abstract can find reward in the performance of the simplest physical acts. The hand-made art object is evidence of accomplishment.

"Self-Actualization Through Macrame" is one of the most popular fiber art books. Weatherby also recommends "Bonsai Your Pet" as another nice home project. "Cuticle Crafts" is another. "Mobiles and Collages With Fetishes" sounds fascinating. "Needlecraft for Junkies" is self-explanatory.

For those interested in travel, there is a handsomely illustrated volume entitled, "The Northern Detroit Guide to Bad Taste."

March 3, 1981

We, the enemy

CONFRONTATION.

When was it we started trying to solve our problems by confrontation? It must have been back in the 1960s. It got to be quite the thing for groups to hurl insults at each other as a means of expressing anger and frustration with the shortcomings of our system.

Out of this, the nation slipped into the politics of demonstration. Kent State, Watts and the 1968 Chicago Democratic National Convention erupted into death in the streets. John Kennedy, Robert Kennedy, Martin Luther King Jr. and George Wallace were stalked and shot down in ultimate confrontation.

As the language grew more strident, the violence increased. The confrontation became almost a kind of spectator sport. We watched in much the same perverse way that an audience observes a pornographic film. We were repelled by what we saw but were too fascinated by the action to turn away.

I have always felt there is an equation in these matters. As the confrontation escalates and the language become more harsh, the reason for the confrontation tends to be more obscure, regardless of the issue. Participants take an almost animal pleasure in their verbal jousting. People on the sidelines cheer them on.

We have had an entire generation emerge in this climate of confrontation. Compromise has given away to polarization. In so many cases, violence became a consequence of passive resistance. The idea of working together was discredited.

It was a gradual thing the way we embraced the belief that the way to get things done is to take to the streets, to block doorways, to climb fences, to confront authority. We even ennobled the act and made heroes of its leaders.

These thoughts jumbled through my mind as the first bulletin of the attempted assassination of Ronald Reagan came into our newsroom. As the reporters returned from lunch, the telephones started to ring, and our people began to piece together the story of John W. Hinckley Jr., the young Evergreen man who is the alleged gunman.

The story is not yet complete. As preoccupied as we are in these times with the behavioral sciences, it is very difficult to pinpoint motives in this kind of violence: What seems to be obvious often turns out to be something that is actually screening the darker reason.

I don't believe, however, that the adversary climate of these times can be ruled out as at least a contributing factor to what happened Monday in Washington. It is cheap and easy to blame the event on "society." That's a popular way of handling these matters. We talk of "society" as though it were some kind of external force, forgetting that society is really everyone.

Pogo, the late Walt Kelly's little cartoon characer, put it this way: "We have met the enemy, and they is us."

And so, if we are going to indict society, we are going to have to file charges against ourselves.

The gun will be blamed for the crime. But the gun is only an instrument by which man is able to extend his violence beyond his reach. In many ways, it is the weapon of the coward.

All of us will filter the information through our own prejudices, and we'll decide individually why Reagan was shot. We'll put ourselves at as much distance as possible from the crime.

The 1980 presidential election campaign was one of the dirtiest on record. Each side responded to the other's verbal barrages in kind. The public decried the mudslinging but secretly enjoyed it.

The residue of all this has not gone away. There is anger and frustration beneath our national surface, and they sometimes manifest themselves in outrageous individual behavior.

Is that what happened Monday in Washington? Was the use of that gun a logical next step from the violence of our language, our recent history of angry confrontation, our acceptance of angry conflict?

March 31, 1981

A closet Trekkie

LIVE LONG AND PROSPER.

That's exactly what it says on the little pink slip of paper. It is addressed to me and signed by Leonard Nimoy, the man who plays Spock.

The sentiment, of course, is the traditional Vulcan greeting. My autographed copy of it is the most important part of my "Star Trek" collection.

Unfortunately, I didn't get it from Nimoy personally. It was my daughter, Muffy, who met him and asked for the autograph.

It was several years ago. She was working as a hostess in a downtown Denver restaurant when Nimoy came in for dinner. He was in town to appear in a play about Sherlock Holmes.

Knowing of my addiction to the old "Star Trek" television reruns, Muffy decided to seize the moment. After seating Nimoy, she worked up her courage and popped the question.

"Mr. Nimoy," she ventured, "I wonder if I might ask a favor."

Nimoy flashed a smile and said, "Of course. What is it?"

Muffy remembers squirming a little bit when she asked, "Would you mind giving me your autograph?" She then explained hastily, "It's for my father."

As Muffy recalls the incident, there was a Spocklike arch to Nimoy's right eyebrow. He told her that parents often ask him for an autograph for their children. This, he said, was the very first time an offspring had requested his autograph for a parent.

I have lots of other things in my "Star Trek" collection. There are calendars from STAR-DATE 3150.10 to the present. I have a bound copy of the Star Fleet Technical Manual TM:379360.

Also in the collection is the complete set of 12 authentic blueprints of the U.S.S. Enterprise, Constitution Class. I have virtually everything one can have in a "Star Trek" collection, with the possible exception of pointed ears.

Goofy? Probably. I have been a closet Trekkie for years. I have seen all of the original TV "Star Trek" programs many times. I actually have memorized much of the dialogue.

My favorite is the one where Spock gets the seven-year itch. Vulcans, as any Trekkie knows, are able to mate only every seven years. If they don't, they go insane.

In that episode, Spock overcomes great difficulties, and with the help of Kirk and "Bones," manages to reach his home planet just in time. But when he gets there, he finds that not only does his wife have a headache, but a new pointed-ear boyfriend as well. Talk about frustration.

As you can imagine, when "Star Trek — The Motion Picture" came to town, I was down there standing in line with the rest of the kids. I saw it in one of those shopping center theaters with sticky floor and small screen. Didn't matter. I loved every minute of it.

The old gang was back together — Spock, Kirk, McCoy, Scotty and the rest. I didn't even mind the two newcomers to the crew, Commander Decker and Lila, a bald-headed celibate woman from one of the Delta planets.

The space hardware in the movie was much more sophisticated than in the TV series. The plot was typical "Star Trek," though. I did think that "V GER," the deadly probe at the center of the dark cloud, must have been a distant relative to "Nomad," an errant space vehicle in one of the TV episodes.

It is just as well they don't let me review movies around here. I don't go if they are about Vietnam, incest, nuclear power plants, divorce and all that other good stuff. For old shallow me, I get enough real life out of real life. "Star Trek" made me feel good.

So good, I set my phaser on "stun" the next day.

January 3, 1980

Coming out

BILLIE JEAN.

Saying she was acting against the advice of her lawyers, tennis star Billie Jean King acknowledged that she had a lesbian affair with her one-time secretary, Marilyn Barnett. Her admission came Friday at a Los Angeles press conference.

Barnett had filed a "palimony" suit against King a week ago, alleging that the tennis star had promised to take care of her financial needs for life. Standing beside Larry King, her huband of 19 years, King admitted the relationship but denied the promise.

She said she decided to make the announcement because "I've always been honest ... I've decided to talk with you as I've always talked — from the heart." She said she hoped her fans would "try to understand" the situation. Her biggest concern, she added, was for her family and friends.

If there is a positive side to this personal tragedy, it might well be in increased public enlightenment of the dynamics of homosexuality. While King represented only herself, she spoke for many others who are hoping for the same kind of compassion.

For some reason, male homosexuality is more acceptable behavior abroad than it is in the United States. We severely denounce it, often violently. Not so with female homosexuality. While it is condemned in other nations, we give it only token disapproval. In study after study of our culture, it is revealed that men feel more threatened by male homosexuality than women do by female homosexuality.

King has that going for her. But there is something more significant here. By making her admission, she becomes an example of something few people like to admit — that there are homosexual tendencies in most people.

There are many theories concerning the dynamics of homosexuality. Most of them center on heredity, environmental influences or an imbalance of sex hormones. Homosexuality, however, is neither a character disorder nor a patriotic deficiency, as many of the emerging religious moralists are preaching these days.

As I read King's admission, I was reminded of a soldier with whom I served during World War II. I'll call him "Bobby." He was a homosexual and one of the bravest men I ever knew.

Bobby had been raised by two maiden aunts in the South. He was very effeminate. Although he made no attempt to disguise his sexual preference, he never made so much as a single homosexual advance toward anyone in our unit.

He was accepted on his own terms much more quickly by his fellow enlisted men than by the officers. He was uncomplaining about all the dirty jobs he had to do. When we were finally committed to action in Normandy, Bobby was always given the most hazardous assignments.

I can't say that the officers were trying to get him killed. They probably felt that he was more expendable than the rest of us because he was "queer." But Bobby survived. He was wounded repeatedly and often recommended for decorations. At first, these requests were rejected.

I once heard a captain say, "No damned sissy in my outfit is going to get a medal." But Bobby's heroism triumphed. His exploits could not be denied. Before the war ended, he had won the Silver Star and several Bronze Stars. He deserved more. The last time I saw Bobby, he was on his way back to the life he had known before. I'll never forget his courage.

Billie Jean King has courage. She has her family and her husband's love. Like Bobby, she will survive and we shall honor her.

Quote: *Oh, Great Spirit. Grant that I may never find fault with my neighbor until I have walked the trail of life in his moccasins.* — Cherokee Indian prayer.

May 5, 1981

This winning thing

THE BLAME.

Ken Milano is being made the scapegoat for all of us. He is the Overland High School football coach who was suspended on grounds that he abused members of his team. The Cherry Creek school board will probably follow the recommendation of Superintendent Richard Koeppe that Milano be fired.

He should be, of course. There is little doubt that he forced a member of his team, Ben Warrington, to run through a gantlet of others players for breaking training rules. Warrington also charged he was punched by Milano.

Until the board acts on the dismissal recommendation at its Oct. 12 meeting, Milano is suspended with pay from all teaching and coaching duties. Koeppe ordered administrative actions be taken against other members of the coaching staff for permitting the violence.

Somewhere in all of this, it is hoped there will be some sort of realization that Milano, as well as Warrington, has become a victim of the sports system. That system, as the legendary Vince Lombardi once put it, is one in which "winning is not everything. It is the only thing."

Our devotion to victory comes early and stays late in life. It frequently supersedes reason and humanity. It exposes the worst in us, and it causes us to reach out and hurt those we love the most.

There are a lot of reasons for this. I discovered many of them during the years my sons were growing up and were participating in football and baseball programs. I let myself get involved to the point where I was operating a summer baseball league for 500 boys.

I came away from the experience with real doubt in my mind of whether the activity had been organized for the benefit of the boys or for their parents. After coping with the problems of organized athletics at that level, I concluded that our kids were acquiring a sick set of values from us.

Any doubt I had about this was dispelled the day a young pitcher told me he wanted to quit baseball. He explained that his coach, the father of one of the other boys on the team, had ordered him to throw at the head of a batter during a league game. The coach admitted it.

On another occasion, one of the coaches had to be physically restrained from attacking one of the boys on his own team. And I don't know how many times I have seen umpires spirited away from angry parents.

It is not fair to generalize, but I found many volunteer coaches were not there to teach skill and sportsmanship. They were rather using coaching to gratify a personal need to win. I became convinced that many of them were losers in life and were trying to compensate for personal failure by becoming winners in kid baseball.

A friend of mine was one of the most successful high school football coaches in the Denver Public Schools. At the peak of his career he had a nervous breakdown and had to quit coaching. He told me he couldn't handle parent pressure anymore.

He said it got to be too much when he had to meet with the fathers at Monday morning breakfasts. Films were shown of the previous Saturday's games, and he had to face a barrage of angry questions.

Another prominent high school coach complained to me not long ago that good athletes refuse to participate because they are burned out by the time they get to the 10th grade. They have been pushed too hard by their parents.

I thought of all this when Ken Milano was charged with abusing his players. In a way, he probably had come to believe he was doing what society expected him to do — win at any cost because winning "is the only thing."

An aberration? No. The Milano case says a great deal about all of us.

October 1, 1981

Breaking away

Exodus.

There is nothing so "over" as the ski season here in Aspen. The rich are departing by Learjet, and the poor are leaving by thumb.

It doesn't matter how much snow is left on "the mountain," the ski season ends Easter Sunday. In a town that is supposed to be so laid-back about so many things, Aspen is uncompromisingly rigid about its requiem for winter.

You could feel the impatience in the air all last week. "SALE" signs were in almost every store window. Casual wear and ski clothing were reduced an "honest" 50 percent.

Some of Aspen's merchants aren't so sure they'll be back next year. The attrition rate among shop owners is almost as high as the rent.

It hasn't been a good tourist year, and old Aspen hands are wondering if this one-time silver boomtown is losing some of its luster as a gathering place for the world's pretty people.

Sure, George Hamilton still touches up his suntan in Aspen's shorter lift lines. Barbara Mandrell, Jill St. John, Sonny Bono, Cher and Jack Nicholson were here this season.

But the Morgan Fairchilds, the Tom Sellecks, the Jaclyn Smiths and the other new-generation celebrities either don't know about Aspen, or they don't care.

The merchandising of Aspen will change somewhat next year. Lift-ticket prices wil be adjusted so that clubs may obtain group discounts. But it isn't likely fast-food franchises will pop up on South Galena Street. A McDonald's will be built in Glenwood Springs this summer, and Aspenites can't wait to drive 40 miles for a Big Mac.

There is sort of time-capsule quality about life in this never-never land. Nothing much changes, not even the mandatory bored expressions worn by waitresses.

Someone once said that without divorce, there would be no waitresses in Aspen. There is some truth to that. So many of them run here to escape from broken dreams.

As they serve rye toast and Bloody Marys for late Aspen breakfasts, they watch for Mr. Wonderful to come through the door.

But he won't. The fast-lane guys in the designer jeans and the short leather jackets are interested only in one-night stands, not cookie-cutter condos in the suburbs.

Hope may spring eternal, but youth does not. And for those who choose to stay yet another season, there will be deeper wrinkles and lonelier nights.

But on the last day of the season, there is not much thought of that. There will be the usual banter about "how drunk it was" last night. The Wienerstube will have its obligatory array of magnificent strawberry confectious.

The morning on the slopes will end at Bonnie's. The show-and-tell gathering starts there at 1 p.m. It's a time to size up prospects for the rest of the day.

The next stop is the Tippler at the bottom of the mountain. The action lasts from 4 p.m. until 6 p.m. Last chance for the unattached is at Andre's from 1 p.m. to 2 a.m.

And that's where hopes will either live or die.

Tomorrow is next year.

April 11, 1982

Home, apple pie and the Avon lady

APPLE PIE.

Let me tell you something. There is nothing better than coming home at night, opening the front door and being greeted by the aroma of home cooking. Makes a fella glad the day's work is over and dinner's on the table.

Happened the other night. Gee whiz, was I ever bushed! Not much had gone right that day. Nothing really big. Just a lot of small annoyances. So you can imagine how welcome the aroma of fresh apple pie was when I opened the front door.

I just stood there for a minute, closed my eyes and imagined what that wonderful pie looked like. I could tell it was a deep-dish beauty.

Lattice top, all right. Probably made with those tart, crisp little Jonathan apples just coming in the stores.

As I continued to savor the aroma, I could almost see that cinnamony apple syrup bubbling out over the golden, flaky crust. The pie was probably sitting on a wire cooling rack on the kitchen counter top. It was still warm, I could tell that.

Decision time. After dinner was over and I was ready to enjoy a wedge of pie, would I top it with a very sharp cheddar cheese? Maybe it would be better with a scoop of Haagen-Dazs vanilla ice cream. Ever watch melting vanilla ice cream swirl around apple slices? What the heck, I'll go for both the Haagen-Dazs and the cheddar.

"Trish! Trish! I'm home!"

"I gathered as much. Why don't you come on in and sit down instead of standing there in the door with your eyes closed."

"Gosh, Honey. I was anticipating the first taste of that beautiful apple pie that just came out of the oven. You know something? You are really some kind of gal. I mean that, Trish."

"What are you talking about?"

"It's the apple pie. That wonderful lattice-topped apple pie you baked for me."

"There is no apple pie."

"No apple pie?"

"No apple pie. What you smell is Avon's new 'Country Baker Apple Pie Room Scent.' The Avon lady brought it today. Like it?"

Ever see a man when all his hopes and dreams turn to ashes? His shoulders slump and the color drains from his face? His palms become sweaty, and great salty tears begin to streak down his cheeks? Ever see that?

"Oh," I managed to say.

I don't know why it is my wife doesn't like the natural smell of things. She is the world's No. 1 consumer of deodorants of all kinds. Open the door in the downtairs john and what do you smell? "Amber Lace." The front bedroom is "Fragrant Florabunda."

I can't be sure, but I think she may have even sprayed the garage with "Lemon Verbena." Not even my old dog, Yazzie, is safe. When the other pups come trotting up to him in the park to exchange whiffs, they get a snootful of "Hello Spring!" When they do, it's "Goodbye Yazzie."

Of course I know better than to say anything. But I am putting the Avon people on notice. If they come up with a room freshener called "Granny's Chicken and Dumplings," or one named "Hot Pot Roast and Gravy," I'm filing a class-action suit.

October 3, 1982

Unburdened at last: Updike's unbearable

SURRENDER.

I have been trying to read John Updike's books for 20 years. He has won every major literary award. His "Rabbit is Rich" is the first single work of fiction to win the American Book Award, the Pulitzer Prize and the National Book Critics Circle Award.

Like "Rabbit, Run" and "Rabbit Redux" that preceded it, "Rabbit is Rich" is the continuing story of Harry Angstrom, nicknamed "Rabbit" because of the way his upper lip curves over his two front teeth.

Updike follows Rabbit with meticulous detail from high school to middle age — from failure as a linotypist to inherited success as a Toyota dealer.

If Updike has omitted a single sensation, a tiniest detail, a smallest element in Rabbit's tawdry life, I can't imagine what it is. Strike that. I don't want to know what it is.

That's my problem with Updike. He gives me more detail than I want or need. His sentences are of interminable length. Example from "Rabbit Redux":

"The walls hold tinted photographs of himself and Mim in high school, taken he remembers by a pushy pudgy little blue-jawed crook who called himself a studio and weasled his way into the building every spring and made them line up in the auditorium and wet-comb their hair so their parents couldn't resist two weeks later letting them take in to the homeroom the money for an 8 by 10 tinted print and a sheet of wallet-sized grislies of themselves; now this crook by the somersault of time has become a donor of selves otherwise forever lost: Rabbit's skinny head pink in its translucent blond whiffle, his ears out from his head an inch, his eyes unreally blue as marbles, even his lower lids youthfully fleshy; and Miriam's face plump beneath the shoulder-length shampoo-shining sheaves rolled under in Rita Hayworth style, the scarlet tint of her lipstick pinned like a badge on the starched white of her face."

That is good writing because The New York Times, New York

Magazine, the Boston Globe, Newsweek, Time and other prestigious publications say it is.

We are all supposed to look at Rabbit and see ourselves. He peers back from the mirror and we behold what one critic called, "a symbol of mature, mellowed-out middle America."

Not this kid. When I look at Rabbit, I see a man preoccupied with every charmless bit of minutiae in American life. By comparison, James Joyce's Leopold Bloom is Little Merry Sunshine.

But I'm wrong, I must be. Perhaps it is a blind spot. I am uneducated, insensitive, lacking in intellect and perception, unable to concentrate, unappreciative of stream-of-consciousness writing, flat-out dumb.

I tried again last week to read John Updike. My legs twitched. I wanted to run out in the street and scream. For me, reading John Updike is like passing a kidney stone.

But at least I have been able to admit it. I am out of the closet. Think of me what you will. Take my name off your list of trendies. Call me a clod.

But, Pal, I feel better now.

March 13, 1983

If those spats fit, then wear them

SPATS?

I am glad to see Cottrell's is advertising men's hats again. "The Man's Store" is pushing a Stetson broad brim that can be worn downturn or regular. It is called "The Ark." It comes in fur felt and sells for $42.50.

When I was a punk kid and had plenty of hair, you couldn't get me to wear a hat in any kind of weather. I believed going hatless gave me an image of youthful bravura.

I remember one bitter December day when I ran into Nelson Hicks on Stout Street. He was president and general manager of Gano-Downs Co., that wonderful old department store next door to the radio station where I worked for $27.50 a week.

Hicks, a feisty old guy, was bundled against the cold. He peered out between the top of his muffler and the brim of his hat and shouted: "How come you don't have a hat on? Come on with me right now!"

He grabbed my arm, spun me around and pushed me through the Gano-Downs door. He marched me over to the hat department, went behind the counter and kept jamming hats on my head until he found one that fit. "Wear that!" he ordered. "Don't let me ever catch you without a hat again."

I learned later that Hicks had a thing about hats. Just couldn't stand to see a man not wearing one. He would stop strangers and give them the same treatment.

His concern for headwear was not confined to colder months. "Straw Hat Day," the ritual time when men switched from felt to straw hats in Denver years ago, ranked up there with Thanksgiving and Christmas, as important observances in Hicks' life.

"Five more days until Straw Hat Day!" he would shout as I walked along 16th Street. That meant I had better get my rear in the store and pick out a straw skimmer before the deadline.

If conventional men's hats are to be fashionable again, I hope bow ties can also make a comeback. There is something open and boyish about a man who wears a bow tie.

I prefer the thin, small-figured ties like my dad wore. Polka dots and small paisleys were my favorites. Some men prefer wider, square bows like the ones Ben Blackburn, our managing editor, fancies.

Playboy magazine recently published instructions on how to tie a bow, as did our Style section here at the News. Not much to it. Same as tying shoe laces.

I gave up wearing bow ties when the stores stopped selling them. I notice some of the older judges in our courts have stubbornly refused to give them up. NBC-TV correspondent Irving R. Levine still wears bows, as he did more than 30 years ago. Columnist George Will prefers short, stubby models.

We will have come full circle when spats come back. They were the pearl gray "ankle pants," as we called them, that men wore to cover their shoe tops. They were troublesome to put on, but they did keep the ankles warm, even though they tended to make the wearer look like Jiggs in the old cartoon strip.

Spats probably wouldn't go well with jeans, though.

March 29, 1983

Only in Boulder

PIZZA DELICTI.

Judge Marsha B. Yeager needed more than the wisdom of Solomon in the baffling case of the shrunken pizzas. In a recent Boulder County Court decision, she required the pizzas themselves.

The mystery began when Kent M. Keener ordered a 17-inch pizza from Dante's, a popular Boulder pizzeria that delivers. It ended in a dramatic court confrontation between Keener and Jay Carter, owner of Dante's.

Keener sought $100, alleging that two 17-inch pizzas he had purchased from Dante's really were only 14 inches. Dante's was guilty of fraudulent advertising, he charged.

Carter based his defense on the contention that his pizzas are sold by the size of the pan in which they are baked. He admitted that some shrinkage may occur during baking, but certainly not to 14 inches.

"And shrinkage I can see to a certain extent," Keener shot back, "but, I like checked out Domino's Pizza and their 16-inch is like 15 and three-quarters. It only shrunk a quarter of an inch. Their pizza went from a 17- to a 14-inch. And I don't believe that it is a 17-inch pizza and I think it's a fraud, myself."

Keener's case appeared at first to be a strong one. He submitted two pizza boxes as evidence. They were measured and found to be 15 inches across.

"To me that's fraud," Keener testified. "It's not a 17-inch pizza when it comes in a 15-inch box. When we measured it it was 14 inches, which means it shrunk more than three inches."

Keener said he called Dante's and reported the discrepancy. He was given credit of $2.90 on a second 17-inch pizza he ordered. Keener testified that it, too, was only 14 inches.

It was Carter's turn to testify. "If you have ever had a pizza, you know you cut it in slices and the slices can move in or out, and if the slices happened to be moved in, you could probably get 14 inches. But it's hard to measure the diameter after it's been sliced because it does shuffle a bit during the delivery process," he said.

"How could you get a 17-inch pizza into a 15-inch box?" questioned Judge Yeager.

"Well," answered Carter, "because when you cut the pizza and you close the ends in, the ends kind of curve up a little bit on the side of the box. The dough is actually still a little bit flexible.

"Basically, what it is, is that the pizza is a little bit squished into the box. It is still 17 inches — or, roughly, maybe 16 by the time it shrinks after cooking, and then the extra half inch is kind of absorbed as it kind of bends a little bit."

In a final statement, Keener said he was not questioning the quality of Dante's pizzas, only their size. "He must have rolled it up like a carpet to put it in there the way he is talking. If it was 17 inches, or even 16 inches, it wouldn't have fit in the box," he said.

After a short recess, Yeager handed down her decision. " ... the court is unable to tell by measuring the box how big the pizzas were, nor can I tell how big the pizzas are from other places — that is, 17-inch pizzas after they have been cooked."

She dismissed Keener's case, leaving open his option of refiling and submitting evidentiary pizza.

Deputy District Attorney Lawrence F. King commented, "This whole scenario is something that could only occur in Boulder, but in fact it probably just shows how litigious we've all become as we've become more aware of our rights as consumers."

One more point. Out of all of this, Keener did manage to get two pizzas, measuring somewhere between 14 and 17 inches for a total of $10.50.

That's not too shabby.

September 23, 1980

Hold the sprouts

VEGGIES.

That's a cutesy-poo word for vegetables. You see it on more and more menus these days, particularly at those Capitol Hill fern bars.

A fern bar is a place 28-year-old people go to eat, drink and, as Andy Griffith used to say, "adjust themselves around one another."

My experience with fern bars is somewhat limited. Peter Blake, one of our assistant city editors, took me to one the other night.

Peter's wife was out of town, and I didn't finish work in time to get home to dinner.

He didn't exactly take me. I met him there. We figured we'd have more flexibility by taking separate cars. Hang the energy crisis. Besides, some of us have to get to bed earlier than others.

The parking lot was filled with Datsuns. Small groups of young men were lounging around, laughing and talking. One bearded youth was standing by the door. He was swinging an imaginary tennis racket. I think he was working on his backhand.

I waited for the imaginary ball to go by before I stepped inside. Peter hadn't arrived. I tried to be as casual as I could, athletically shifting my weight from one foot to the other.

No one paid the slightest attention to me. I was just beginning to feel like the bastard at a family reunion when Peter finally arrived. It was a good thing he did. Another two minutes and I was going to get the heck out of there.

Peter told me to follow him. He pushed through the crowd and found a table that had just been emptied. The waitress was wearing a tight Danskin top and a denim skirt.

"Hello," she said brightly. "My name is Sunshine. I'll be with you in a minute."

I think that's what she said. I couldn't be sure because of the music. We were right under a loudspeaker. Loud it was, too, and it wasn't the Ink Spots. It was a tape of a rock group called Electric Grandmother. It was made up of three guitars and a 105mm howitzer.

Sunshine did indeed return in a minute. She gave us our menus. I don't remember what Peter ordered. I think it was a granolaburger with sprouts. I had the filet of sole. The veggies were chopped zucchini, garbanzo beans and sprouts. You get sprouts with everything. I wondered whatever happened to corn on the cob and string beans with bacon.

Everyone seemed to know everyone else. People drifted by our table and stopped to talk for awhile. John Ashton, one of our feature writers, sat down for a couple of minutes.

I have no idea what anyone said. It was the music and an old problem I have from hearing too many mortar shells. When people seemed to be speaking to me, I would smile, nod and sometimes chuckle. When asked a direct question, I would mutter knowingly, "My uncle died in the bathtub this morning."

I learned to do that years ago at weddings. In passing the reception line, I would smile and use that line when introduced to the bridesmaids and ushers. It's a good, durable sentence. You might want to try it the next time you are at a wedding or in a fern bar.

I made my way through about half my veggies and sole when I decided to return to my home in sophisticated Bear Valley. Just as I was leaving, a reporter from the Denver Post showed up. He and Peter are friends.

I left a lavish tip for Sunshine, hoping that she would overlook the fact that I didn't finish my veggies and that I was not precisely 28 years old. As I was going out the front door, I ran into Tim McGovern from our paper. He seemed surprised to see me.

"What the hell are you doing here?"

"My uncle died in the bathtub this morning," I said.

October 14, 1980

Un-Raveling 'Bolero'

"BOLERO."

In the motion picture "10," Dudley Moore copes with his midlife crisis by chasing Bo Derek to Mexico. The pursuit ends in her bed.

For some activities, Bo explains, she prefers the accompaniment of music by Prokofiev. But when it comes to making love, she wants to hear a recording of Maurice Ravel's "Bolero."

Since "10" has become popular, classical music radio stations around the country have been deluged with requests to play "Bolero." Many of them come in late at night, and quite a few are received during the early morning hours.

A surprising number of people want to hear "Bolero" at noontime. Needless to say, the composition has been a runaway best seller in record stores.

For whatever else may be said of it, "Bolero" has become to sex what Rossini's "William Tell Overture" is to the masked Lone Ranger and his "Hi Yo Silver! Away!"

If Ravel were alive today, he would be surprised at the success of his simple one-finger melody. The entire composition is constructed from the most meager of materials.

He referred to it as "the longest orchestral crescendo ever written." There are two 16-bar phrases, played at the beginning by the flute and joined gradually by the other instruments.

If "Bolero" has a quality of hypnosis about it, it is because it is played mostly in the key of C major. It lurches briefly near the end into E major, only to return again to C major at the strident close.

Ravel was never very fond of the piece. He told a friend that "Bolero" consisted wholly of "orchestral tissue without music." He said the themes were "altogether impersonal" and he left it to the listeners "to take it or leave it."

It was really an accident that Ravel composed "Bolero." The dancer, Ida Rubinstein, had commissioned him to orchestrate "Iberia" by Isaac Albeniz for a ballet performance she was to make at the Paris Opera.

As he was beginning his work, Ravel was told that Enrique Arbos, a Spanish musician, had tied up the copyright on "Iberia."

"Who the hell is this Arbos anyway?" Ravel demanded, "And what am I to say to Ida? She will be furious." The pressure was on Ravel. He responded by composing "Bolero."

Ravel met the deadline, Nov. 22, 1928. Rubinstein's dance was choreographed by Bronislava Nijinska. As the curtain rose, the audience saw Rubinstein alone in a smoke-filled tavern.

She was dressed as a Spanish Gypsy. As the music began, Rubinstein's body swayed to the relentless tempo. The orchestra became more threatening and Rubenstein was gradually joined by other dancers.

When the crescendo finally came, the audience sat in stunned silence. A woman's voice cried out, "He's mad!" Ravel later commented on her outburst by saying that she understood his piece perfectly.

The critics of the time agreed with both Ravel and the woman. One wrote that the "Bolero" was "the most insolent monstrosity ever perpetuated in the history of music."

Ravel was not particularly offended by the judgment. He confided to fellow composer Paul Honegger, "Alas, it has no music."

Ravel probably never anticipated that "Bolero" would be used in the manner it is today. He did specify, however, that it should be performed in precisely 17 minutes.

For some, Ravel's timing may be too short, or too long, as the case may be. It is interesting to note that modern performances rarely last that long.

That's the way it is with so many thing these days. People seem to be in such a hurry.

March 15, 1980

4

DERELICT DIALECT: INNER DIALOGUE

Derelict dialect

Readers of Garry Trudeau's "Doonesbury" cartoon strip have been getting introduced to what is known as "mellow-speak." It is a California-oriented method of communication involving the use of such expressions as, "I know what space I'm in."

This kind of talk has caught on here to a limited degree among bureaucrats, legislators, lobbyists, patrons of single bars and other rascals.

Politicians are among the better practitioners of mellow-speak. When cornered, an elected official often will tell a constitutent, "I hear what you are saying to me."

Roughly translated, this means, "I understand your position. However, I am not necessarily symphathetic with your views. I consider it politically inadvisable to take a public stand at this time."

Another popular phrase, particularly at the Statehouse, is, "I'm not up to speed on that." The inference here is that the speaker hasn't had time to properly research an issue. It can also mean, "I don't know what the hell you are talking about."

Another negative response is, "I have no feel for that." Approval, on the other hand, is suggested by, "I know where you are coming from."

Mellow-speak, as with other subculture languages, is not meant to clarify. It is rather a jargon spoken by insiders to each other so that those on the social periphery will not completely understand.

Is there a Colorado-speak? Yes, but it doesn't have as much to do with how ideas are expressed as it does on how words are mispronounced.

We are democratically impartial about this. Coloradans are just as likely to butcher a Spanish word as a French one. We particularly are inept at pronouncing Indian names.

The town of Saguache is a good example. We pronounce it Suhwatch. It was once a Ute Indian encampment called Sa-gua-gua-chippa. The word meant "water of the blue earth." Fur trappers couldn't pronounce the Indian word and had to settle for Suh-watch.

Fortunately, there is a book available that gives local phonetic pronunciations of Colorado counties, communities and mountain peaks and passes. It is "Colorado Place Names" by Geo. R. Eichler, a former Denver newspaperman.

Buena Vista, meaning "good view," ought to be pronounced Bway-nah Vees-tah. But that's not the way residents there say it. Eichler gives the local usage pronunciation as Byoo-nuh vihs-tuh. Just plain Byoo-nee also is acceptable.

Del Norte residents say Del Nort, not Del-Nort-ay, as would be the correct Spanish pronunciation. Same thing with Rio Grande. Most people say Ree-oh Grand, not Grand-ay. On the other hand, local usage of Mesa Verde has swung away from MAY-suh Vurd to Vaird-ay.

Pueblo presents a particular problem. The Spanish pronunciation would be poo-ay-blow. Eichler gives the local usage pronunciation as Pweb-low. In practice, however, many people call it pee-eb-luh.

Denver streets are tricky. Tejon should be Tay-hohn. We say Tee-hohn. In Colorado Springs, it is OK to say Tay-hohn. Umatilla isn't pronounced Oo-mah-tee-yah. Local usage is You-mah-til-uh. Acoma should be AH-cohma. We say Ah-COH-muh.

We do fairly well with the Spanish pronunciation of the letter "j." La Jara comes out as Lah-Har-uh. We say La Hun-Tuh for La Junta. It should be La Hoon-tah, but we get the "j" right.

Those wishing to master Colorado-speak should be aware that the letter "j" isn't always given the Spanish "h" sound. There are exceptions.

It isn't Grand Hunk-shun.

June 27, 1979

Wha'd he say?

No VERBS.

That's an amusing sequence in the "Doonesbury" cartoon strip in which Sen. Edward Kennedy is conducting a news conference. There are no verbs in his rambling answers.

Kennedy is becoming famous for his ambiguity. That CBS television interview he had with Roger Mudd was typical of Kennedy's inability to speak extemporaneously.

It is filled with "ers," "ahs," "uhs" and "moreovers." Sentences are rarely completed. They sort of trailed off, sometimes ending with a nervous clearing of the throat.

Kennedy compensates in public appearances by shouting and by using such buzzwords as "leadership," "crisis" and "aggression."

Political incomprehensibility is not necessarily a drawback. It may even be a asset. Reporters find it very difficult to deal with politicians whose responses to questions are vague and obscure.

American voters have often given political figures higher marks for style than for substance. That was certainly the case with Dwight Eisenhower. It is irreverent to suggest that he was the Casey Stengel of American presidents.

Ike's campaign headquarters for both of his successful candidacies were in Denver. I attended most of the press conferences he had here. I'm not sure I understood any of them.

One of Eisenhower's favorite political gambits was the off-the-record news conference. He would call reporters together and would give them information for which he did not wish to be held personally accountable. He would preface these sessions by saying, "Boys, this is off the record."

Reporters hated this because they felt they were being compromised. It was decided that the next time Eisenhower tried this, some would stand up and walk out.

It wasn't long before he did it again. About half the press corps left. Being young, not yet highly principled and mostly curious, I stayed to hear what he had to say.

After it was over, those who had left crowded around those who had stayed and wanted to know what he said. None of us was able to say because we didn't understand anything he said.

The problem of understanding Eisenhower was the logical and reasonable tone of his voice. It really sounded as though he were making sense.

Ike even had problems when he read a speech someone else had written for him. He tended to ramble from the script and lose his timing.

During one of the campaigns, it was decided to have him give a major nationally televised speech from Denver. It originated at the Channel 7 studios. Jim Lannon, who still works for the station, was chosen as the director.

Lannon noted about 20 minutes into the speech that Eisenhower was going to run over his time limit. He calmly alerted his control room crew that he was going to cut the president and end the program on time.

"Cut the president?" Eisenhower's political advisers and White

House staffers were shrieking at Lannon. "You can't cut the president of the United States!"

"I can and I will," Lannon said evenly. "This is a paid political speech. He gets 29 minutes and no more. You will all be quiet or you will have to leave the control room."

Lannon then said to his crew, "Prepare to cut audio and go to black." Lannon waited until Eisenhower's voice dropped and then he commanded, "Now!"

Eisenhower finished his speech in the studio, unaware that he had been cut off. I doubt if anyone ever told him.

Later on, it was generally agreed that it was one of Ike's better speeches.

January 24, 1980

Fairy good idea

CHEAP.

Our features editor, George Kane, took me aside when I started to work at the News and told me never to write a column about writing a column.

"That's cheap journalism. Don't do it. Ever!" George said firmly. He added that there is never an excuse for the practice. Not even on those days when the writer is completely devoid of ideas.

"Not to worry, Mr. Kane," I said. "I don't have a problem that way. I always know exactly what I am going to write about. I will never resort to writing a column about writing a column because it is tacky to do so."

He wanted to know what made me so sure I wouldn't do such a thing. George said that all columnists complain bitterly about the lack of ideas.

Little did he know that I have my very own Idea Fairy. She has been giving me material for years. That's why I have never stooped to writing a column about writing a column.

I was rather surprised at her appearance. I had somehow expected she would look like Tinker Bell. You know, wings, little tiny fanny, a wand, the whole shot. Uh uh.

She isn't the fairy godmother type either. She is about 8 inches tall. Almost the size of a Barbie Doll. A little heavier.

I don't know how much she weighs. She usually wears a simple little tweed suit. She doesn't like pants outfits. Almost always wears a rust-colored scarf, tied at the neck.

When she first appeared, I said to her, "What do I call you? Are you a Miss, Mrs. or a Ms?"

"I don't have any hang-ups about that," she said. "Just call me 'Idea Fairy.' My marital status, or lack of it, has nothing to do with my work."

I think she has children. Sometimes she complains about driving in the car pool when it is stormy. Actually, she talks very little about herself.

Idea Fairy is quite attractive. Nice smile. Very bright eyes. I mentioned this to her once. She bristled at the compliment. "Don't get any ideas, Buster," she said. "It would never work."

She explained that she had been assigned to me and that our relationship would be friendly, but not personal. I said that was OK by me. I told her I meant no offense when I commented about her eyes.

She usually sits on the typewriter cover. Sometimes she taunts me a little while before she gives me the idea. "What's the matter, Buster, mind gone blank? Those nimble fingers aren't exactly flying over the keys."

After she makes me wait a little while, she motions for me to lean over. Then she whispers the idea in my ear. And then she disappears. Poof. Just like that.

Idea Fairy has a temper. Sometimes she doesn't like what I do with her ideas. That happened the other day. It was the column I wrote about how Jimmy Carter, Ted Kennedy and Jerry Brown reminded me of characters in a soap opera. Her idea.

"Trash. Just trash. You blew it, Buster. You took a perfectly good idea and blew it. Shape up, Buster."

I don't know why she calls me "Buster."

She has calmed down since then. She has been coming up with some really good ones. Until today. As a matter of fact, she didn't even show up.

I waited right up until an hour before deadline. Checked the phone messages, even though she never uses the telephone. Too heavy for her. Darned if I know where she is.

Hope she is all right.

November 15, 1979

Press briefing

JESUS IS COMING.

"Ladies and gentlemen. Over here, please! May I have your attention? Thank you. I am Gabriel. I want to thank you people from the newspapers and radio and TV stations for coming out here this morning to Stapleton Airport.

"Can you all hear me over the Hare Krishna chanting? It isn't too loud for you, is it?

"Good."

"As you know, flight schedules are running late-ish because of 'chicken feed' fares. We now expect Him to arrive in about 20 minutes. I thought we might use some of this time for a little briefing.

"Everybody have press kits? We have a few extras. Inside is the official itinerary for His visit to the Mile High City. You'll also find copies of His airport statement and tomorrow's sermon. There's also a brief biographical sketch. As most of you know, He is the Son of God.

"The ceremony here will be brief. Listen, we know you are all busy and that this is Orange Monday. We also understand that Patty Schroeder is having a little lollipop rally down at Larimer Square later this morning. Some of you have indicated you have to cover it, too. Don't worry. We'll get you out of here on time. We love Patty. We love everybody.

"As soon as He deplanes, we're gonna try to get His luggage off the carousels and through customs so He'll be able to come directly here.

"As I said, we won't be here very long. Public Works Manager Harold Cook is representing Mayor McNichols. Mr. Cook will present the Saviour the 'Denver Dollar.' And yes, it will be one of the new Susan B. Anthony dollars from the Denver Mint.

"After Mr. Cook's remarks, two members of the Pony Express will present Him with an official Orange Crush T-shirt.

"No, He won't put on the T-shirt. Not here.

"After the Pony Express bit, He'll read His prepared airport statement. You have copies of that. You television people will note that certain paragraphs are underlined. Each of them will time out at around 40 seconds.

"We've done this for your convenience so you don't have to film the entire statement. We figure that any of those paragraphs will make a complete story. All the TV stand-up reporter has to do is make a brief intro and a kiss-off and you got yourself a film package that will run just over a minute. This will free your cameras to shoot general airport cover stuff and crowd reaction shots. Nice, huh?

"Channel 9 will cover the motorcade live from its helicopter. We're hoping Channel 7's Insta-Cam has been fixed so it can pick up the arrival at the Hilton. And does anybody know if Channel 4 is back from the Western Slope? They've been in Grand Junction all week covering the apple harvest story.

"There are only one or two changes in the itinerary. He will do guest shots on Beverly Martinez's show on Channel 2 and a "Noonday" on Channel 4. But He will not, repeat, will not do a phone show with Alan Berg on KHOW. We've canceled out on that and won't have any further comment.

"I guess most of you know that we have changed the location of tomorrow's sermon. We've moved it from Boettcher Hall over to the old Auditorium Theater. They've had some problems with the PA system in the new concert hall. That's why we're moving to the old auditorium. We know it's not as fancy, but He wanted to be sure that His word isn't misunderstood.

"Also not on the itinerary is the shtick with Howard Cosell. Roone Arledge has set up a drop-in promotion on Monday Night Football. The Messiah will chat with Howard, Dandy Don and the Giffer in the booth at Mile High Stadium during tonight's game between the Broncos and the Chicago Bears.

"That's about it. Oh yes. He won't be meeting privately with Ted Strickland. He's not meeting with Gov. Lamm either. The Lord doesn't take sides in these matters. He doesn't want to mix religion with politics.

"They've just announced His plane's arrival. We'll see you all down at the hospitality center in the press room of the Hilton.

"Go Broncos."

October 16, 1978

Small lies

WINNIE.

The British Broadcasting Corp. ought to keep its mouth shut. There are some things in life that people are better off not knowing. That Winston Churchill used an impersonator is one of them.

We expect a little deception from our public figures. It is too much, however, to learn that Churchill had a stand-in when he told the world, "We shall fight on the beaches, we shall fight on the landing grounds, we shall fight in the fields and in the streets. . . ."

The BBC confirmed last week that it was really actor Norman Shelley who had made that speech on the network's overseas service. Churchill did make the original speech in the House of Commons, but was too busy to record it for later broadcast.

It sort of makes you wonder how many great quotations were uttered by imposters. As the American ship Bonhomme Richard was sinking in its battle with the British Serapis in 1779, John Paul Jones was supposed to have shouted, "I have not yet begun to fight!"

Maybe it was just a yeoman third class look-alike who actually hollered at the British. Could it be that Commodore Jones had not yet begun to fight because he wasn't even on board?

There is no question that it was Neil Armstrong who said, "That's one small step for man, one giant leap for mankind." But where was he when he made it?

Was Armstrong really on the moon, or did the TV networks and the government conspire to stage the whole thing in the desert outside of Las Vegas?

Even today, how can you be sure it is Jimmy Carter who is running the country and not Rich Little?

There is nothing new in media deception. There was a time when a small group of Denver radio entrepreneurs "re-created live and direct," whatever that meant, broadcasts of New York Yankees baseball games.

They sounded as if they actually were coming from Yankee Stadium. They weren't. Using guile, imagination and sound effects, the announcer gave his "play-by-play" account of these games from a Stout Street studio.

No permission was obtained to make these broadcasts. A New York bookie telephoned the station at the end of each three innings with just the barest of detail on what had happened to each batter.

The information quickly was typed out and handed to the announcer. He then fleshed out the account of the game by having imaginary dogs run out onto the field and by taking note of the wind direction from the center field flag.

When listeners thought they were hearing the sound of the bat, the sportscaster really was flicking his forefinger against a matchbook.

Sports broadcasters encouraged that sort of thing. The two sportscasters who covered the games of the old Denver Nuggets basketball team almost 30 years ago once had to call a poorly attended game on Christmas night.

To relieve their boredom, they took Nugget players Leonard Alterman and Kenny Sailors out of the game and put in "Donner and Blitzen."

Donner netted only three points that night, all free throws. Blitzen was credited with four rebounds. The broadcasters who perpetrated these frauds will not be identified here. They are now in their declining years and have reformed somewhat.

The networks still use canned laughter on their situation comedies. This is supposed to encourage the viewer to laugh at material that really isn't funny.

It is a well-guarded secret that some "direct reports" heard on radio newscasts are telephoned "direct" from the next studio.

Quote: *"There are a terrible lot of lies going about the world, and the worst of it is that half of them are true."* — Winston Churchill.

October 9, 1979

Scientific verbiage

AN AFFAIR.

Trish has a crush on Carl Sagan. Trish is my wife. Sagan is the hotdog creator, chief writer and host-narrator of "Cosmos," the new public television series on Channel 6.

He is a professor of space sciences and astronomy at Cornell University, where he also is director of the Laboratory for Planetary Studies.

Sagan has been on the cover of Time magazine and is a frequent guest on Johnny Carson's late-night TV show. Trish thinks he is some punkins because of the way he looks in his corduroy jacket and turtleneck sweater.

The attraction is more than physical. Trish likes the patient way he explains such things as terrestrial and extraterrestrial intelligence, whatever that means.

No telling how serious the romance is. I don't think they are seeing each other. My best bet is to just play it cool and hope the infatuation passes. I have wondered, however, what life for Trish would be like if she had married Sagan instead of me.

"Trish, why did you open the window?"

"It's hot in here. The place needs airing out."

"You must understand that by opening the window, you are admitting colder air into the room. This condition does not, as you suggest, actually cause the room to become cooler. Quite the reverse is true.

"The cooler air has a profound effect upon the bimetallic thermostat that controls the heating system in our home. The thermostat operates by the expansion and contraction of metal."

"I just . . ."

"Inside the thermostat are two strips of different metals that have been bonded together. When the temperature changes, the two metals expand or contract unequally. This causes the bonded strip to bend in the form of an arc."

"I'm sorry, I . . ."

"The bending of the strip establishes or disconnects an electrical contact that either closes or opens an electric circuit. The electric circuit controls the heating unit."

"That it, Carl?"

"Hardly. It is just the beginning, if we can contemplate a beginning in our infinite universe. The world is very old, and human beings are very young. Significant events in our personal lives are measured in years or less, our lifetimes in decades, our family genealogies in centuries and all of recorded history in millenia."

"Please."

"But we have been preceded by an awesome vista of time, extending for prodigious periods into the past, about which we know little — both because there are no written records and because we have real difficulty in grasping the immensity of the intervals involved."

"But the window."

"When the cold air is impacted upon the thermostat, the furnace is activated to produce more heat. Since the window is open, and there are other apertures in our house, the heat goes out into the wonderous atmosphere."

"OK, OK."

"Our plucky little Lennox forced-air system tries to heat all of Bear Valley, Denver, Colorado — even the United States. We must ask ourselves, Trish, what imbalances are we imposing on the cosmos and what are the consequences."

"But . . ."

"It is only the last day of the Cosmic Calendar that substantial abilities have evolved on planet Earth. Thought waves, like heat waves, radiate out. Is their destination the mysterious planet Mars? Will they speed to Jupiter with its colorful storm clouds? And Saturn."

"Shut up, Carl."

Illiterate that vanity

MAL A PROPOS.

That's the French term for "inappropriate." We have Anglicized it and have given it a slightly different meaning. We define "malapropism" as the humorous misapplication of a word.

The queen of verbal goofs was Mrs. Malaprop in Richard Brinsley Sheridan's play "The Rivals." She said such things as "Illiterate him, I say, quite from your memory."

I wish I could illiterate from my memory a malapropism that appeared in this column recently. In commenting on an amateurish song lyric I had written years ago, I said I thought I was protected by the "Statue of Limitations."

I wasn't aware of my boo-boo until I got a letter from Garrett W. Ray, editor and publisher of the Independent Newspaper in Arapahoe County.

He wrote, "I'm puzzled by the reference to the Statue of Limitations, which apparently provides protection a la Roman Catholic saints.

"I've been to all the best statue places — St. Peter's in Rome, the Great Buddha of Kamakura, and the Statue Farm in Englewood —

and have never seen the statue you mention.

"What does it look like? Something like the armless Venus de Milo?"

No, Mr. Ray, it bears little resemblance to Venus. The Statue of Limitations is a male figure. He is crouched over a typewriter and his foot is in his mouth.

The Statue of Limitations doesn't offer protection against anything, not even the pigeons.

Heck, I don't know why I wrote "statue" when I meant "statute." Maybe I didn't. It could have happened at the copy desk. Maybe in the back shop.

If I actually did make that mistake, it wasn't my first malapropism. It probably won't be my last.

Early in my career as a radio announcer, I committed a real doozie while reading a commercial about a medication for the common cold. In my firmest baritone, I asked, "Do you suffer from annoying postnatal drip?"

Of course the copy said "nasal." I knew the difference, but somehow it came out "natal." Telephones at the studio rang. People pointed at me on the street. It took me years to live it down.

Some people become famous for their malapropisms. The late Richard J. Daley, mayor of Chicago, was a man who was ambitious to use fine language. However, he was not sufficiently industrious to use a dictionary.

In just one speech, Daley said that he "resented the insinuendos" of his opponents and was speaking "for the enlightenment, edification and hallucination of the aldermen."

On another occasion, Daley predicted, "We shall reach greater and greater platitudes of achievement." Public figures like Daley, according to Bergen and Cornelia Evans, in their "Dictionary of Contemporary American Usage," seem to "soar above their abilities and display, in the malapropism, not only their ignorance but their vanity as well."

I suspect that others use the malapropism deliberately. This must have been the case when novelist Leo Rosten cautioned, "Don't blame God — he's only human."

I have always liked Yogi Berra's "You can observe a lot by watching." That's right up there with Dizzy Dean's "You have to take the bad with the worst."

There is often a lot of truth in the malapropism. It was Sam Goldwyn who warned, "A verbal contract is not worth the paper it's printed on."

My "Statue of Limitations" may have been mildly amusing. But it wasn't up to the malapropism in a Philadelphia Bulletin feature story.

"Beethoven had 10 children and practiced on a spinster in the attic."

November 18, 1979

Keep wishing

FULL OF HOPE.

Readers of this column know how devoted I am to linguistic simplicity. It is frequently alleged my copy reads more like a telegram than a newspaper column. I intend to keep it that way.

There is a lot of competition for your attention in the morning. I do not mean to complicate matters by attempting to write in the style of William F. Buckley Jr.

I learned a long time ago there are many English teachers out there in the weeds. They are thrilled to spot a dangling participle in the newspaper, and they love to call it to the attention of the writer.

While I admire perfection in writing, I make no pretense at achieving it. I just try to keep what I do somewhere in the ballpark of accepted usage.

There are four rules of grammar I try to follow:

— The tense of a column shouldn't wander.

— The subject must agree with the verb.

— Avoid the use of commas. I hate commas.

— Never begin a sentence with the bastard adverb *hopefully.*

I am not alone. Writing in the Harper Dictionary of Contemporary Usage, the distinguished Hal Borland said this about *hopefully:* "I have fought this for some years, will fight it till I die. It is barbaric, illiterate, offensive, damnable, and inexcusable."

Charles Kuralt, the CBS television commentator, is no less opposed. "Chalk squeaking on a blackboard is to be preferred to this usage," he wrote. "I don't accept it, but I fear we are all stuck with it."

The late Walter W. "Red" Smith, the most eloquent of sports columnists, viewed *hopefully* with the same sense of despair. "I deplore it, I curse it and I'm losing the war."

For some strange reason, sports figures are the most common

offenders. "Hopefully," the pitcher tells his interviewer, "we'll beat them Dodgers in the playoffs."

Why is he so wishy-washy about it? He should simply say, "I hope we beat them Dodgers in the playoffs." By starting the sentence with *hopefully*, he suggests it is someone else who is doing the hoping.

Hopefully used in the context of "in a hopeful manner" is OK. "The pitcher strode *hopefully* to the mound to beat them Dodgers" works because the adverb *hopefully* modifies the verb *strode*.

The worst example of an adverb modifying an entire sentence I have ever heard occurred on a recent KOA radio newscast. A fire chief told a reporter, *"Hopingly* we'll have the blaze under control soon." The chief took the verb *hope*, turned it into a gerund by adding *ing*, and by tacking on *ly*, he made it into an adverb. Geez!

I have a theory that sociologists have infected the language with all these suspended adverbs. Attend almost any workshop or seminar, and you will hear the air filled with *hopefully, importantly* and *interestingly*. Show me a sociologist who begins a sentence with *interestingly enough* and I will show you a sociologist who is not interesting enough.

Maybe it is temporary. Fads come and go. Remember how teenagers used the world *really* as a positive response to almost anything? That seems to be passing. Perhaps *hopefully* will meet the same fate.

I hope.

May 4, 1982

Pardon spy mooner

SPOONERISM.

That's when sounds in a spoken sentence are accidentally transposed. While it is true radio announcers are most frequently afflicted with these verbal faux pas, the term actually gets its name from a preacher.

He was the Rev. William A. Spooner, warden of New College, Oxford, England. His first recorded spoonerism was when he smiled at the groom at the end of a wedding ceremony and said, "It is now kisstomary to cuss the bride."

Spooner told his flock one Sunday morning, "The Lord is indeed a shoving leopard." His frequently garbled language even infected ushers in his church. Legend has it that one of them whispered to a woman seated in a pew, "Mardon me, Padam, aren't you occupewing the wrong pie? May I sew you to another sheet?" I don't know whether or not I believe that.

Spooner's classic came during a service when he was asking the congregation to pray for Queen Victoria. He was trying to say, "Our dear old queen." It came out, "Our queer old dean."

News commentator Lowell Thomas once referred to British Cabinet minister Sir Stafford Cripps as "Sir Stifford Crapps." Announcer Harry Von Zell introduced President Herbert Hoover as "Hoobert Heever." And then there is the commercial announcer who was trying to say "The best in bread." His spoonerized version was "the breast in bed."

My vote for the prince of spoonerisms goes to a young announcer I helped break in to broadcasting at Denver's KMYR shortly after World War II. We shall call him Jack because that was his name. He had a fine voice, excellent diction and a solid vocabulary.

During his first night on the job, I was instructing Jack on how to announce a remote broadcast from the old Park Lane Hotel. The copy read: "It's the music of Clyde Comnillo and his orchestra! Good evening, ladies and gentlemen. This is your invitation to join the gay groups at the beautiful Park Lane cocktail lounge."

Jack rehearsed it several times. No problem. He just whizzed right through it. Smooth. It was a different matter when the red light went on. I can still see him holding his ear and saying, "Good ladies, evening and gentlemen. This is your invitation to join the gray goops at the Park Tail cocklane lounge."

Jack kept right on going. He wasn't the least bit flustered. As I sat there watching him, I realized he was completely unaware of what he had said. It was that way throughout his entire announcing career.

He would go along fine for months without so much as a single fluff, and then some unseen force would grip him at the worst possible moment. There would be no warning to these episodes. Jack would hopelessly mangle a perfectly innocent sentence, giving it a new and sometimes embarrassing meaning.

The spoonerism that made Jack a legend in his own time came during a high school basketball game. Despite his problem, Jack was very quick and fluent and had become a play-by-play sportscaster.

The game was being played in the old North High gymnasium.

There was no press box. Jack and the engineer were wedged between students on the balcony. It was a playoff game, and the lead changed almost every minute. The kids were shrieking and stomping their feet, causing the balcony to sway. It was deafening. Jack had his fingers in his ears, trying desperately to concentrate on the game.

There were only a few seconds left. A kid named Schultz from North managed to steal the ball. He quickly dribbled down to the key, stopped, set, shot and hit at the buzzer. The crowd went wild. They didn't hear what the radio audience heard, however.

"Wait a minute! Here comes Schultz. Steals the ball! Only five seconds! Schultz dribbles to the edge of the keyhole. He stops, sets, hoots and sh--s! North wins the game!"

December 14, 1980

5

PATERNITY SUITS: FAMILY MATTERS

Pop

HOTTER THAN A DEPOT STOVE.

That's the way my father would have described last week's weather. Frank Amole's language was filled with colorful little analogies. They were accurate and filled with fun.

He was a salesman most of his life. He "made the territory," as he called it, out of Denver. Back in the '20s, he was "on the road" for Hendrie & Bolthoff, a hardware and manufacturing equipment wholesaler.

The salesmen of that time traveled by railroad. That's why so much of what they said was involved with terminology of trains. Certainly there was nothing hotter than the potbellied stove, on a cold night, in the depot of a remote Kansas town.

Another one I always liked was Pop's way of describing frugality. "Tighter than a Pullman window," he would say. Anyone who has ever struggled to open a painted-shut window on a Pullman railroad passenger car knows all about tightness.

Getting back to high temperatures, another favorite of his was "hotter than a Spanish princess." The connotation was not necessarily erotic. It really had more to do with improving fortunes. It meant having a run of good luck in selling, or perhaps in a crap game. By the way, learning to "talk" to dice was important. When trying to make five "the hard way," it always helped to holler, "Drive up, Wilbur!"

My father always preferred to call salesmen "agents." Theirs was a close-knit fraternity. They were bright, clever and very witty. In every little town, they knew where there was a poker game, or what little restaurant had the best biscuits and gravy. And they knew how to squeeze one more day out of razor blade by rubbing it on the inside of a glass water tumbler.

Mostly, they stayed in hotels near the railroad stations. In Glenwood Springs, it was The Denver. At Gunnison, you put up at The La Veta. And if you could get the narrow-gauge out of Durango, you stayed at the Sheridan in Telluride. The mother house here in Denver was the Oxford Hotel, across 17th Street from Hendrie & Bolthoff and a half block from Union Station.

The agents were important. Consumer goods and technology we now take for granted were luxuries in those small towns then. Salesmen brought these refinements with them. They also were carriers of style, the latest humor and news from the city.

At night, agents would gather in the hotel lobby to work on their "swindle sheets," their term for expense accounts. A certain amount of larceny was expected since salaries were not exactly extravagant. They would laugh and regale each other with the latest jokes. They would say things like, "It would stink a dog off a gut wagon," or, "He was crazier than a peach orchard bull," and then there was the outrageous, "I'll knock you for a row of Hungarian succotash bowls."

I have always thought it was too bad that those times weren't captured by a Damon Runyan or a John Steinbeck. Arthur Miller came along some years later to write his classic "Death of a Salesman." He certainly caught the tragedy and the despair of their lives. Poor Willie Lohman struggled to keep his dignity and his family intact with little more than "a shoeshine and a smile."

All of that was true. But it was also true that their lives were enriched by fun, by personal challenge and by a special kind of camaraderie. Perhaps Miller omitted these things because he didn't want to take the edge from his tragedy.

And so the salesman's special language slips into the past and away from comprehension. People don't know about Pullman windows or depot stoves anymore. With the return of royalty to Madrid, perhaps the temperature of a Spanish princess will again become significant.

It was hot in Denver last week. I thought about my father and how he talked and laughed. His was a very special time.

He was a very special man.

June 25, 1978

Happy birthday, Ma

MA.

It doesn't seem possible that Elizabeth Grace Wilson Amole is 84 today. She's not one to be overly concerned with birthday anniversaries, so I'm sure my mother would rather this one just slipped by.

But it's not in me to ignore her story any longer. She has lived long and well, and I don't know anyone else who is as self-sufficient, energetic and as sharp as she is.

I am reminded of this each time it snows. I call her early in the morning to tell her I'll stop by about 10 a.m. to shovel her sidewalks. "It's all done," she will tell me. "I got up early and have already finished. I just take it a little at a time."

It should be noted that she lives in the house my great-grandfather built around the turn of the century. It is on the corner of a block on the North Side. It has a large yard, and Ma not only shovels her own walks in the winter, but she does all of her own gardening and lawn care in the summer, except for grass cutting.

Born on a farm near Bloomfield, Ohio, she came to Colorado in 1904 with her mother and father, and her older brother, Frank. He had contracted tuberculosis, and the family came west for the state's high, dry air.

They lived in a shack near Limon. Grandpa was a ranch foreman, and as I have noted here before, she and Frank herded about 600 sheep on mules when she was just 7. It was quite a change from the comfortable farm they had left in Ohio.

They later moved to Montrose. That's where Ma grew up. Her mother took in sewing to help give her music lessons and put her through school. Grandpa worked as a carpenter.

My mother took her first teaching job right after she had graduated from high school. It was in a tiny school in Third Park, on a homestead near Nucla. She taught all eight grades in one room, and some of the students were almost as old as she was. Her pay was $65 a month. Ma paid $30 a month for room and board. Lunch consisted of leftover pancakes made into sandwiches.

Shortly after she started teaching, an old rancher in the area died. One of the cowboys came to the boarding house where she lived to take the schoolmarm to the funeral.

As he helped her up on the buckboard, he explained that there was no preacher in Nucla, and she was expected to conduct the funeral. When they pulled up to the church, the coffin had been placed on the porch. It was a hot day, and the body hadn't been embalmed.

Some of the ranch women had done the best they could to prepare the body for the funeral. They had rubbed formaldehyde on the face and had made paper flowers to cover the coffin.

Ma was 18 at the time, and she remembered how frightened she was. "I just got them all to stand up and tell what they remembered about the old man," she said. "And then I sat down at the pump organ and started to play hymns. Everyone joined in the singing. They didn't want to stop. They were having such a good time."

Her second year as a teacher was at Oak Grove, on Spring Creek Mesa. She kept a horse whip hanging on the wall as a symbol of her determination to maintain discipline. And there were days when she had to muster her students to chase rattlesnakes from under the building.

Later, she attended Western State College and the University of Denver to get her teaching certificate. She taught in the Denver Public Schools for 26 years.

Ma didn't believe in retirement. After her teaching years, she sold Literary Guild memberships at May D&F. And then she sold better dresses in the old Forecast Shop of the same store.

There is nothing feeble or senile about my mom. She is in excellent health. She is active with her Clio Club and PEO sisterhood groups. She reads, has a clear grasp of current events, and she is quick to note the occasional grammatical errors that sometimes find their way into this column.

She will be furious with me when she reads this. She is embarrassed by publicity or any kind of notoriety. But let me tell you something, she is a very special woman.

A very special mother.

February 2, 1982

Parenting business

PARENTING.

Today I parent. Tomorrow I shall parent. Often I have parented. Parenting is very difficult.

Psychologists tamper with the language. They take a noun and turn it into a verb. Then they make a gerund out of it by hanging an "ing" on the end.

That's all right. We didn't have a word that covered the everyday business of being a mother or a father. So, for lack of a better term, we have parenting.

There is also malparenting. A young Boulder man sued his folks because he said he had suffered permanent emotional damage as a result of their malparenting.

The judge found the case without merit and threw it out of court. The plaintiff received no damages. He probably felt better, though.

The lawsuit was just his way of telling his parents how angry at them he was.

One of the great misconceptions about parenting is the belief that there is an end to it. There isn't. Once a parent, always a parent. You have to keep plugging away at it until you die.

Another mistaken belief is that parents don't want their children to leave home and get out on their own. Nothing could be further from the truth. It's the kids who don't want to cut the old apron strings.

The reason for this is simple. Instead of teaching their kids to be independent, parents try to win their approval. They shower them with affection and material goodies. Parents do this because they want their children to like them.

The teen years are stressful. Sweaty tube sox always seem to be in the middle of the living room floor. The sound of Fleetwood Mac rumbles up from the basement to the second-floor bedrooms.

There are endless telephone conversations and half-filled pop cans under the bed. The bathroom door is always locked. Don't forget the lollygagging. And then there's waiting up until 3 in the morning, listening to the squeal of tires and the distant sound of sirens.

Then, finally, there's what appears to be a light at the end of the tunnel. The little nippers have grown up and are leaving home. Peace at last.

But it doesn't always turn out that way.

It really doesn't matter how far they go. It could be on the other side of the world. They'll be back. It won't take much to bring them home, either.

Some kids can smell a pot roast all the way across town. Fresh-baked rolls or a devil's food cake will do it every time. Open one bottle of beer, get ready to open another.

Another sure-fire way of having the offspring pop in unexpectedly is to clean the basement or garage. Always works. Just try to give an old toboggan to the Goodwill or throw away a raunchy teddy bear. You better get ready for company.

No telling how many bicycles with flat tires, model airplanes and Barbie's Dream Houses are stored away in this town.

There are darkroom outfits, rock collections, autographed T-shirts and Monopoly games. How about sleeping bags, archery sets, Ouija boards and tissue paper pompons?

It doesn't do any good to try to get the kids to take their stuff with them. They won't do it. They don't want to be bothered with the clutter. They want you to have it.

Home is where the heart is. It is also where the junk is. Parents complain about this condition. It doesn't do any good. They just move the stuff from one basement room to another and then out to the garage. And then back again.

It's a terrible thing how children won't leave their parents in peace. They just keep coming back again and again. If is isn't the pot roast, it's an old catcher's mitt.

On the other hand, it sure beats not having them come home at all. For any reason.

Parenting is very difficult.

April 9, 1979

Phenomenon

I LOVE YOU, GEORGE.

It was about 2 p.m. when Muffy called me at work. She was very upset because she had lost her ride to Red Rocks to see the Beatles. She wanted to know if there was any way I could take her.

Wednesday, Aug. 26, 1964, was a warm day. Muffy told me we had better leave right away. KIMN was saying Red Rocks was filling rapidly and there might not be room for everyone.

It must have been about 3:30 when we got there. People had been waiting all night to get the best seats. Even so, we found two fairly good ones about a third of the way up from the stage.

Muffy is my older daughter. She was 12 at the time. I knew she would have rather been there with her friends. I had purchased tickets days earlier. They were $6.60 each, expensive for the times, but Muffy said it was worth it.

Six teen-age girls and one policeman had been hospitalized earlier for treatment of injuries suffered in a wild welcome for the group at the Brown Palace Hotel. The officer had been bitten on the wrist.

As we made our way to our seats. I thought about the adulation Frank Sinatra received in the early '40s. Same thing for Elvis Presley in 1956. I didn't realize it then, but I was about to witness something much larger.

We settled down for the long wait. I had never seen so many policemen in one place. The crowd was well-behaved, if occasionally quite noisy. Almost everyone was about Muffy's age.

I saw a cowboy hat sticking up above the other heads several rows away. It was Pete Smythe, an old friend. I remembered he had a daughter about the same age as Muffy. And then I began to notice there was an adult male every 20 feet or so. They were the daddies who had driven most of the little girls to Red Rocks.

The sky darkened. Tension began to build. Any movement toward the stage was greeted with screams. The most noise came when the instruments were set up. A woman in her 40s somehow broke through the police lines, ran up on the stage and kissed the bass drum.

I steeled myself against the growing sound as the concert began. The Bill Black Combo opened the show. Then came the Righteous Brothers, the Exciters and Jackie DeShannon.

When they finished, promoter Vern Byers walked out on the stage. He held up his hands. It was suddenly very quiet. Byers stood alone in front of a microphone and said, "And now, the Beatles!"

There was an explosion of sound that lasted 33 minutes. Everyone stood the entire time. The Beatles started with "Twist and Shout" and closed with "Long Tall Sally."

It was almost impossible to hear the music. Only Ringo Starr's drums seemed to slam through. It didn't matter. Everyone could see those thin, black-clad stick-figures. It was everything those little girls had hoped for.

Even though the sound was overwhelming, I kept thinking I could hear a small voice saying, over and over, "I love you, George. I love you." I looked around, and then down. It was little Muffy. She was standing almost motionless. There were tears in her eyes. She was telling George Harrison from the safety of 30 rows up that she loved him. Suddenly, I felt very old.

I have never pretended to understand what the Beatles meant to the children of the '60s. A psychiatrist told me he believed all those protests during that troubled decade had somehow been triggered by their chemistry. Maybe so. My memory is more personal. I can still hear Muffy's voice. It was an innocent moment of poignancy, suspended in a time of chaos.

There is no questioning the importance of their music. It ranged from the earthy to the mystical. It was adventerous and fun. It could be very personal. John Lennon's tragic death will stimulate yet another wave of interest in Beatle music. The younger generations will carry it forward and give it their own meaning.

But there will never be another time like that August night 16 years ago.

December 11, 1980

A banner day

The Idea Fairy wasn't sitting on the typewriter cover when I came into the newsroom. She was pacing back and forth on the top of my desk.

FAIRY — I thought you'd never get here. I am dying to hear all about Brett's graduation from CU. Is it true that he is the first Amole ever to be graduated from college?

ME — The very first.

FAIRY — You must be proud of your son.

ME — You bet I am. A lot of people take higher education for granted these days. We don't at our house. Brett really worked hard for his degree. He overcame more than his share of obstacles. And he helped support himself by working in a beer joint and a bakery. As you said, I am very proud to be his father.

FAIRY — Was the commencement ceremony impressive?

ME — Yes and no. There was some hooting and whistling during the long-winded award speeches. It didn't seem to matter to the speakers, though. They just kept droning on and on.

FAIRY — Those things do tend to drag. I have always thought there ought to be two ceremonies. The first one would be to confer the advanced degrees. It would also give faculty members, regents and alumni a chance to tell each other how great they are.

ME — And the second?

FAIRY — It would be for the kids getting baccalaureate degrees. The speeches would be short and snappy. The diplomas could then be handed out, everybody would sing, "Hail, all hail our alma mater!" and then people could go home.

ME — I must say, Fairy, that is truly one of your better ideas. Would there still be banners?

FAIRY — Banners? What kind of banners?

ME — The kind that popped up Friday at CU.

FAIRY — What did they say?

ME — The graduates from the School of Education held one up that said, "Teachers Do It With Class." You couldn't miss it. The letters were in different colors and the banner was at least 40 feet long.

FAIRY — That is kind of funny.

ME — I'm not so sure about the banner the pharmacists held up.

FAIRY — What did it say?

ME — I can't tell you. We have never discussed things like that, and besides, this is a family newspaper.

FAIRY — Buster, I am getting the feeling that you didn't quite approve of the banner, the whistling and the hooting. Anything else?

ME — The firecrackers, the balloons and the squirting of beer and champagne at each other. I thought it was a little inappropriate, considering the seriousness of the occasion.

FAIRY — Oh, come off of it! You know something about you? If there was ever a way of getting that phony stuffed shirt off you, I think we'd find a real stuffed shirt inside.

ME — That's not fair. It's just . . .

FAIRY — It's just that you don't really understand. You talk about seriousness. Let me tell you about seriousness. Those kids have the rest of their lives to be serious.

ME — But . . .

FAIRY — But nothing. There's nothing wrong with seizing that last moment to have a little fun. There will be time enough tomorrow for inflation, recession, Mount St. Helens and the hostages. By the way, what is Brett going to do?

ME — He's going to be a newspaperman.

FAIRY — Did you give him any advice.

ME — I told him to write short sentences.

FAIRY — Good.

May 25, 1980

Tube sock crisis

ONE SIZE FITS ALL.

That means everyone else can wear your clothing. This is particularly true of tube socks. They are the white over-the-calf athletic stockings with colored stripes at the top.

I wear tube socks all the time. They are comfortable and cheap. One shoe store packages six pairs for just $9.97.

I have never worn out a pair of tube socks. That's because members of my family are a pack of common thieves. They steal my tube socks. If I buy a six-pack of tube socks in the morning, they will be gone by night.

All I have in that stocking drawer of my dresser are mismatched singles. There are no two socks alike. The stripes don't go together.

I have to go to work in the morning with purple and yellow stripes on one leg and red and blue on the other. I know, it is true most people will never see the tops of my tube socks.

But what happens if I am injured in an automobile accident and rushed to Denver General Hospital? You can imagine the humiliation of lying on a table in the emergency room and hearing a nurse whisper, "My God, it's Gene Amole. He has holes in his underwear and his socks don't match."

I have told my wife, Trish, that when I topple over and go to the great newsroom in the sky, she ought to marry a man with one leg. The lucky devil would come into a lifetime supply of single tube socks.

It always has been a mystery as to why only one sock disappears. Where does it go? Why don't both socks get lost? What are you supposed to do with the one that is left?

After years of patient research, I have found the answers to these questions. The automatic washing machine is the culprit. It has to be. If you throw two matching tube socks in the washing machine, only one comes out.

Not many people know this, but there is a "destruct" cycle. It is between the "wash" and "rinse" cycles. It is during that function that the machine quickly sorts through all the laundry, finds one sock, chops it up into little pieces and flushes it out with the rinse water.

The machine is clever enough to either destroy or disguise all that remains of the sock. What doesn't go out with the rinse water will wind up as lint in the filter at the top of the machine.

More sophisticated laundry equipment is on the way. I have it on the highest authority that the new 1980 models will perform a revolutionary new function.

It will occur during the last three minutes of the "spin-dry" cycle. Science and technology actually have developed a machine that will automatically remove all the buttons from your shirt and will then shoot them through your socks.

I have considered other explanations for the missing tube socks. Perhaps the cat is dragging them behind the lilac bush. Maybe there is a Tube Sock Fairy and I have somehow offended him or her.

Meanwhile, my wife and children continue to steal my tube socks that do match. Trish wears them when she jogs around Harvey Park Lake. I have noticed that Susan wears my socks while watching TV and scarfing junk food.

My other daughter, Muffy, lives in Aspen. It is sort of exciting to realize that my tube socks are in the same town as John Denver, Claudine Longet and Hunter Thompson.

Brett is the oldest living senior at the University of Colorado at Boulder. He is wearing my tube socks to Spanish classes and I hope he will graduate in them some time in 1979.

I believe Jon lives somewhere between Denver and Aurora this week. I have no idea where he wears my tube socks. It probably is just as well I don't.

If you have been touched by this story, bundle up your clean single tube socks and send them to me. You will get nothing in return. I will try to match them with what I have. That way I won't be embarrassed at Denver General Hospital.

July 9, 1979

Holey situation

A PERSONAL MATTER.

I hate to have to bring this to public attention, but something must be done about my wife, Trish. She is a compulsive throwerawayer.

That's right, she throws away possessions of mine that are perfectly serviceable. Trish does this without telling me and without replacing what she has thrown away.

It must have something to do with this thing she has about neatness. You know, a place for everything. Everything in its place.

She never checks to see if there is just one more squeeze of toothpaste in the tube. If it appears empty, out it goes. Same thing with the old Converse basketball shoes I use when I have to do some painting around the house. I have to wear them all the time, otherwise, she chucks them into the trash.

I have hidden my old Harley Davidson motorcycle jacket. She has been itching to get her hands on it for years. I have also had to stash away my yellow baseball cap — the one I wear when I drive my pickup. It says CAT on the front.

You should have heard me complain when she threw away my

perfectly good World War II tanker coveralls. Trish displayed absolutely no remorse. "You spend too much time living in the past," she said.

That may be, but it was the future that concerned me early this morning. Sentiment was not involved. It wasn't a matter of not being able to knock around in some comfortably old and familiar clothing.

It was my jockey shorts.

My day starts at 3:30 a.m. It is dark and lonely then. When the clock alarm goes off, I slip through the early morning gloom into the bathroom for shave, shower, shampoo and you-know-what.

Then, with wet towel clutched around my middle, I tiptoe back into the gloom of the bedroom. I feel my way over to the bureau, slide open the second drawer and slip my hand inside to get a clean pair of jockey shorts.

Nothing.

Almost. There is an old Mozart T-shirt in there. That's all. No jockey shorts. Not a single pair. Zero.

"Trish."

"What is it?"

"Where the hell is my underwear?"

"I threw away everything except your Mozart T-shirt."

"You what?"

"Keep your voice down. You'll wake up the Haggertys next door. Everything was worn out. I don't want you to go to work with holes in your jockey shorts."

This is ridiculous conversation to be having at 3:30 in the morning. I am standing there like some kind of wounded stork.

"What difference does it make if I have holes in my jockey shorts?"

"It is just the idea of the thing. Besides, you might be injured in an automobile accident. They would take you to Denver General Hospital. When the nurses undress you, they would see holes in your jockey shorts. I can't have that."

"Goddammit, why didn't you tell me you were going to throw away my underwear so I could have bought some more?"

"You would have put it off. You would have just kept wearing those old jockey shorts until there was nothing left but a few strings. I know you. This way you will have to go out and buy some new jockey shorts."

I rummaged through the rag bag. Nothing but some torn up old pillow cases. No jockey shorts. Time was running out. I had to get to work. Trish went back to sleep.

She was right. I did go out later in the day and bought some new jockey shorts. Good thing, too. Did you ever try to put your legs through the arm holes of an old Mozart T-shirt?

October 2, 1980

Paternity suits

I'M PREGNANT.

Wonderful words. They were said to me the other day by a young friend. She had been married last summer. When she told me she was going to have a baby, there was nothing but happiness in her eyes.

That was when I decided to write something about having babies. Not much is said about it anymore. Abortion seems to get all the publicity.

That's a subject I have tried to avoid. I guess I have reached that point in life where I have been convinced that there are no absolutes and that there is a lot more gray in this world than black and white.

Is that wishy-washy? Maybe? It is perhaps more a recognition on my part that we all don't share the same truths.

I don't know what it is like to carry a child. But I have been a father four times and I guess that qualifies me to be at least an expert witness, as the lawyers might say.

From my own experience, and from watching others, I don't believe there is a time in marriage when husband and wife are any closer together than during pregnancy.

It is a time of sharing and learning. Not always easy, though, what with touches of morning sickness, dieting and those long last weeks of waiting.

Men sometimes feel a bit useless during this period. It seems as though all they do is get up a lot at night, help the wife in and out of the car and take up some of the housework slack.

Even so, the great miracle would be impossible without the man. Believe it, there will be opportunities later to make sacrifices only he can make.

I have heard that some women try to disguise their pregnancy in the belief that it makes them unattractive. I can only speak for myself, but I have always thought women are more beautiful and appealing during pregnancy than at any other time. It is something in the eyes. The way they smile.

I'll never forget the day Susan as born. It had been a long and difficult labor for Trish. The family was crowded around the nursery window. We were pointing and laughing and sharing a precious moment.

I looked over in the corner and there was the doctor, Dave Blanchet. He was laughing, too, and doing a little dance by himself. That's what I mean when I talk about a contagious enthusiasm for life.

Some parents feel guilty that they are not instantly in love with their baby. We have been conditioned by motion pictures and romantic literature to think that the birth of a child is some kind of quick bliss.

It takes time for parents to really love their children. It is a gradual process. There are long and colicky nights and the sobering realization that the little rascals can't do anything for themselves.

Worth it? You bet it is. I don't love one of my four any more than the others. Each is special to me in a unique way. And as difficult as being a parent often has been, I wouldn't give up even an instant of the experience.

I wish, though, that I had been able to profit from my mistakes. Doing it again, I would try not to be so uptight. In being overly protective, I failed to understand that children are not so much taught to be independent as they learn it from experience.

Relax. Enjoy every minute of childhood. In the long stretch of things, it is over almost before it begins.

That is as it should be.

January 22, 1980

Trish takes off

FANTASY FLIGHT.

Trish is one of those people who is not able to hurry. In all of the 15 years we have been married, I have had to accept the fact that the more I try to get her to hurry, the more slowly she moves. If we are running late, it is as though she were in a slow-motion film.

It was that way last week when she was getting ready to go to Phoenix to visit her parents. Even though she started packing three days before she was to leave, I still had to drive like a maniac to get her to the airport on time.

Just as we approached the mousetrap, where I-25 intersects with I-70, she fell silent.

"Are you all right?" I asked.

"It was such a wonderful thing for them to do."

"What are you talking about?"

"My third-grade class at Laura Rathman Elementary School. They raised enough money to send me on my trip."

I realized Trish was having another one of her fantasies. Sometimes she pretends I am Carl Sagan. She often spots an interesting-looking person at the supermarket and makes up a big story about him. "He's an anthropologist at the University of Chicago. Visiting his sister in Denver. She's a nurse at Mercy Hospital," Trish will whisper to me confidentially.

"The children must think a great deal of you."

"Oh yes. The mothers had a bake sale. There were chocolate chip cookies, zucchini bread, whole-wheat muffins — lots of lovely things. The children also had a 'Run for Peebles' fund-raiser. They got people to pledge money for the number of times they could run around the playground."

"Your name is Peebles?"

"Yes. Virginia Peebles."

"Mrs. or Miss?"

"Ms. But you can call me Virginia. Do you like my outfit?"

"It's very nice."

"Thank you. I thought brown corduroy would be suitable for my trip. I got it on sale at Joslin's. I managed to find this little tote bag. It coordinates pretty well. I hope it fits under the seat of the plane."

As we drove along I-70, Trish continued to flesh out details of her new fantasy life as Virginia Peebles. Laura Rathman Elementary School is a three-story, red-brick building. It still has the old kind of children's desks that are bolted to the floor. The desk tops tilt up, leaving room for Big Chief tablets, books and other supplies. "It is one of the last of the lovely, old schools," she explained, a note of melancholy in her voice.

Virginia Peebles lives alone in a little carriage house in the University Park area. She has an orange calico cat. Never wanted to marry. Spends her leisure time doing crewel work. Is a member of the Friends of Chamber Music. "I never married. My fulfillment is in teaching," she smiled.

I could hardly get a word in edgewise. Virginia chatted happily about her third-grade class. The classroom has high ceilings. There are travel posters on the wall. "That's what gave the children the idea for my trip," Virginia said.

I dropped her off on the ramp, instructing her to check in while I parked the car. I told Virginia I would meet her at gate C-21, where her flight was to leave. As I walked rapidly along the concourse to the gate, I wondered if it would be Trish or Virginia who would be there.

And then I got to wondering who would get off the plane when I pick her up next week. Will it be Virginia, or will Trish adopt yet another identity? And what about me? Will I have to be Carl Sagan again? Should I wear my turtleneck sweater?

I told her I would be waiting when she came back. She paused briefly before she entered the plane and turned around. I shouted, "Goodbye, Virginia."

I couldn't hear her reply, but I watched her lips, and I thought she said, "Goodbye, children. It was so nice of all of you to come out to the airport."

March 17, 1981

A matter of training

BEDTIME STORY.

I have begun to wonder lately who are the masters and which are the pets at our house. That thought occurred to me as I was telling CAT his favorite bedtime story the other night. CAT, of course, is our· cat. We have a poodle named Yastrzemski and a hamster we call Butterscotch. They run things.

We have planned our lives around them to such an extent that Trish, Susan and I haven't been out of town together on vacation for years. Since we are planning a little holiday in April, we had to confront the problem of what to do with our animals.

There was a sensible solution. Trish's parents, Roger and Kay Conner, are flying up from Phoenix to take care of them. That may not sound sensible to you, but it is either that or stay home and spend another vacation in Bear Valley.

Five years ago, we put CAT and Yazzie in a boarding kennel for a few days. It was a disaster. CAT lost weight, developed bald spots on his rear and was disoriented for weeks. Yazzie didn't fare much better.

Trish is in the process of planning a color-coded master schedule of how to take care of the pets. They eat breakfast at 5 a.m. Yazzie has to have his nap at 11 a.m. CAT has a snack while he watches the noon news on TV. That kind of thing.

I don't know why we let them manipulate us this way. We just made some small concessions at first. Before we realized it, CAT was demanding and getting smoked sturgeon instead of chopped mackerel.

Yazzie is also particular. He won't settle down after his evening walk along Bear Creek until he has had a chocolate chip cookie. He prefers red to white wine.

There is no problem with his sleeping at night, however, so long as you lift him up on the bed and set the control on his heating pad at the second click. Yazzie doesn't want it too hot.

I didn't like CAT at first. He wandered up to our door about seven years ago. Against my judgment, he finally worked his way inside, despite an allergy I have for cats. I have to scrub my hands with soap and water after I so much as scratch his ears. Otherwise, I get itchy splotches.

This presents some obvious problems at night when it's time for CAT's bedtime story. He insists on hearing it about 8 p.m. Paces around the kitchen and cries until I finally go in the family room and sit down.

CAT flips up on my lap, parks his hind legs under his fanny and digs his front claws into my chest. There are several stories he likes, but his favorite is the one we call "Deprivation."

I tell him about how he had run away from where he was living because the people didn't care about him. When we get to the part about how they slammed the door on his tail, CAT purrs softly and sinks his claws deeper into my chest.

Yazzie also likes the story. Problem is he tries to get on my lap with the cat. There is usually snarling, hissing and growling. Splotch city.

I am typing up CAT's favorite stories on little cue cards for Roger. He won't have to follow them exactly, referring to them only in case he forgets something important.

Butterscotch won't be much of a problem once Roger and Kay get used to hearing him run in his little exercise wheel all night long. Cute little bugger, if you can stand the smell.

I am really looking forward to the vacation. There'll be a surprise for the pets when we get back. I am going to learn a new trick for them.

I am going to sit up and beg.

February 17, 1981

J'accuse

CIRCUMSTANTIAL EVIDENCE.

My wife rarely telephones me at work. That's why I was so surprised when she called me at the newsroom. I could tell she was upset. Something serious, I thought.

"I don't quite know how to tell you this. It was terrible, just terrible."

"For God's sake, what is it?"

"Well — Messy got out of his cage, and CAT killed him. And, oh, Geno, he ate little Messy."

That was serious. Messy is one of our two pet hamsters. CAT, of course, is our cat. The idea that one would kill and eat the other was disgusting.

Trish described the opened door on Messy's cage and the blood spatters on the floor and wall. But there was nothing left of poor little Messy. Not a tuft of hair.

"What happened to CAT?"

"I don't want to talk about CAT. I told him to get out of here, that I never wanted to see him again."

I tried to calm Trish. I told her that CAT is a predator, and it was natural for him to kill Messy. To CAT, Messy was just an oversized mouse.

"I don't want to hear that. CAT goes to the Dumb Friends League. And besides, what shall I tell Susan when I pick her up from school? It is just too awful for her."

We left it at that. I went back to work, but the whole bloody scene was never really out of my mind. I dreaded going home. I didn't want to confront Susan or home. And I didn't want to see CAT, either.

The moment of truth came when I got home at 6:30. Trish met me at the door. "Susan is in her room," she whispered.

"What did you tell her?"

"I told her that Messy's cage was left open. When he crawled out, he must have fallen to the floor. When I found him he was alive but couldn't move. I rushed him over to Anderson's Animal Hospital, and the doctor said he had probably broken his litle neck.

"I told Susan the doctor said there was no hope, that he might have had a heart attack, and the kindest thing to do was to put Messy to sleep. I told her the doctor said he would try to keep Messy alive until Susan could see him. I told him she wouldn't want him to suffer — to go ahead with whatever. ... "

"Did she buy that?"

"Yes, but she is very upset. She'll be OK, though. I'm just sick about this."

Dinner was quiet. Susan ate only one plate of spaghetti. I tried to get CAT to come in, but he wasn't having anything to do with me. I told Susan we would get another hamster. "Not yet," she said.

I had just taken our dog, Yazzie, out for his late evening patrol when I heard a really terrifying scream from our house. There was more screaming. And still more.

Trish was standing in the door, tears streaming down her face. Susan was crying. And there in Trish's hands was little Messy. He was alive, well, not a mark on him. His eyes were open and bright, and his little nose was sniffing away like crazy.

When Susan had gone back to her room to finish her homework, there was little Messy, scampering across the floor. She thought she was seeing a hamster ghost. That's what all the screaming was about.

It took some doing to explain Trish's elaborate fabrication of Messy's demise. Susan now understands about the broken neck, the heart attack and all the rest. CAT came back in the house. The blood spatters?

We still haven't figured out that part.

March 2, 1982

Exotic shades

AGENT ORANGE.

"You look like a nerd in those shorts," Susan said.

"That's no way for a daughter to talk to her father on the first day of our Hawaiian vacation," I replied. "What's the matter with these shorts? They don't fit?"

"Actually, it's not the shorts. It's your legs. They are not only too skinny, they are too white. You look like a nerd," she repeated. "Look around. You don't see anyone else with legs that white. You have to get a tan."

I have never been one to lie around in the sunshine. I don't know what to think about as the sweat drips from the tip of my nose. And besides, I don't tan. I get sunburned.

That's why I decided to take a shortcut. No one wants to embarrass his daughter by looking like a nerd on Kaanapali beach, so I bought a bottle of InstaBronz® — "Bronzes Instantly. Tans for Days. Moisturizes."

The directions were simple. "Shake well. Squeeze small amount into palm. Using fingertips, apply a light, even coat of Insta-Bronz®, blending carefully to avoid streaking. Let dry. For darker tan, apply 2 or 3 times. Wash hands after each application."

"Daddy!" Susan shrieked, "Your legs have turned orange. Get back in the condominium before somebody sees you. You look like a nerd with orange legs."

She was right. But as I examined myself in the mirror, I nearly resembled the great whooping crane preparing for flight than I did a nerd. Either way, I knew I was really an endangered species with those awful orange legs.

Standing in the shower trying to remove InstaBronz®, I wondered why everything always turns orange, no matter what color you try to dye it. And then I had a terrible thought. I wanted to lock up Ronald Reagan for two weeks to see the real color of his hair.

But you don't take a vacation in Hawaii just for the tan. There is more to it than being lulled by hypnotic sounds of the sea. More than the *mahi-mahi* and the *mai tais*. Even more than the string bikinis and the glorious sunsets behind Molokai. More than watching the great whales in Lahaina Bay.

There is shopping. It is the reason women go on vacation. They spend most of their time buying souvenirs to take home to relatives and friends.

I learned how to shop many years ago at Montrose from Grandpa Wilson's dog, Old Poodge. When Grandpa and I walked over to Main Street from his house at 525 N. Fifth St., Old Poodge would pad ahead and wait for us in a shady spot. Once we passed, he'd run to the next shady spot.

That's the way I shopped with my wife, Trish, on our vacation. I waited in shady spots while she picked her way through endless racks of identical *aloha* shirts, *muumuus* and T-shirts that said, "Just Maui'd."

During these excursions, man's only function is to carry the credit card. He is self-propelled money. Don't think. Don't feel. Don't speak. Spend and look for the shady spots. But perhaps the best travel advice of all comes from Britain's Prince Philip.

Quote: *Never stand when you can sit and never, never pass up an opportunity to go to the bathroom.*

August 5, 1982

Being of sound mind

WILL AMOLE.

My grandfather. I thought of him the other night as I watched a rerun on Channel 7 of "The Night They Panicked America."

The program was a fictionalized television account of Orson Welles' sensational 1938 Mercury Theater radio drama, "The War of the Worlds." It was based on an H.G. Wells fantasy about a Martian invasion of Earth.

I remembered Grandpa because he was the one who introduced me to radio. It must have been about 1926. I was just a little bit of a kid and I spent a lot of time at his house at 64 W. Maple Ave. It was around the corner from the old Webber silent motion picture theater. My mother, father and I lived nearby on West Bayaud.

I still can see him there in the dining room. He was a big man. Stern face. Black moustache. Grandpa worked for the railroad, once as station master of what we used to call the Denver Union Depot.

Anyhow, Grandpa would spend hours with his crystal set. I would watch. When he finally was able to wiggle the cat's whisker just right, his eyes would light up, and I knew he had heard something.

He then would take off his headphones, adjust them for me and hold them over my ears with his big callused hands. There might be music or a tiny voice. Grandpa would say, "That's Cincinnati. Think of it. Cincinnati. All that way."

I didn't know about Cincinnati. Grandpa did. Being able to hear it in Denver was one of the great miracles in his life. Radio triggered his imagination then, as it later would mine.

He had run away from his home in Ohio when he was 15 and had come to Denver in the early 1880s. He was able to keep himself going by doing a variety of odd jobs, one of which was planting those beautiful elm trees that used to stand around Courthouse Square.

Grandpa mined gold in the Cripple Creek-Victor area for a time. He was active in the early Colorado labor movement and was an avowed socialist, atheist and, unaccountably, Christian Scientist.

I have thought a lot about why Grandpa loved radio so much. It must have had a great deal to do with travel. When he heard the announcer say, "This is WLW, Cincinnati," he wasn't just listening to a radio station.

The sound was so much more than that. In that eye of his mind, he was able to see rails spanning out across the wind-punctured plains of eastern Colorado and Kansas.

In the static of that faint radio signal, Grandpa could hear the long-forgotten sounds of St. Louis. He could see that great Ohio River and imagine that the sound was taking him home to the little house where he was born so long ago.

Someone once said that radio was the "theater of the mind." It was. Gifted writers like Arch Oboler, Norman Corwin and Willis Cooper gave us a new art form. They shaped sound and silence into an experience of spectacle, excitement, beauty and terror.

Orson Welles practiced the art with greater skill than most. The television program Wednesday night about the invasion from Mars was accurate. The sound effects, the equipment and the studio technique were authentic. Take it from someone who worked in radio during what is now called its "golden years."

Grandpa died before we had television. I used to wish he had lived long enough to see it. Maybe not, though. It probably would have taken away the old man's imagination.

He might have died with none.

Quote: *"Across an immense ethereal gulf, minds that are to our minds as ours are to beasts in the jungle — intellects vast, cool and unsympathetic — regarded this Earth with envious eyes and slowly and surely drew their plans against us."* — Orson Welles in "The War of the Worlds."

June 1, 1979

Farewell Josie; hello sorrow

JOSIE.

Actually, her name was Josephine. We called her Josie most of the time. Josephine seemed like such a long name for such a small dog. She was a little black poodle, sister to our dog, Yazzie.

When Roger and Kay Conner — Trish's parents — come up from

Mesa, Ariz., in the summer to visit, they bring along Josie. She always loved it here. I don't think she ever got used to desert heat. The first thing Josie would do was go out in our back yard and snuggle down in the cool grass.

She and Yazzie got along so well. They'd sleep together, eat at the same time, and I loved walking with them along Bear Creek in the early evening. They would scamper along in tandem, as though tied together by an invisible leash.

Josie didn't look quite right when she arrived last week. Her back feet sometimes slipped out from under her. I thought it was strange she didn't want to come with Yazzie and me to the park.

Roger and Kay had written a couple of months ago that Josie was ill. The veterinarian had thought she might have a tumor. Another doctor said she was OK.

But she wasn't. Looking back, I guess we all knew that. She ate very little. We tried some baby food, cottage cheese, cat food. Nothing worked. Trish noticed a strange odor about her.

In the meantime, Roger and Kay were off to Hawaii Wednesday to celebrate their 50th wedding anniversary. I told them not to worry. We would take good care of Josie.

By coincidence, Trish had planned to go to Chicago for a weekend reunion of her nursing school class. Susan, our daugther, tagged along. She loves Chicago.

I took them to the airport the afternoon this was written. Before we left, Trish told me she was quite worried about Josie. She didn't like that odor. Nurses know about smells. I told her I would take Josie to Anderson's Animal Hospital.

On the way to the airport, Trish started to cry. I knew it was about Josie, but we kidded about something else and she started to laugh. After I got them on the plane, I went home to get Josie.

Dr. John Albers had seen her last week. He said he knew then that the cancer had spread from the tumor on her breast to the rest of her body. I asked the inevitable, "Should we have her put to sleep?"

"It would be a kind thing to do. She is terribly uncomfortable. There is no hope," he said.

He left us alone for a couple of minutes. I took off Josie's collar, petted her and said goodbye from all of us. She was trembling.

Dr. Albers came back in the room, picked up Josie very tenderly and said, "There, there, little girl. You'll feel a lot better in just a minute."

I tried not to cry when I paid the bill. I don't do well at that kind of thing. Trish and Susan will call. I am going to lie and say I left Josie at the hospital for observation. I don't want to spoil their weekend.

I'll tell them about Josie when they get home Sunday night. I'm not looking forward to that.

Or telling Roger and Kay.

June 12, 1983

6

WHO GIVES A BEEP?: NEW TECHNOLOGY

Who gives a beep?

BEEP.

Show me a man with a little black radio paging gizmo on his belt and I'll show you someone who takes Di-Gel. Those little beepers are becoming a menace.

Unfortunately, they also are a status symbol among business-types who fancy themselves as big hummers. You can't go anywhere these days without hearing a lot of beep-ah-dee-beep all over the place.

It all started with the doctors. There probably was some justification for wiring physicians so they could be reached in cases of medical emergency. It is my view, however, that about half of those calls really dealt with matters like picking up a loaf of bread on the way home.

Now, everybody is getting into the act. Lawyers, insurance agents, storm window salesmen and other busybodies are carrying beepers.

They love to be beeped in public. It is supposed to give them an aura of mystery and importance. To be noticed is to be admired. Or so they think.

We all have had the experience of seeing someone beeped in a restaurant. Beeping etiquette calls for the individual to feign embarrassment, smile, briefly excuse himself and then walk swiftly from the room.

This is supposed to leave the rest of us in a state of wonder and respect. Who called? What was the message? Is everything going to be all right?

Some of the new beepers are more sophisticated. They actually speak. Sometimes you can hear the voice of a little mechanical woman. She'll say something like, "Barney Dolan must reach you by 12:30 or the deal is off."

Mountain Bell is marketing a long-distance pocket pager. You can be beeped almost anywhere along the Front Range. Service is available in Denver, Boulder, Colorado Springs, Pueblo, Fort Collins and Greeley.

Some people probably get beepers because they are heavy into electronic gadgetry, like CB radios, digital wristwatches and pocket calculators.

Most have them, however, because they seem to bolster one's

151

sense of self-importance. Beepers convey the notion life and commerce will not continue unless a key person is beeped.

The greatest annoyance for the rest of us is the person who is beeped at lunch. No one wants to hear someone else's electronic sounds while rendering justice to a hot corned beef sandwich and a glass of cold beer.

It is my suspicion that some people who carry pocket pagers are really cheapskates. They arrange to have someone beep them at about the time the check is to be paid.

But, assuming that is not the case, it just isn't healthy to be interrupted by a beep at mealtime. As a matter of fact, people shouldn't even discuss business while dining.

Business and food don't go together. Improperly combined, they produce heartburn and other stress-related ailments. One thing leads to another and pretty soon the beep becomes a burp. That's when the busy executive starts popping those antacid pills.

Maybe the restaurant ought to have beep and non-beep sections. Sort of like areas for people who still are foolish enough to smoke and those who do not.

That way, the more civilized among us could be protected from all that confusion and noise. That would leave the high achievers to themselves. They would feel free to be beeped as much as they like, and even to beep each other.

Hypertension doesn't always have its consequences in the upper digestive system. It can affect the heart. If that happens, the guy who thinks he is so important that he can't be out of touch will find himself with the ultimate beeper.

The electronic heart pacer.

July 18, 1979

Don't call me

Dial 9.

"What hath God wrought?" wondered Samuel F.B. Morse as he tapped out his first telegraph message. I have given it some thought and have concluded God hath wrought more than I can handleth.

My problem is not with the telegraph, but with the modern

telephone. I liked it better when I could pick up the phone and the operator would say, "Number, plee-uz."

I would say, "Let me talk to Keystone 7924." She would ring the phone, and my call would go through. Simple.

But not anymore. Here at the Rocky, we have something called the DIMENSION PBX, and I haven't figured out how to call Trish to see if she wants me to pick up a loaf of bread on my way home.

To complicate matters, a note on my desk the other day said: "We no longer have the 'call forwarding all calls' ability on our phone system. Instead, this feature has been changed to 'call forward busy don't answer.'

"To activate this new feature you will hit *3, listen for the dial tone and dial the four-digit extension, hear the confirmation beeps and hang up."

Hang up? I'm sorry I picked up the darn thing in the first place. I don't want any calls forwarded. I have never had any good news on the telephone, and I certainly don't want bad news beeped forward. Just let it die right there on the line.

As if this weren't enough, I was out of town for a few days, and while I was gone, the dunderheads who own the radio station where I moonlight had Ma Bell install the HORIZON® CS system.

Since I returned, I have been trying to assign my FLEX DSS/OUT button, whatever that is. I don't FLEX as well as I did as a younger man. My FLEX went shortly after I became short of breath and my knees buckled.

I did stumble upon something interesting. When I try to hold a call, I DEPRESS SWITCHHOOK, and my phone beeps out four notes of Beethoven's Fifth Symphony. It won't do Yankee Doodle, though.

It must be my age. I have a 13-year-old daughter who is a virtuosa on the telephone. I have known her to set up conference calls and call collect from the shopping center. Her greatest achievement was to get Mountain Bell to use a 20-cent stamp to refund a dime she claimed she was overcharged.

Ma Bell lost me by initiating all-digit dialing. I loved the old exchanges. Remember Spruce? Gallup? Tabor? Telephone numbers had personalities in those days. Not anymore. You know the lady who comes on the line to tell you the number you have dialed is no longer a working number? She is not a real lady. She is a computer lady. You can tell by the clipped way she says her numbers.

I don't know if Mountain Bell deserves the $127.4 million rate hike it has requested from the Colorado Public Utilities Commission. That's a bundle. The company cited inflationary pressures as the reason for the increase.

But from where I sit, Ma Bell's services have been inflated beyond my ability to use them. Until I come to terms with the new equipment, please don't call me.

I'll call you.

April 15, 1982

Computer-think

A BAD DREAM.

The most terrifying of nightmares is the one where you are about to be overwhelmed. It might be water. Sometimes you feel buried in sand. It could be anything.

Whatever it is, it keeps coming at you. There is nothing you can do to stop it no matter how you twist and turn and scream.

In this case, it's information. We are all waking up to find that our bad dream has come true. We are swamped with data and it is about to smother us.

Technology is the culprit. It's another case of our inability to deal with the consequences of machines.

It isn't so much a matter of what they are doing for us. It is what they are doing to us that is so bad.

Pop sociologist Marshall McLuhan saw it coming. He said. "The Xerox machine has made every man a publisher." He was referring to the photocopier device developed first by the Xerox company.

Instead of just sparing typists' fingernails and saving their time, the photocopier has glutted our lives with printed matter that we have no hope of ever reading.

Same thing with those frightening word-processing systems. They print material at thousands of words a minute. The machines don't give a hoot whether anybody ever actually reads the stuff. They just keep spewing it out until somebody pulls the plug.

People in business do their best to read the mounds of material relative to what they do. It's a lost cause. Trade journals are stacked on top of industry association reports and interoffice memoranda.

The poor wretch who tries to keep up with all of this will find that he can't. He gives up reading altogether. The job of data processing is given to a computer. It's just another machine that couldn't care less whether the material is ever read by a human being.

Of all of these devices, the photocopier probably is the most misused. It is too simple to operate. Any boob can push a button.

The result has been a floodtide of printed matter, most of which did not deserve duplication. File clerks cram it away in sliding drawers where it will stay forever.

The business of bureaucrats is paper work. That's why they love the photocopier. It permits them to seem busy and productive. With only the slightest bit of effort, the bureaucrat can use the photocopier to make himself appear to be significantly involved in important materials.

The bureaucracy is not happy just to inundate itself with printed matter. It imposes these same requirements on industry. Reports, applications, studies, evaluations, reviews and action programs are exchanged and filed away without anybody ever reading them, let alone comprehending their contents.

We have come around to the point of believing that if we throw enough information at a problem, it will somehow be solved.

But instead of dealing with solutions, devices like the photocopier only help us cope with some degree of personal frustrations. When the problem seems to defy our first efforts at logical resolution, we turn to our loyal photocopier.

We push the button. Little lights flash. The machine buzzes and whirs and printed material slides out into the tray.

We are no closer to solving the problem. But the machine gives us a false sense of accomplishment. Each time the button is pushed, another paper slides out.

We stack up and file away duplicated materials. They become bulk and tangible evidence of our commitment to problem solving.

Quote: *"The real danger is not that computers will begin to think like men, but that men will begin to think like computers."* — Sidney J. Harris.

June 8, 1979

Cut the cacophony

ONE MOMENT, PLEASE.

The switchboard operator then puts you on hold. Immediately, the late Guy Lombardo's orchestra swings into a peppy little arrangement of "Tipi Tipi Tin."

It is the same kind of music you hear in hotel lobbies and while you are getting a root canal at the dentist's office.

Our Frances Melrose complained that she had to listen to "two Spanish songs before the taxicab would come down here to pick me up and take me home."

I agree with Frances that music doesn't belong on the telephone. It is bad enough to be a part of a captive audience in an elevator, but everyone should be entitled to a little peace and quiet on the telephone.

Society has become addicted to noise. I guess people just have to hear something all the time. It must be a fear of being alone.

I welcome a little silence when the operator puts me on hold. Gives me a chance to collect my thoughts and plan the bottle of beer I'll have when I get home.

It can be too much of a good thing, though. You have to wonder sometimes if the operator has decided, in the memorable language of John Ehrlichman, to "let him twist slowly, slowly in the wind."

Sooner or later, someone is bound to be curious about that little pulsating light on the telephone and will ask, "For whom are you waiting?"

You barely get the name out before the voice comes back, "I'm sorry. He just left for lunch and won't be back until 2:30."

My pet peeve with the telephone is that I don't understand what the switchboard operators say. They speak in a monotone, go too fast and run their words together.

"Gerd merning. MingusRaffertyandBloom. Wern mermernt, pleez." That's when you are put on hold and Guy Lombardo does his thing.

You try to go back in your mind to reconstruct what the operator said. This is difficult to do while tapping your foot to "Tipi Tipi Tin."

It is one of those coordination things like simultaneously patting the head and rubbing the tummy.

I hasten to add that the operators here are certainly not guilty of going too fast and running their words together. They enunciate "Rocky Mountain News" very carefully, and with considerable feeling.

Some switchboard operators answer by just reciting the last four digits of their telephone numbers. Law firms and doctors' offices follow this practice.

It is unsettling to hear someone say, "Seven-four-three-two" when you are expecting to hear the name of a person or a company.

When someone does that to me, I have been known to reply, "This is Nine. May I speak to Seven, please." If that doesn't work, I usually holler, "Hut! Hut! Hut!"

The worst of all switchboard operators is the one who isn't there. You know what I mean. The tape recorder that answers the phone.

"This is the law firm of Marvin Whiplash. I am out of the office at this time. Please leave your name and telephone number. You will have 15 seconds to state your message at the sound of the tone."

It is demeaning to have to talk to a tape recorder. Orwellian nonsense. Sometimes I say, "Marvin, you can take that trick tape recorder of yours and put it where the sun doesn't shine."

Lately, though, I just wait for the tone and whistle a few bars of "Tipi Tipi Tin."

November 29, 1979

On colorations

MAUVE-ISH.

I hate it when we redecorate. It isn't having the house messed up that bothers me, nor is it the smell of the paint that annoys. It is being involved in small decisions. I decide the big things in our family, like American policy in Central America and grain sales to Russia. Trish takes care of choosing the color to paint our living room.

Only she won't let it go at that. "We want colors that are restful, not dull. Stimulating, not excessively vivid. The colors and textures we select will make a very important statement about our family and our lifestyle," she said.

"Hey, whatever."

"Don't say that. This is very important. We are going to have to live with these colors. Certainly we must have contrasts, but they must be subtly defined. There must be harmonious ambiance. Keep in mind that we are talking total experience here. I need your input," Trish said earnestly.

"I am inputing the money. You input the color."

"Wait. Come over here," she said, ignoring me completely. "What I think we're going to do is try to pick up the color in this picture. Look at it very carefully It's mauve. At least it is sort of mauve-ish.

"And then we'll use a kind of a heather-gray-ish in these cushions. The print in the chair upholstery is almost hyacinth. I like that, don't you? Or maybe you would prefer something plum-ish."

"Heck if I know. Go ahead and do what you think is right."

"We are going to have to have the dining room chairs recovered. The oatmeal clashes with the off-charcoal. I don't think a cream or a khaki would work either. Cognac would be a bit much."

"Taupe-ish?" I volunteered.

"Of course not. That would be as tasteless as using, say a chamois or a sand. We don't want to get into the butter colors either. I rather like the putty and okra tones, but I suspect they are too green-ish for what we are trying to accomplish here. We might keep them in mind for the basement, though."

I tried to slip out to the kitchen to get a beer, but her hand tightened firmly around my wrist. "The hallway is important because it is transitional from the living room to the stairway."

"Like the knee bone connected to the leg bone," I said, snapping my fingers in tempo.

"We'll use a fine-print floral wallpaper, picking up quiet suggestions of the downstairs colors and those we'll be using upstairs. By the way, that avocado capeting in the guest room will have to go. So will those pumpkin-ish rugs in Susan's room."

"Yuuuck. Barf. Barf." I shuddered in agreement.

"You see," Trish said brightly. "I knew you could do it. All I wanted was just a little help."

She picked up her carpet swatches, fabric samples and color charts, leaving me standing in the hall. There was only one question left in my mind:

Whatever happened to the good old red-ish, white-ish and blue-ish?

August 7, 1983

Lament of the inept

HE'S GONE.

The plumber just left. He was here about 30 minutes. It didn't take him any longer than that to "snake out," as he put it, a stopped-up drain in the basement bathroom.

I don't know how much it cost. My wife, Trish, gave him a check. I was not available at the time beause I was hiding upstairs in the bedroom.

You are thinking that I should have been able to unstick that drain. You are absolutely right. Easy little job like that. Anybody could do it.

Almost anybody.

Not this kid. Not only am I unable to make the simplest mechanical repairs, I will break anything that is working properly simply by touching it. I ought to be committed to the Colorado State Home for the Inept.

It must be some sort of family curse. My father once confessed to me that he had manual dexterity roughly equivalent to that of a bear cub. My sons are similarly afflicted.

I have always envied the guy who has natural mechanical skills. He is the sort of smart alec who squints his eyes as he looks at your busted power lawn mower and says, "It is obvious that the cable to your fistarus is malfunctioning. That's why the kranastan won't open."

It isn't that I don't try. Over the years, I don't know how many times I have tried to fix that little valve in the toilet tank.

You know the one. It's at the bottom of the tank. After the toilet has been flushed, water flows back into the tank, raising the float ball to the top, automatically closing the valve.

That's the way it should be. But it doesn't work that way in our biffy. The water just doesn't push the float ball high enough to turn off the water. It comes close, but not close enough.

The valve stays open and the water continues to run, it runs night and day. God only knows how many thousands of acre-feet of precious Colorado water have been lost because of my leaky john.

I try tightening the ball by turning it clockwise. That doesn't do it. Then I twist it the other way. The valve stays open.

Fury begins to replace reason. I try to bend the rod that holds the ball so it doesn't have to rise so high to shut the valve. That doesn't work either. I bend it the other way.

If anything, even more water escapes. I jerk the float ball so hard that it comes off in my hand. What had been the simplest of home repair jobs has become a major plumbing disaster.

The only thing to do is call the plumber. The operator at the answering service reminds me that because it is the weekend, the cost will be $46 an hour — plus parts.

I don't have any choice. The plumber arrives in about 30 minutes. He is wearing a leisure suit and he is irritable because he has been called in on his day off. While the plumber fixes the toilet, I hide in the bedroom. Trish writes him the check.

It isn't just plumbing. I can't repair anything. I long ago gave up trying to replace light switches and furnace filters. When I try to fix a screen door closer, the door either slams shut or the stubborn s.o.b. won't close at all.

If something happens to the automatic dishwasher, I immediately know what to do. I call GE. They send out a nice little lady repairwoman who can fix it in a jiffy.

I try to be away from home when she is scheduled to be there. If not, I hide in the bedroom and Trish writes her a check.

Oh, I've tried. Really. I have all those Sunset "how to" handbooks. My basement and garage are filled with tools. I have a belt sander and a three-eighths-inch reversible, variable speed drill. I have a radial arm table saw and three sets of socket wrenches. I don't know how to use any of them.

I just hide in the bedroom while Trish writes a check.

September 16, 1979

7

GOOD MEMORIES: PERSONALITIES

Because he has to

The first sketches of the murals in the rotunda of the Colorado Capitol building were made by poet Thomas Hornsby Ferril at a knife-throwing party.

It was the evening of June 8, 1935. Ferril and several friends had gone out to dedicate artist Allen True's new studio on Little Dry Creek.

In addition to Ferril and True, the distinguished gathering included architects Burnham Hoyt and G.B. Kaufman. The latter designed Hoover Dam. Also on hand were sculptor Arnold Ronnebeck and Robert Edmond Jones of the theater.

As the tempo of the party increased, the celebrants began to throw knives, hatchets and ice picks at the door of True's new studio. "As a lifelong knife thrower," Ferril recalled, "I'd let the wagering suckers win a few pots, then move in for the kill when the kitty was high enough.

"Several drinks later, along toward sunrise, we bogged down in harangue about art, everybody arguing, nobody listening.

"We got hungry. Allen sent his son out for hamburgers, which we gobbled up. I salvaged the greasy paper bag the hamburgers came in. Then I held forth eloquently on why water was the great theme of the West."

Only True was listening at that point. It was getting very late. "I began drawing pictures on the hamburger sack, telling Allen he could make murals out of them," Ferril said. "He saved the sack and painted the murals. I had agreed to write poetic texts.

"All eight murals were ready to go up in the rotunda in 1938. Allen had painted them in a greenhouse at City Park. But I hadn't written the poems. Our dear friend, Charlie Bayly, so generous to the Denver Art Museum, said if I didn't write the poems, he would.

"Much as I loved Charlie, I wasn't about to let him do the poems. Charlie was expert at other things, such as driving his mother's electric automobile to East High and running bullfighting shows in Central America.

"So I got up early one morning and wrote all the poems at one sitting. The lettering was done by Pascal Quackenbush. When the government money ran out, the generous Boettchers footed the bill. The job was completed in 1940."

Tuesday, Gov. Richard D. Lamm will officially designate Ferril poet laureate for the state of Colorado. The honor is as richly deserved as it is overdue.

It is my view that Tom Ferril is one of this nation's great poets. Not just for Colorado. Not just for now. His greatness extends beyond region and time.

In a television program now being prepared about Ferril and his work, he is asked about the poet's relationship to nature. The answer will surprise some.

"A poet should never let the environment boss him around, no matter how magnificent or overpowering," Ferril said. "He should never let scenery take the upper hand. That's why good English poets wrote bad poetry in Switzerland.

"I love our great mountains and rivers, but they are only tools for implementing the meaning of life. After all, man is the subject of poetry, and man alone. We must never forsake the play for the setting."

Ferril likes to describe poetry as a "passionate apprehension of experience." He believes it should cover the whole range of life from agony to ecstasy.

At 83, Tom Ferril is now at work on his sixth volume of poems, "Anvil of Roses." He says he writes poetry "because I have to."

Thank God for that.

Quote: *"I have held rivers to my eyes like lenses, and rearranged the mountains at my pleasure, as one might change the apples in a bowl."* — Thomas Hornsby Ferril.

September 30, 1979

Wrestling with fate

BRUNO.

That wasn't his name. I see him on the streets every now and then. I'd rather not use his real name. You'll understand later.

I thought about him the other day when I saw a story about the remodeling of old Mammoth Gardens. It took me back more than 30

years to the time I worked there as a ring announcer for the Monday
night wrestling matches.

Tom Zaharias hired me. He had been a prominent professional
wrestler. His ears cauliflowered and his belly too ample for the ring,
Tom retired and settled back to promote matches.

I got 15 bucks a night. It was always in cash. I was the guy who got
up in the center of the ring, took the mike that was lowered from the
ceiling and hollered, "And in this corner weighing 257 pounds, is Mad
Man Mullins! He is wearing black trunks and is the Great Lakes
defending champion."

I liked working with professional wrestlers. Contrary to their
outrageous public behavior, I found most of them to be kind, generous, decent people.Those I remember with particular fondness were
Danny Loos, Mr. America, the Angel, Gorgeous George and Bad Boy
Brown.

Bruno was different. A loner, he hardly spoke to anyone, and he
created problems for Tom. Wouldn't follow the script. The other
wrestlers didn't like that. He was mean and vicious. He really tried to
hurt his opponents, and he often succeeded. But the crowd came to
see blood, and Bruno gave it to them.

The other wrestlers decided to take matters into their own hands.
They set him up in a match with the Angel, a brute of a man with a
large misshapen face. Like most of the others, he was really a gentle
man, but he was extremely strong.

Tom instructed Bruno and the Angel to go the full three falls.
Mammoth Gardens was sold out and Tom didn't want to disappoint
the fans. When I came into the ring, they were screaming at the top
of their lungs. After the introductions, I ducked under the ropes to
watch.

To everyone's astonishment, the match was over almost before it
began. The Angel grabbed Bruno's right arm and immediately
wrenched it out of the shoulder socket. Bruno screamed in agony.

We carried him downstairs to the locker room and put him on a
bench. While Bad Boy sat on him, Mr. America and I pulled his arm
hard, and we finally got it back in the socket. Bruno groaned and
cursed. He managed to dress himself and leave.

Bruno was off the circuit for weeks. When he finally recovered,
Tom booked him back into Mammoth. When he climbed into the ring
that night, he took one look at me, jerked the microphone out of my
hand, ripped it off the cord and slammed it across the side of my
head. I don't remember much else; I quit the next day.

That was the last I saw of Bruno for five years. The next time was
at a charity telethon. I had just done my pitch when a group of

children in wheelchairs were being pushed onstage by their parents.

There was Bruno. His daughter was a small, frail, blonde child. I could see by her tiny legs she would never walk. The Bruno I saw then was not the one I remembered. He was quietly attending to someone he obviously loved very much.

As I watched that pathetic parade before the TV cameras, I began to understand the other Bruno — the one in the ring. His fury was not really against me and the wrestlers. It was against what fate had done to his daughter.

Yes, I still see Bruno occasionally. We don't speak. He doesn't wrestle anymore. Too old. But I'd be willing to bet he is still taking care of that little girl.

November 3, 1981

A letter to Starr

DEAR STARR:

It's a free country. Relatively so. I guess the big corporations have a right to make bonehead mistakes. But I couldn't believe it when McGraw-Hill broadcasting announced that you were being put on early retirement at Channel 7.

You were too popular. Is that the way it was? They had to get you out of the way so the new guy coming in would have a shot at higher audience ratings. Would CBS fire Walter Cronkite so Roger Mudd would be better-known?

It's a crazy business. You and I came into broadcasting about the same time. How long has it been? At least 37 or 38 years. We've been friends most of that time. What is happening to you now hurts me almost as much as it must be hurting you. A lot of your friends feel that way.

I have never had any quarrel with the notion that the young have to replace the old. But dammit, Starr, I think they ought to have to prove they are better.

You've probably said the same thing to yourself. Listen, buddy, the whole town knows you are really No. 1. It doesn't matter how many of those pearly-teethed androids they parade in front of the camera, they'll never replace you.

Since the news broke that you would be leaving Channel 7, I've been having all sorts of Starr Yelland flashbacks. They begin with your salad days at pre-World War II KOA radio.

Remember old Studio D on the third floor? On a clear day you could look across California Street and see through the dressing room window at Montaldo's.

Laughs. Lots of them with Bob Young, Tor Torland, Bill Balance, Milt Shrednik, Gil Verba, Ivan Schooley, Bill Day, Evadna Hammersley, Happy Jack Turner and Frances McCoy.

There were Ed Brady, Chuck Collins, Bob Palmer, Eddie Bowman, Clyde Davis, Shorty, Sue and Sally and Cecil Seavey. Remember Mozart's? That was the little joint down the street where everybody drank beer after work.

The first time we actually worked together was in 1948. I had a show on KOA called "Breakfast at Baur's."

I was the emcee, you were the announcer and Lenny Baylinson played the novachord. It was a terrible program. Not your fault. Not mine, either. Not Lenny's. It was just a bad show. I was fired and you were sympathetic.

Most people think of you only as a TV personality. I always thought you were great on radio. You weren't afraid to do anything. You practically invented talk-radio with "Party Line."

I'll never forget the night you called W.C. Handy at his home in Memphis. It was his birthday. He must have been near 90. You talked him into getting out his old cornet and playing his own composition, "St. Louis Blues," over the telephone. Starr, you are incredible.

People don't know how tough it is to go on television sometimes. When things aren't going right and your heart is breaking, you somehow have to get your act together and go on anyhow. I don't know how many times I have seen you do that.

I will never forget how brave you and Helen were when your son was injured in that roller coaster accident. There were those long months of treatment and then he died. I will never understand how you managed all that. I couldn't.

We've all taken our lumps along the way. I can remember trying to put my life back together. When Trish and I got married in that little Point Loma chapel out in San Diego, you were there. You and Helen.

And then there was that day when Helen and I stood outside the Coronary Care Unit at St. Joseph's Hospital. We could just see your face through the crack in the door. I have to tell you this, I really didn't know whether you would make it.

You made it. Boy, how you made it. You have never looked better and your work has never been better.

Well, that's about it. No room here for the flood of all those good memories. You'll take this in stride. You are tough and talented and resourceful. I know that because I know you.

When things cool down, you and I and Carl Akers, Dusty Saunders, Tom Pade and some of the others will find a corner at the Press Club and hang one on.

Geno.

January 8, 1979

Gilda in her glory

BUMP AND GRIND.

Watching the TV Home Box Office special "Top Banana" the other night, I thought of a burlesque act in 1956 that closed in Denver after just one show. The audience was small. There were only three people, including the performer.

Gilda's claim to fame as a striptease dancer was that she had been one of the original "Our Gang" comedy kids in the movies. She was the one with the blonde hair and bangs. I met her when she was just beginning a six-week stint at the old Tropics nightclub on Morrison Road.

The first morning she turned up at the radio station where I did early morning news, Gilda was carrying a sack of doughnuts. She was wearing a prim-looking cotton shirtwaist dress and low-heel shoes. Her long hair was gathered in a modest bun at the back of her neck.

She explained she had insomnia and had come to the station after her last show. She said she enjoyed the clowning around Lloyd Knight and I used to do on his "Clockwatcher" radio program. It reminded her of her burlesque days.

Gilda would come out most mornings, always plainly dressed. No makeup. She would stay around and shoot the breeze between records until 9 a.m. Then she would get sleepy and go home to bed. That's about all there was to it. Neither Lloyd nor I ever saw her perform at the Tropics.

Lloyd was one of the most naturally funny men I ever knew. He was impulsively explosive at times. But there were other times when he would make elaborate preparations for his mischief. The years we worked together on the radio were the best either of us ever had.

It used to amuse him to try to make me laugh during my

newscasts. He would go to almost any extreme, sometimes setting fire to my copy or pantomiming the stories I was reading.

The 7 a.m. news was 15 minutes long. I would do the headlines and break for the first commercial at about 7:02. Then I would read the rest of the newscast until 7:12. There was a break for a second commercial. I would come back with the weather to finish at 7:14:30.

I got through the first commercial with no problem. As I started the center section, I heard the faint strains of Dave Rose's recording of "The Stripper" in the background. Lloyd must have been playing it on the cue monitor. I could hear it, but it wasn't going out over the air.

The door opened slowly. I glanced down and saw Gilda's leg. I looked back at the copy, knowing what was to come. To the insistent tempo of the music, Gilda danced into the newsroom.

I looked up again. She was pulling the hairpins out of the bun. All that blonde hair began to tumble down around her shoulders. After the next paragraph, I sneaked another look. Gilda was bumping and grinding around the newsroom, only this time she was starting to unbutton the top of her shirtwaist dress.

I knew that if there was any chance at all I was going to finish that newscast, I had better not look up again. It was about then I first began to hear Lloyd wheezing. He must have been standing in the doorway.

Even though my eyes were rivited to the copy, there was an occasional bare shoulder or knee in the periphery of my vision. I could smell perfume. At one point, there was some kind of cloth draped around the back of my head. I knew it had to be the skirt on that shirtwaist dress.

It was 7:11. I almost had it made. Lloyd began to cackle. My voice started to rise as I fought to keep from laughing, but it got higher and higher until it became a falsetto. I knew I was whipped. I shrieked, "I can't stand it! I can't stand it!" I started to pound my fists on the desk. Lloyd's face was crimson. Tears were streaming down his face. I looked at Gilda. She had crumpled to the floor and was giggling hysterically. She was fully clothed.

You believe that?

June 2, 1981

A triumph shared

BEN.

There's going to be a big birthday party for Ben Bezoff April 18 at the Regency Hotel. He will be 65.

About 400 are expected. Past and present members of Congress will be on hand. So will a couple of former governors and Mayor Bill McNichols, one of Ben's closest friends.

Newspaper reporters and broadcasters will be there to hoist a few. The politicians will turn out, some of whom may even be Republicans.

I have known Ben longer and better than most. He gave me my first regular job in broadcasting 37 years ago and we have been close friends since that time.

He taught me how to edit wire copy for radio newscasts and how to say "nyews" instead of "nooz." I worked hard to pattern my broadcast delivery after Ben, and I always was flattered when people said we sounded something alike.

If you want to understand Ben, you have to know something of vodka martinis and corned beef sandwiches. You must have seen him, telephone balanced on his shoulder, wheeling and dealing with Democratic district captains.

Your picture of Ben is not complete unless you share his love of Chopin and are tolerant of his addiction for old postage stamps. It is important that you see Ben through the eyes of his lovely wife, Cherie, and their daughters, Naomi and Manya.

Not enough space for all of that here. But maybe there's enough room left in this column for a story.

It was the summer of 1948 and I was out of work. I had wound up on the wrong end of a union dispute. There wasn't a radio station in this town that would hire me.

Ben was operating a little one-man advertising agency at the time. Even though he really couldn't afford it, he hired me to do a few advertising and public relations odd jobs.

You'll recall that 1948 was an election year. The Republicans had nominated Thomas E. Dewey and Earl Warren. That was the year the Democrats split. Former Vice President Henry Wallace and

Glenn Taylor were the Progressive Party standard bearers. Strom Thurmond and Fielding L. Wright splintered off into the States' Right Party.

What was left of the Democratic Party reluctantly nominated incumbent Harry Truman for president and aging Alben W. Barkley for vice president.

None of the big advertising agencies wanted any part of the Colorado Truman-Barkley campaign. No money. Truman was supposed to lose. Ben volunteered to handle the campaign, and I was his $200-a-month assistant.

We worked night and day. There was no money for political advertising, so we had to razzle-dazzle our way into newspapers.

It was announced Truman would whistle-stop through Denver and wanted to see as many people as possible. We couldn't afford to rent a hall so we used the west steps of the Capitol for a speech by Truman.

We staged a parade up 16th Street. At least 100,000 people turned out to cheer everything Truman said and did. It was a tremendous success.

Ben and I were exhausted. We rode in the motorcade to the Denver Union Station in the back of a borrowed limousine with Charlie Ross. He had been a Pulitzer Prize-winning columnist for the St. Louis Post Dispatch and was Truman's press secretary.

Ross thanked us warmly and said, "Boys, if there's ever anything you want in Washington, I want you to come and see me personally at the White House."

In later years, both of us realized that Truman would have swept Colorado anyway. We never went to Washington to ask for anything. That triumphant moment in the back of that old Cadillac was enough for us.

Ben has been ill. He doesn't know how much longer he will live. But then that's true for everyone. However much time there is for us, Ben and I have a wonderful memory to share.

April 4, 1979

Memories of Darlene overshadow sorrow

OBITS.

The first thing I do when I come to work is look at the obituaries. If my name isn't there, I go ahead and write a column. Not much point if I won't be around to get paid.

The problem is I keep seeing names of old friends. It is depressing to learn people you have loved are gone. Oh, sure, I am sorry for them, but it is more a matter of self-pity because I have lost my pals.

And so it was when I read of the death of Darlene Wycoff Robinson. Heart attack. Happened Jan. 12 in Hawaii, where she and her husband, William "Buzzy" Robinson, were vacationing.

The tragedy was compounded Monday noon when Buzzy killed himself. Family friends said he was just too overwhelmed with grief to go on. I can understand that.

Let's get the sad stuff out of the way so we can go ahead and remember the fun times. And fun times they were. I don't think I ever saw Darlene, or "Baby," as many called her, when she wasn't laughing.

I first knew her in late 1945 when she was club editor here at the News. She became society editor a year later. She was good because she never broke a confidence or betrayed a source.

Darlene didn't sit around wringing her hands about the First Amendment. Her journalism was gossipy, frothy. It was sometimes funny — funnier than she intended.

We still laugh about the time she wrote of a very important society wedding, "The marriage was consummated at the altar of St. Martin's Episcopal Chapel before 200 delighted guests."

And then there was her classic, "The newlyweds will spend their honeymoon fishing and hunting bare."

The result of these unintentional gaffes was usually a parade of stern-faced ministers, irate fathers and hysterial mothers into the office of editor Jack Foster. They usually got a stock apology from Foster but very little contrition from Darlene.

She never took the whole la-dee-da business of society too serious-

ly, not even after she became part of it. That happened when Darlene
and Buzzy were married in 1951. He was a member of one of
Denver's oldest and wealthiest families.

There was quiet grumbling among some who thought Buzzy should
have married within his "class" rather than to someone who worked.
But the whispers never bothered Darlene. She drifted easily into the
Circle Drive aristocracy, becoming a wonderful wife, devoted mother and friend.

But she never forgot her old buddies who remained on the other
side of the tracks. Her roots were here. The last time I saw her she
was having lunch with former Rocky staffers Sam Lusky and Leonard Tangney. They were in a booth at Copperfields, across the street
from Mother News.

I could hear her infectious laughter before I saw her. Wearing a
very chic black dress, she was never more beautiful. That's the way
I'll remember her — in good company, in good health, in wonderful
spirits.

We loved you, Darlene.

January 23, 1983

No regrets

H.

"This is Preparation H.," the voice on the telephone said. "I was
wondering if we could have lunch next Tuesday at Mission Trujillo."

It was H. Ray Baker. I have never known what that first initial
stood for. Hannibal? Horrace? Heathcliff? It doesn't really matter.

H., as most people know him, was an artist and editor of Empire
magazine at The Denver Post for years. He chucked the whole thing
about 15 years ago to embark on an odyssey that took him to Greece,
Taos, N.M., and points between.

When I arrived at Mission Trujillo, a nice Mexican restaurant in
Littleton, I spotted H. at the bar. I hadn't seen him in years. His hair
had turned almost white, and he was sporting one of those little Van
Dyke beards that are so popular these days.

He said there were others coming and that John Trujillo had set
aside a table for us in the back. I wandered over and was pleasantly
surprised to see a half-dozen cronies from the old days. A couple of

newspaper-radio types, a dentist, a retired huckster and even an editor emeritus.

When H. sat down beside me, I asked him what the purpose of the occasion was. "I just wanted to see how many of you are still alive," he said.

John put a couple of large carafes of margaritas on the table. We all settled back to laugh and talk of years that had slipped by so quickly.

H. is 69 now and not in the best of health. He walks with a cane and has had to quit painting. He lives in a retirement community near Mission Trujillo.

He said his 7-year-old son had visited him from California recently. A couple of ladies where he lives took note of the lad. One of them sweetly told H. what a fine-looking grandson he had.

"Grandson, hell," H. exploded. "He's my son." The woman appeared flustered at first, then shocked. She sputtered a bit and then scolded H., telling him that he ought to be ashamed of himself.

"I told her, to the contrary, I was very proud of myself. As a matter of fact," H. said indignantly, "I am more proud of that boy than anything else I have ever done."

H. has certainly done a lot of things. He wrote a book called "Mountain Men." He can't remember how many paintings he has done. H. does recall how many times he has been married, however, although the figure eludes me. His eldest son is 42. It might be said that H. has touched most of the bases in his time. As a result, he is admittedly somewhat chipped around the edges.

H. hasn't mellowed any. He is a forthright and crusty as ever. In talking about the radio station where I also work, H. said, "I can't stand that supercilious, condescending sonofabitch who is on your station at 10 in the morning."

I forgot to ask him what had happened to all those paintings he had done, particularly the ones of some well-known Denver ladies who had posed for him *au nu*, as the French would say.

I still have the painting he gave me in 1964. It is titled "The Debutante." It is done is shades of blue and pink. The young woman in the foreground has a pretty, but pointless, face. Her mother is standing behind. The family resemblance is there, but the mother's face has become hardened, not so much by years as by ambition and greed.

I suppose the painting is more of a caricature than anything else. It is both funny and tragic. People who have seen it tell me it makes them uncomfortable. I like it, though.

During lunch, H. told me he has no regrets and no apologies.

We went our separate ways about 2 p.m. As we left the table, I noticed one of the carafes of margaritas was only half-empty, indicating that some of us had slowed down some.

Quote: *"Old age and treachery can overcome youth and skill."* — H. Ray Baker.

November 13, 1980

War buddies

ESPY IS DEAD.

I just found out about it, even though he died back in 1976. Lung cancer. They think it was caused by some sort of industrial fumes he had inhaled at work. He was 54.

Reuben Espinosa and I became friends back in World War II. There were just a handful of Denver guys assigned to what had been a Missouri National Guard battalion. You know how those things can be. We were a minority. Had to stick together.

So long ago.

Now, here I sit, trying to sort out some very painful personal feelings about my friend. A lot of it has to do with coincidence. No, it's not really coincidence. It is more than the random way life seems to bring people together.

A letter came to the News Friday, asking my help in running down a "letter to the editor" that had somehow become lost. It was signed by a Reuben Espinosa.

There was a telephone number listed. After finding out what I could about the missing letter, I called this Reuben Espinosa. As I dialed the number, I had a feeling he was the son of my old friend. He was.

When I asked about his father, I learned Espy had died. I was shattered. It was very difficult to talk. Have you had that happen to you? It was all so sudden — so unexpected. Even though I had not seen Espy for many years, I had a profound feeling of loss.

While I was bumbling on the telephone about how sorry I was and how I wished I had known, young Espinosa remained composed. He explained about the lung cancer and what sort of redress the family hoped to attain.

Espinosa reminded me of another chance touching of our lives. He and my older son, Brett, had met while both were attending the University of Colorado at Denver.

If you are still reading this, you may be wondering why the name Reuben Espinosa seems to familiar to you. You have read it in the newspapers. His uncle, Arthur Espinosa, was one of two men shot to death in an ugly confrontation with police in Curtis Park a year ago. Young Reuben Espinosa has been the family spokesman during subsequent events.

Do you remember seeing him on television? You may recall how calm and well-spoken he was. His statements to the press were articulate and sincere. That's the way he sounds on the telephone, too. There's a kind of steadiness about him.

We didn't talk much about the Curtis Park incident. I think I said that "some good can come out of all things" and that I hoped his life would somehow benefit from the experience.

He said he hoped so. And then he added, "You know, I'm really a very moderate person, but sometimes — sometimes, it is very hard to keep the lid from blowing off."

I told him that I had tried over the years to contact his father. Somehow, I wasn't able to bring it off. I remember seeing him years ago in front of his house, down at 20th and Champa. He was in construction work at the time.

I asked Reuben why Espy never tried to get in touch with me. He said he felt his father was embarrassed because he was so poor. That hurt. We had so much in common and had been through so much together. The memories. I can still see him grinning, with that muddy steel helmet pushed down over his eyes. I remember when he was wounded and how he bounced back up and went right back into action. I wonder if he ever told his family.

He's gone now. My thoughts are like some sort of crazy montage of Bear Valley and Curtis Park. Of Denver and Bastogne. Of Brett and Reuben at UCD.

It would have been great to see Espy before he died. We could have had a couple of beers and laughed and cried about what had happened to us.

I guess I'm angry at myself for not trying harder to find him. I'm mad at Espy, too. He could have trusted me more.

That's it, I guess. Personal accounts like this are very difficult for me. Draw whatever conclusions you wish from them, I just wanted it known that Espy was a fine, decent man.

August 14, 1978

The other paper

Ep.

Gravel-voiced Edwin Palmer Hoyt has always preferred that nickname. That's what he said when he blew into town back in February of 1946 to become editor and publisher of The Denver Post.

Ep Hoyt also wanted it known that he was going to shake up the stodgy old Post and also make some changes in what we were then calling the Queen City of the Plains. He was right on both counts.

The Post dropped its old pink front page and adopted a new type style. Hoyt gave the newspaper an editorial page, something it never had before. Reporters were ordered not to include editorial bias in their stories. The practice of "jumping" stories from one page to another was ended.

Hoyt then spent $2 million for a new plant and presses at 15th and California streets, the Post's present location. The move was made from the old Champa street site in 1950.

While he was doing all this, Hoyt moved swiftly to annex 13 Western states into what he proclaimed the Rocky Mountain Empire. He then declared Denver the capital and the Post the voice of the empire. Hoyt never publicly named himself emperor of the domain, but few doubted that was what was really in his mind.

There was understandable grumbling from those who resented this new citizenship being imposed upon them in such an arbitrary way. It isn't enough to say that other newspapers, particularly this one, were indignantly aggrieved. Not nearly enough. No sir.

Hoyt didn't mind. He went right ahead with is broad-brush plans to change the way news was reported and published in this town. He beefed up staffs in all departments. Hoyt imported talented journalists like Dick Dudman, Fred Colvig, Bill Hosokawa, Don Sterling and Thor Severson. He made Ed Dooley managing editor and Bob Lucas head of the editorial page. The third man in the operating troika was business manager Chuck Buxton.

Gifted writers like Bob Stapp, Jack Frank, Ken White, Jim Kelly, Red Fenwick and Larry Tajiri came to the Post. Will Haselbush and Don Davis were on the desk, Bernie Kelly, Olga Curtis, Tom Watt, Eva Hodges, Frank Haraway, George McWilliams, Buzz Larsen,

Tom Gavin, George Brown, Bill Beardshear, Bob Bowie, Mort Stern, Harry Farrar, Paul Conrad, Pat Collins, Orin and Ira Sealy, Ralph Baird, Ed Maker and so many more were there.

Ep Hoyt recognized that there was a lot of little boy in grown men. He got stuffy business leaders to dress up in cowboy clothes to ride the Post's train to the annual Cheyenne Frontier Days.

The Post opened a Washington Bureau under Barney Nover and sent its reporters on junkets all over the world.

He had his detractors. Gene Cervi, publisher of Cervi's Journal, would bitterly say, "Ep Hoyt is a sonofabitch." And then he would add, "But by God, he's a good newspaperman."

Hoyt helped engineer the defeat of Mayor Ben Stapleton's 20-year political machine. Handpicked to replace him was Quigg Newton, an apple-cheeked lawyer who really knew very little about the city or its problems. The new mayor supposedly got his instructions directly from Hoyt over a private telephone line.

Ep Hoyt's empire began to crumble as earnings on Denver Post stock started to decline rapidly. Hoyt was shoved into retirement in 1970. He was unjustly blamed for all of the Post's economic problems.

Somewhere the record ought to show that the coming of television had a great deal to do with those declining revenues. Afternoon newspapers in other cities were going broke. But the Post weathered the storm and also attempts of publisher S.I. Newhouse to gain control of the paper. Much of the credit for survival is due Palmer Hoyt. He was bold and imaginative.

Ep's health has been failing. He's now at home, recovering from recent surgery. He hopes to be up and around in a few weeks.

Hoyt is one of a kind, and our city is richer because of him.

November 12, 1978

Real stars on TV

PRIME TIME.

It's good to see Jimmy Hawthorne doing weather reports on television. Channel 4 ought to pay him a lot of money and put him in prime time so the station would get higher audience ratings.

Hawthorne has made weather fun again. Part of it is the way he appears. He's not one of those plastic-looking glamor guys. He wears big round-eyed, thick-lens spectacles. They make him look like Kermit the Frog.

Jimmy doesn't bore you with a lot of low-pressure system and upslope nonsense. I was watching him last weekend. He jabbed his finger at Illinois on the weather map and shouted, "Look at that! The Midwest is going to be wet, Wet, WET! Talk about wet, they are really gonna have a big chunk of wet!"

Hawthorne sometimes talks to himself, using different voices for each side of the dialogue. He was like a man possessed. He whirled around and said. "I am now going to conduct the chorus of the National Association of Weather Singers."

At that point, we could hear the KOA radio weather jingle. Hawthorne was waving his arms in tempo with the music and was mouthing the jingle lyrics.

I have know Hawthorne for many years. We are both graduates of the old KMYR radio station, sometimes known as the F.W. Meyer Home for Bad Little Boys Who Want to be Radio Announcers.

Jimmy has since been a major radio personality in California and a broadcast executive in Hawaii. His late night radio show on ABC was a coast-to-coast hit. He was one of the really funny guys on Hollywood television back in the early '50s.

Hawthorne is now radio promotion manager at KOA. I suppose the reason he doesn't perform much anymore is because he doesn't want to. Still, it would be nice to see him regularly.

Television weathercasting in this town has gone downhill since KOA put the skids under Ed "Weatherman" Bowman some years ago. He was the greatest, bar none.

Bowman really knew his meteorology, or so he said. But that didn't keep him from using some non-traditional weather forecasting methods.

My favorite was his way of figuring the chances of rain. Bowman would drive around the edge of town until he found a field in which cattle were grazing. He would compute the percentage of cows lying down to those standing up and that was the precipitation probability.

When Bowman and I worked together on television, he used to frequently inquire how my left knee felt. It has one of those Joe Namath joints. The cartilage had been surgically removed.

Bowman would tell the audience that the pain in my "old war wound" indicated that we were going to have a storm.

After we got off the air, I said, "Eddie, I didn't hurt my knee in the war. I came through without a scratch. I bumped my knee on the kitchen floor."

"I know that," Bowman said, "but it sounds better if I tell 'em you were wounded in the war."

Psychiatrists had a field day with Bowman's weather maps. One of them told him that his jet stream arrows were really aggressive phallic symbols and that the cloud puffs were representative of great, pneumatic bosoms.

Bowman denied that his drawings were anything but weather maps. "I can't help it if psychiatrists have dirty minds," he said.

He had a rustic approach to weather reporting. He would say, "You better throw your slicker on the tractor seat tomorrow. It looks like we are going to have a real frog-strangler."

Eddie is a pilot. He used to fly an ancient open-cockpit Ryan. He wore scarf, helmet and goggles, riding boots and whipcord breeches. He looked like a short version of Waldo Pepper.

Bowman still lives in Denver. He does weather reports for out-of-town radio stations. Eddie is an authentic folk hero. He, like Hawthorne, ought to be on television regularly.

August 29, 1979

Billbarker recalled

BILLBARKER.

That's the way I'll remember him. Not Bill Barker. Billbarker. People always used both of his names together, as though they were just one name. I have heard people talk to him that way.

—"Billbarker, I loved your program last night," or "Billbarker, when is your new book coming out?"

I guess I always called him "Bark." But when H. Ray Baker telephoned me Monday, he said, "I just heard Billbarker died." I was saddened at the news but pleased he didn't linger in pain and discomfort. He had been a close friend for many years. His life disproved the old saw that "anyone can be replaced." There is no replacement for Billbarker.

I always admired the relationship he had with is wife, Lydia. They were very close. It is somehow appropriate that his last book, "The Whole Famn Damily," is about their life together. It will be in the bookstores in May.

There is one story about Billbarker I don't think has ever been written. To my knowledge, it was never in any of his Denver Post or Rocky Mountain Journal columns, and I don't think it was in his books, "The Wayward West" and "Denver," the latter written with Jackie Lewin. I know it wasn't in "The Search for Bridie Murphy."

He told it to me one night at the Press Club. The Western Slope resort of Aspen popped up in our conversation. I told him how impressed I was with the quality of participants at the Aspen Institute of Humanistic Studies, the Aspen Design Conference and the Aspen Music Festival. Billbarker smiled. "Would you like to know how all that really began?" he asked.

Certainly. He was witty, articulate, and he knew how to build his story to an unexpected climax. That's what he did with his Aspen yarn that night. I wish I had a tape recording of it.

As I recall the account, Billbarker said he had hired on in 1949 as a press agent for Walter Paepcke, the wealthy Chicago industrialist. It was Paepcke who is generally credited with converting Aspen from a sleepy, almost-deserted former silver boomtown, to the ski and culture mecca we know today.

Paepcke told Billbarker to find some kind of publicity stunt to promote Aspen's image as a think tank. After pouring over books at the library, Billbarker discovered that 1949 also was the 200th anniversary of the birth of the German poet-philosopher Johann von Goethe.

He suggested to Paepcke that Aspen ought to have a Goethe bicentennial convocation. According to Billbarker, Paepcke had never heard of Goethe, but the idea appealed to him anyhow. He told Billbarker to find out who was the top Goethe scholar in the world.

It was back to the library again. Billbarker learned that none other than Albert Schweitzer, the renowned physician, musician, philosopher and author, was then regarded as the No. 1 Goethe scholar in the world.

"Get him!" ordered Paepcke, even though he had never heard of Schweitzer either.

Since Paepcke had never heard of Schweitzer, Billbarker reasoned that Schweitzer hadn't heard of Paepcke. So the invitation was sent in a letter from Robert Hutchins, president of the University of Chicago, a friend of Paepcke's.

To everyone's astonishment, Schweitzer accepted. He made the 7,000-mile trip from his beloved jungle hospital in French Equatorial Africa to tiny Aspen, to make a speech about Goethe and to play Bach organ fugues. In 56 years he had seldom ventured from his isolated hospital at Lambarene.

Billbarker topped his story that night by saying: "When Schweitzer arrived here, the old boy thought he was in Illinois. He figured that since Hutchins' letter was on the University of Chicago stationery, Aspen must also be in Illinois."

Quote: *God bless.* — Billbarker.

April 5, 1981

Old-fashioned

JUNE, JULY AND AUGUST.

Three good reasons for being a schoolteacher. There was much more to it than that for Gene Albright. He won't be returning to teach fourth grade at Utah Junction School next month.

Albright was stifled by bureaucracy.

"I was going on until I dropped," he said, "but little Utah Junction dropped before I did. The school probably will last one more year. I just didn't want to be there when the end came."

Utah Junction is a tiny, old two-story public school at West 56th Avenue and Pecos Street in suburban Adams County. The name of the school goes back to Denver's earliest years when the stagecoach was the main transportation and communication link between what was then Auraria and the rest of the world.

Westbound coaches used a northern route to Utah, through southern Wyoming. After the Sand Creek Massacre, Indian raids in northern Colorado forced stagecoaches to travel a more difficult western route. The first stop was called Utah Junction, now the location of the school Albright is so sad to leave.

He had taught the fourth grade there for 23 years. It doesn't seem enough to leave it at that. More accurately, Albright presided over a priceless educational experience for some 600 9-year-olds.

Now it's over.

He waited until the last day of school in June to say he was leaving. The official reaction of the Adams County District 50 administration was predictable. "The personnel director said to me, 'Why didn't you let us know earlier so you could have gone to the retirement tea?' " Albright shuddered as he thought about it. "There is nothing more ghastly than a retirement tea," he said.

Watching Albright teach was like being present at a miracle. The air was always charged with excitement. The children seemed in a joyous race to keep up with their own minds. They studied the stars, milkweed pods, Cervantes, kinnikinick, James Thurber, field mice and Mozart. Albright rarely worked at the head of his class. Watching him, it seemed like he wasn't teaching the children at all, but rather involved in a learning experience with them.

Together, they made a "nature trail" in a vacant lot next to the school. In industrial Westminster, the children learned about Albert Schweitzer's "reverence for life." They didn't pounce on snakes and horned frogs. Instead, they would stand quietly to watch nature's tiny dramas.

Albright didn't believe in textbooks. He saw them as limitations to learning. Each student would write his own textbook each year. They were crammed with information about science, music, the graphic arts and nature.

While Albright never presented himself as an authority figure, they always called him "Sir." The respect clearly was not imposed on them. It was more something that Albright had earned. While his teaching methods seemed bold and adventurous, he was old-fashioned enough to swat the bottom of an unruly student.

Albright was good at involving others in his innovative teaching. Poet Thomas Hornsby Ferril and composer Cecil Effinger have visited his classes. Once, the entire 40-voice Classic Chorale came to Utah Junction, just to sing for the fourth grade.

That's all over. It is not too comfortable to think that this year's class won't know what it is missing. Some 30 bright-eyed kids, mostly Chicano, will get a routine fourth-grade education.

Albright thinks old Utah Junction will close in another year. The pressure of bureaucracy seems inexorable. "New people are coming in. They're nice enough, but they want to reduce learning to statistics. The system tries to make everybody the same, so everybody reads the same and is on the same page. That's not important. They don't read alike any more than they write alike, or have the same color eyes."

And so Gene Albright has refused to surrender to conformity. He insisted on freedom. This remarkable man would rather not teach at all than surrender to the system. It's such a shame.

He seems so alone.

August 17, 1978

Good memories

THE FUN TIMES.

Geo. R. Eichler died alone this past weekend at Golden. He was 63. Funeral services are being planned by a Jefferson County public administrator. There are no close family survivors.

Denver Post columnist Jack Kisling said a neighbor found Eichler's body. It was seated in a chair near his collection of Western history books.

George and I had been friends for many years. I knew him first as a reporter for the Post. In more recent years, he worked in advertising and public relations. George was a researcher and wrote Western history.

He was competent in all areas. George's best work, however, was as historian. He wrote history people could actually use.

His book, "Colorado Place Names," was unique. He carefully researched how Colorado communities, counties, peaks and and passes got their names, and how local custom dictated their proper mispronunciation.

That's the sort of information people really need. The book ought to be required reading for the waves of radio and television reporters who constantly pass through local broadcasting's revolving door.

It is so sad that George died alone. I am certain his buddies from the Press Club's Deadline Room feel the same way.

I am not going to remember George the way his neighbor found him. My memories of him will have more to do with the fun times. One of the best of these took place about 25 years ago when Lloyd King was putting together his King Soopers grocery empire.

George was handling much of the advertising. King had hired Chuck Collins and me to do a series of radio promotional broadcasts for the grand opening of the Mayfair store.

Collins was blind. He worked for many years in Denver radio as what was known in the trade as a "song and piano man." The two of us did a total of 20 cut-in broadcasts during the three-day opening celebration.

Broadcasters hate this kind of work. It is boring. There is never any place to sit and people stare at you as though you had top billing in a freak show.

George stayed with us the entire time. Between broadcasts, George and I played the card game of hearts with the engineer. Collins listened. It was remarkable how, by listening, he could remember who had what cards.

As the weekend began to wind down, King thought it would be a good idea to start giving away free grocery samples. The word spread quickly and the crowds became larger each time we went on the air.

I remember one wiry, gray-haired woman particularly well. She was small and wore rimless glasses. As we began to give away the samples, she would push her way to the front and grab everything that was held up.

When it came time for the last broadcast, King brought out a case of refrigerated cans of Reddi-Whip, the whipped-creamlike dessert topping. It was a new product then and everyone wanted a sample.

As usual, the aggressive little woman was right there, only this time she was grabbing every can as quickly as I could hold it up. Something inside me snapped. When I got to the last can, I shook it a couple of times, flipped off the red cap with my thumb, and I squirted the entire contents right on the top of her head.

People gasped. George turned white as a sheet. Chuck began to shout, "George! George! What the hell is going on?" George composed himself and began to give Chuck a play-by-play account. He sounded like a sportscaster.

Everyone started to laugh. The woman said nothing. She turned and walked away. There was Reddi-Whip all over her. George, Chuck and I went to a bar and had some beers.

Those were the fun times.

May 8, 1980

High flying

EDDIE.

He was Waldo Pepper, Don Rickles and just a little bit of Ernest Hemingway all wrapped into one.

Ed Mack Miller died this week out in north Denver at the age of 56. That's what it said in the paper. It is more likely he is up in the sky somewhere in one of those ancient open cockpit jobs. Can't you just see him? That craggy face is out in the slipstream as he pushes the old crate into a joyous chandelle.

Eddie could fly anything from a glider to the big jumbo jets.

A few years ago, Miller became infected by the tennis virus. It became an obsession. Almost impulsively one day, he and his son, Mike, decided to play tennis around the world. With little more than racquets and a change of clothes, they left by the front door of their old house at 3420 W. 46th Ave. and went straight to the airport where the odyssey began.

Around the world they went. In every country Eddie would simply walk up to the door of the most exclusive tennis club he could find. In tennis shorts and with racquet in hand he would say, "My name is Ed Mack Miller. My son and I are playing tennis around the world and we want to play here. Will you please show us to a court?" That would usually do it. Finally, they got back to Denver and went home. They were careful to enter by the back door of the house so that the circle of the world would be complete.

Miller wrote five books and hundreds of articles. He loved the world of writing almost as much as he did flying. And he would often combine the two. I figured in one such event about 25 years ago. He called me on the telephone one Sunday morning just at dawn. I can still hear his voice, "Wake up Gene! This is Ed Mack Miller. Take a shower. I want you to be out at Ruby Hill at precisely 9 o'clock."

Ruby Hill was the location of the old KDEN where I worked. I got there about five minutes before 9. There was Ed, dressed in his Air National Guard major's uniform — 100-mission crush hat, silver wings, the works. We stood there and talked for a few minutes and then he pointed up toward the northern sky. I couldn't believe it. But here they came, the "Minute Men" precision jet flying team of the Colorado Air National Guard. They were screaming overhead, and as they were right over Ruby Hill, they wrote the word GENE in smoke. Incredible! I couldn't speak.

Miller hardly looked up. And then, in his most off-hand way, he said, "That's it. Gotta be getting along. See yuh." Then he got in his car and drove away, leaving me standing there with my name in smoke, breaking up in the morning breezes.

Miller never mentioned the incident until some years later. It turned up in his book, "Exile to the Stars." In the fictional version, I was Gene Aden of radio station KMOL. He always denied that Amole and Aden were the same.

Eddie's fictional characters were believable. Miller wrote the dialogue in his study, acting out all the parts into a tape recorder. Then he would transcribe what he had ad-libbed.

Ed Mack Miller was at his best at the Denver Press Club. He didn't just come in, he made an entrance. One night, he, his wife and three of their 11 children came in for dinner. They were all wearing wooden shoes. They just clumped in, sat down and ordered dinner. Miller had picked up the shoes in Norway where he had been writing an article on NATO military maneuvers.

Everybody kept up with the Miller family at Christmas time. Almost every year, Ed and Cathy would announce the arrival of a new Miller. They are all beautiful children and most of them have learned to fly. Cathy was as perfect for Ed as he was for her.

It didn't matter how far apart they were, they were always so very close to each other. Ed might be off flying the "hump" in Asia or clowning around with Pat Coffey and Pat Oliphant in London or looking at an old Eagle Rock with Dave Scherer in Kansas, but he was never more than a thought away from Cathy. Really.

So, he's not gone. He's up there somewhere and he's having a wonderful time.

January 12, 1978

Irreplaceable

STORMY PETREL.

I miss Gene Cervi now as much as I did that cold night 13 years ago when I was an honorary pallbearer at his funeral. Not wanting to say goodbye, his old pals lingered in front of the cathedral after the services. We agreed there would never be another Cervi.

I thought of that the other day as I was jostled on the 16th Street shuttle by one of those junior-executive-on-the-make types. "Anyone can be replaced," he confided to another clone.

Gene Cervi was irreplaceable. There is a void where he was. It will never be filled. There is no way to take the place of his species of stormy petrel.

That's what the press called him in the turbulent '40s when he was state Democratic Party chairman, "because no one else would take the job," Cervi explained.

Ed Johnson, against whom Cervi unsuccessfully ran for the 1948 Colorado Democratic senatorial nomination, held a another view. "He's the worst state chairman in the United States," Johnson said.

If Cervi seemed quixotic, it was because he was politician, journalist, father, liberal and knight in shining armor. He found a way to do all these things well.

After a career as reporter for both the Rocky Mountain News and The Denver Post, he founded his own weekly newspaper, Cervi's Rocky Mountain Journal. While the circulation rarely exceeded 5,000, it was must-reading for Denver's power structure. "I read it in self-defense," one 17th Street banker angrily said.

Cervi perceived as public enemies 17th Street, Public Service Co. of Colorado, publisher Palmer Hoyt, The Denver Post, Safeway Stores, the Denver Water Board and other "political eunuchs," as he called them. If he looks down on us today, I wonder who the enemies would be now.

The old 17th Street power structure is back in Delaware or up in Canada, Public Service Co. has seen better days, Hoyt is dead, the Post is fading and Safeway is being pushed around by King Soopers. Only the Water Board prospers.

My favorite time with Gene Cervi was the afternoon we sat together in an auditorium on the University of Denver campus. We were covering a lecture by Ashley Montagu, the pop anthropologist.

It was during the '60s when Montagu was preaching his screwy brand of revolution on college campuses. The speech was running overlong. Cervi was becoming restive at Montagu's outrageous opinions.

I was facing a deadline back at the radio station, and knew I would have to leave before the speech ended. Quietly, I rose to a crouch, whispered my apologies and started to tip-toe for the aisle.

Behind me, I felt Cervi also getting up. And then the auditorium was split with the rasp of his voice. "You are a liar, a cheat and a fraud!" Cervi thundered, "And Gene Amole and I are walking out of here."

By the time we got to the parking lot, Cervi's face was crimson with laughter. Tears were rolling down his cheeks. He could hardly breathe. And then I started to laugh. I missed my deadline.

And I miss my friend.

August 4, 1983

Godspeed, Lamb Chop

LAMB CHOP.

I don't remember exactly when I gave that nickname to Sister Mary Louise. It wasn't right away, certainly. Not being a Catholic, I suppose I viewed all nuns with suspicion mixed with fear.

It must have been about 30 years ago that she called and asked if I would speak at a Loretto Heights College conference of high school newspaper editors. I didn't really want to, but she persisted, and I finally agreed.

When I walked up those long stairs in front of the old brownstone administration building, I was astonished when a tiny nun stepped from behind the door to meet me. She seemed no more than 5 feet tall. Her face was bright and pretty, and there was a small widow's peak of hair showing on her forehead under the hood of her habit.

"I'm Sister Mary Louise," she beamed, grasping my hand firmly.

We were instantly friends. She was so open and filled with fun. She taught in the English Department at Loretto. I learned later she was one of the nation's leading authorities on Shakespeare.

As the years slipped by, we stayed in touch, usually because she kept tapping me as a resource person for what seemed an endless succession of conferences. I didn't mind, though, since we always found time to talk. She had strong Republican views, and I was an Adlai Stevenson disciple.

As we became closer friends, I learned there were three important men in her life — Jesus Christ, her father and William Shakespeare. She never really told me that, but she didn't need to.

We rarely discussed religion. I can't think of a single time when I felt she was trying to convert me to her belief. She accepted me as I was.

She talked about her father a great deal. She loved him very much. Lamb Chop, as I then bagan to call her, told me she had wanted to write a book about him. "I have a title for it," she said, "I want to call it, 'The Greatest Christian I Ever Knew — My Father, the Atheist.'"

She explained that he had lived an exemplary life, had loved his wife and children, was a devoted father, but never had come to grips with his faith. "He was an outstanding Christian, but he just didn't know it," she told me.

She may write the story yet. I hope so. Mary Louise did write a book. It was an account of her life as a nun. But it was at a time when religious orders were more rigid. Her mother superior ordered her to destroy the book. She did, and she told me it was without any bitterness.

She is an excellent writer. Her undergraduate degree is from Webster College, and her M.A. and Ph.D. are from St. Louis University. She has done post-doctoral work at Oxford University in England, and she has studied at Stratford-on-Avon. She has received research fellowships at the Folger Shakespeare Library in Washington.

I asked her once if I should call her Dr. Sister Marie Louise. "Stick with Lamb Chop, Geno," she said. "Don't pay any attention to that doctor stuff."

The two of us did a yearlong series of radio programs on Shakespeare's plays in 1964 in celebraton of the 400th anniversary of the bard's birth. I actually did nothing. She was the show. We played recordings of every Shakespearean play. She loved it when I picked her up in my white Corvette convertible to do the programs. We'd drive along Federal Boulevard, her black habit snapping in the wind.

She traveled a great deal, teaching for a while in the Arab nations and also at Santa Clara in California. She studied at the British Museum in London.

It was there she had a small walk-on role in one of Elizabeth Taylor's many romances. Mary Louise was staying at the Dorchester Hotel in London at the same time the actress was having an affair with Michael Wilding.

Mary Louise was walking down the hotel's back stairs one evening when she encountered Wilding climbing the stairs. In that impish way she has, Lamb Chop popped in front of the startled actor and said. "I know where you are going, Michael, and so does God." She winked and scurried away.

There are a lot of other Mary Louise stories I could tell, like when her Jewish doctor told her he didn't believe in a hereafter. She grinned and told him, "Boy, do you have a nice surprise coming."

Lamb Chop is leaving Denver June 13. She's moving to the Sisters of Loretto Mother House in rural Kentucky. Her health has been fragile in recent years. "Sticky blood," she explains. I know she'll receive excellent care in Kentucky, but I will certainly miss her.

I wanted her to know that before she leaves town.

June 3, 1982

Right words

The ability to say the right thing at the right time is a rare talent. It is the other way around for most of us. I am one of those. If there is a way to put my foot in my mouth, I'll somehow find it.

It is either that, or my clever rejoinders occur to me long after the fact. I hate being a witness at a trial. The lawyers have a field day. I stumble through incoherent testimony, and I am made to look the fool. It is on the way home I think of the snappy comebacks.

I'm not much better at parties. There's always a slick dude who grabs control of the conversation early. He guides it skillfully through familiar territory — familiar to him, that is.

I have to sit there and admit I haven't read the books he has. I somehow never made it to those small foreign films he finds so stimulating. The names he drops aren't the ones I know out in Bear Valley.

At a dinner party the other night, I met a psychologist I really envy. On at least one occasion in his life, he was able to say precisely the right thing under the most difficult of circumstances.

Dr. Roy Yamahiro is manager of education and training at Martin Marietta Aerospace — Denver Division. A nisei, or second-generation Japanese-American, he was born in Oregon.

But much of his childhood was spent in an Idaho relocation camp. He and his family were among the many loyal American of Japanese ancestry who were unjustly confined in the West during World War II.

In his position with Martin, Yamahiro helped plan an Outward Bound wilderness program for company employees. "The idea was to give them a challenging experience. We wanted to improve their self-confidence," he said.

As a part of the program, the employee is placed alone in a wilderness area for 54 hours with nothing but a canteen of water and a bedroll. When Yamahiro took the course, he was plunked down along the Green River, downstream from Echo Park, Colo.

"My project was to see if I could chip out an Indian arrowhead. I figured I was a soul brother to Indians since both of us have

Mongoloid roots." And Yamahiro thought he might even be able to use the arrowhead to get some food.

"I hadn't had a bath in a long time, so I took off all my clothing except my tennis shoes and hat. I waded in the river, took a bath and found a rock I thought I could chip into an arrowhead."

Just as he had managed to make a big rock into a little one, two raftloads of tourists suddenly floated around the river bend. Yamahiro was stark naked, and he had no chance of getting to any kind of cover.

"Those people couldn't have been more suprised. There was a naked Japanese-American man standing in the river in the wilderness. I was pretty surprised myself. There didn't seem to be anything to do, so I just waved at them.

"They were only 10 or 15 yards away. They were so shocked, none of them even smiled. There were men, women and children. I knew I had to say something."

Yamahiro did say something. And it was just the right thing at the right time.

"Is the war over yet?"

March 7, 1982

8

SUPER BOWL SOUP
& OTHER RECIPES

Super Sunday dinner

POT ROAST 1 — SUPER BOWL 0

Has it occurred to you how much better off we are here than down in New Orleans for the Super Bowl?

Believe it. As a matter of fact, we'll be watching the same game and seeing it better. And we'll be getting the instant replays they won't see at the Superdome. Professional football without replays is like a day without sunshine.

And wouldn't you know it, they've been beaucoup days without sunshine down in Cajun country. It's been cold, wet and clammy all Superbowl week.

Accommodations haven't been all that great. Dispatches from the front indicate the Royal Orleans has been booked up for some time and dinner reservations at the Crescent City's fabled eateries are hard to come by.

Some Denver Bronco fans are being put up in Baton Rouge and others at the Knotty Pine Tourist Court at Biloxi, Miss. They're nice rooms, too. Some have shower curtains and linoleum floors. The wall heaters may be a little noisy, but they sure do smell of propane gas. Biloxi is a great little town, if your idea of a big evening is to hang around the pop cooler.

One of the problems of watching a game in the Superdome is noise. It overwhelms and there is no way you can turn it down and listen to Bob Martin and Larry Zimmer instead. There are also the pigeons.

Woody Paige confirms that pigeons still live in the Superdome. They subsist on spilled popcorn and the other abandoned refreshments. An attempt was made last year to exterminate the birds but the Audubon Society stepped in. And so the pigeons live and perform the usual bodily functions wherever.

Getting into New Orleans was difficult. Getting out will be a miracle. Fans have been arriving all week. But once the game is over, they're all going to want to leave at once. Can you picture that airport? A zoo. People will be surging through the wrong concourses, getting on the wrong planes at the wrong time.

Compare all of this to your Super Sunday. You were able to sleep in a little. You've had a chance to read the funnies or go to church.

You can catch all the pre-game hoopla on TV which they'll miss down there.

Just before the game starts, put on the pot roast. A 3- or 4-pound chuck will be fine. Flour and season it and then brown it in bacon grease. Drain off the grease and pour in two cups of cheap, red jug wine. Cover the top of the roast with sliced onions and chili sauce. Cover and simmer in the oven or in an electric skillet until the second half of the game is about to begin. Then add peeled and quartered potatoes, sliced carrots, coarse-chopped celery and parsnips, if you like them.

By the time the game is over, your dinner should be ready. The vegetables ought to be well browned and almost candied in that rich sauce around the edge of the roast. You may have to add some more wine if the juice starts to cook away. You might want to have a little nip for yourself, too. Whatever.

Remove the vegetables and keep them warm in the oven. Use a spatula to lift the roast out onto a cutting board. Then add flour and water to the juices to make the gravy. You won't believe that gravy. It is so rich! Well, it would be what with the wine and chili sauce. Right? Right.

Slice the roast into strips, against the grain. Serve with the vegetables and drizzle that magnificent gravy over everything. And there you have it — a super dinner for Super Sunday and you haven't missed so much as one minute of the game.

Now, you can see why you are so fortunate to be in Denver for the Super Bowl instead of New Orleans. You haven't had to put up with missed buses, people who drink too much, baggage carousels, lost ticket stubs, crowded freeways and cigar smoke.

And you've had a marvelous dinner with the greatest gravy ever. It will sure beat whatever they serve on the airplane or is available at the airport snack bar.

As for the Broncos, they'll blow Tom Landry's plastic Cowboys away. Believe it.

January 14, 1978

It's Super Bowl Soup

NEXT SUNDAY.

Super Sunday? Not exactly. Super Bowl XIV in Pasadena promises to be the most one-sided confrontation since the 1864 Sand Creek Massacre in eastern Colorado.

Terry Bradshaw's Pittsburgh Steelers will have an easier go of it against the Los Angeles Rams than Col. John Chivington's "blue belly" cavalry had against a handful of unarmed Indians.

Most of us will watch Super Bowl XIV on TV anyhow. This leaves us with the problem of how to keep the day from becoming a dead loss.

As you have come to expect, I have a plan. What we are going to do, gang, is make up a kettle of Super Bowl Soup! Once you have tasted it, you will say that you have never had a more super bowl of soup.

Longtime readers of this column will recall the now-famous pot roast recipe printed here for the Super Bowl XII game in 1978 between the Denver Broncos and the Dallas Cowboys. Dallas won 27 to 10 and many people wrote in to say that the pot roast was better than the game.

Next came the World Series brisket recipes for last year's October classic. You enjoyed drizzling that marvelous gravy over thin-sliced beef, potatoes, carrots and parsnips while the Pittsburgh Pirates were coming from behind to beat the Baltimore Orioles.

Flushed with success, I have decided to share with you my mother's recipe for vegetable soup. You will love it because it is simple to make, inexpensive and probably nutritious. I guess it is, although I am not one of those granola and yogurt types.

There is an old saying that "cheap meat ain't good and good meat ain't cheap." That's generally true. It doesn't apply to beef shank, however. The shank is from the front leg of the animal. The last time I looked, cross cuts of the shank were going at about $1.03 a pound.

Use one or two pounds, depending on the size of your brood. Cover with about 3½ quarts of salted water in a large pot. Add a pound of peeled and cored fresh tomatoes, or use a can of generic tomatoes at about 33 cents. Whack up one medium white onion and throw it in.

Bring to a boil and then back off to a simmer and let cook for a couple of hours or so. You'll know when to put the rest of the stuff in when the meat starts to get tender.

Keep breaking up the tomatoes with a wooden spoon. This will give you an excuse to keep going to the pot and enjoying the aroma. The next thing that goes in is one-half cup of medium pearled barley.

Peel and cube one good-sized red potato and coarse-chop some celery. Stir it in with the meat, barley, onion and tomatoes. Cook another half hour and start to taste.

The final ingredients are corn, green peas, carrots, green beans and baby limas. The easiest and cheapest way of doing this is to simply use a 10-ounce package of mixed frozen vegetables at about 39 cents.

You can add other vegetables if you like. I would advise against using cabbage, however, as it will make you gassy. Once these last vegetables have been added, your Super Bowl Soup will begin to assume its real character. You can adjust the taste by adding salt and pepper.

The recipe has been modified so there are XIV ingredients. Put a bottle of Tabasco on the table for those who like their soup zingy. Have ketchup available for the shank, which may be eaten separately.

This is family soup. It will bring you all closer together. Serve it with mixed green salad, hard crust bread and Monterey Jack cheese. Super Bowl Soup is even better the next day.

Oh, yes it will be Pittsburgh by XIV.

January 13, 1980

Something to relish

CRISPY.

Pencils and papers ready? Good.

Here is another recipe of Uncle Geno's not-so-famous recipes for robust appetites. It is called "Sweet and Sauer Holiday Relish."

At a time when some have become captivated by *nouvelle cuisine,* mandarin cookery and other equally exotic bills of fare, it is important to occasionally stand up for meat-and-potatoes-type food.

We don't just pay lip service to culinary fundamentalism around here. No sir! Readers of this column know well of our contributions to the preparation of such hearty favorites as pot roast, vegetable soup, beef brisket and that marvelous chili sauce we put up last summer.

Those who seek thoughtful analysis of world affairs, informed political commentary and an incidental touch of satire are sometimes disappointed at what they read here. Not so with the recipes.

They have been roaring successes. I learned early in the game that a sure way to the reader's heart is through the stomach.

"Sweet n' Sauer Holiday Relish" is so easy and quick to prepare that it is almost cheating. Any boob can do it. I know this from personal experience.

The nice thing about it is that the results suggest long hours have been spent in the kitchen. Not so. It takes only a few minutes. If your guests choose to be deceived, let them.

The basis for this crispy relish is sauerkraut. It doesn't even have to be the good stuff your grandma stomped in the bathtub. Any kind will do. Get a 16-ounce can, the cheaper the better.

Open it and put the content into a mixing bowl. Don't drain. Throw it in the whole works. Break the kraut apart with a fork, nibbling some of it as you go.

Kraut is such honest food. It is wonderful as the basis for a *Choucroute Alsacienne,* into which *kassler ripchen,* pig's knuckles, Polish sausage, bacon, frankfurters and other smoked meats are baked. It is a delight when served with boiled and buttered potatoes, garnished with parsley and washed down with a good *spatlese.* But that is another story.

Getting back to the relish, chop up one white onion and add to the kraut. Don't use a yellow onion. Unless cooked, I find yellow onions a bit stout for my taste. Good, firm white ones are the best.

One cup of chopped celery is next. No leaves. For the sake of appearance, try to keep the ingredients chopped to the same size. Pretty food tastes better.

The original recipe for this relish didn't call for green bell pepper. I impulsively added some and have found the results pleasing. A half-cup of chopped pepper is just enough for color and taste.

Beginning to look pretty nice? You bet. But wait until you add the pimento. Yes. Get one of those little four-ounce jars of chopped pimento, drain off the juice and add to the bowl.

You are almost there. Combine three-quarters cup of sugar and a like amount of white vinegar in a sauce pan. Heat until the sugar has dissolved. Don't boil, just stir.

Pour liquid over other ingredients. Mix again. Carefully spoon everything into a one-quart glass jar. Screw on the top and refrigerate 24 hours.

After you have made your first batch, you may want to change the sugar-to-vinegar ratio. Try adding a tablespoon of either caraway or celery seeds. For a little more authority to the relish, splash a little Tabasco into the liquid.

"Sweet and Sauer Holiday Relish" is a name I made up. The green pepper and red pimento give it a nice holiday appearance. It goes well with meats and cheeses.

Be sure to get up in the night several times and go to the refrigerator to keep sampling the relish. Take note of how it improves with each tasting.

November 18, 1980

Take this bird and stuff it!

STUFFING.

Don't get me started on why Thanksgiving Day is my favorite holiday. I go on and on about how people don't have to buy each other's affection with useless gifts. It's keen for the family just to be together for a nice dinner. Mine are the simple tastes. Except when it comes to turkey stuffing.

Right! I am about to slip you a recipe for Capt. Sunshine's Incredible Everything-but-the-Kitchen-Sink Turkey Stuffing. It is a marvelous mosaic of taste and texture.

This recipe is really an evolution. I have been fooling around with it for years. What follows not only has superb flavor, but it also produces an exotic mixture of aromas.

Stuffing is important. As Gertrude Stein might have said, "A turkey is a turkey is a turkey." But what goes inside gives the old bird character. It is a part of the Thanksgiving feast we all remember. Mine is unforgettable.

First, open a bottle of Harvey's Bristol Cream Sherry. Actually, any brand will do, but Harvey's is the best. Have yourself a little nip and then pour exactly 8 ounces into a measuring cup. Put it aside while you prepare the other ingredients.

Take 17 slices of dry white bread and 3 slices of dry pumpernickel. Cut into crouton-size cubes and place in a large mixing bowl.

Sprinkle with 1 teaspoon pepper, 1 tablespoon salt and 1 tablespoon sage, thyme or poultry seasoning. Marjoram works OK, too.

Brown and crumble in a skillet one-half pound of bulk breakfast sausage and one-quarter pound of Italian bulk sausage. After thoroughly mixing the sausage, remove with slotted spoon and put in the big bowl.

Add 1 cup each of chopped celery, chopped onion and chopped walnuts. Throw in 3 tablespoons of parsley and 2 cups of sliced fresh mushrooms. Add 1 tart crisp apple, peeled, cored and chopped. Granny Smiths are nice. So are Jonathans and Newtons.

I know what you are thinking. You are concerned about the pumpernickel and the Italian sausage. Just seems out of character, doesn't it? Trust me. And you probably want to saute the onions and celery. Don't.

Everytime I make this stuffing, I am reminded of Chinese philosopher Lao-tse's observation about bean sprouts. "They should be firm but yielding," he wrote. So should the celery and onions in this dressing. The nuts and apple will retain a nice crispness, too.

Heat 1 cube of unsalted butter in 2 cups of chicken broth until the butter melts. Campbell's works fine. Pour the liquid into the bowl. Do not mix yet. There is one more important ingredient.

Right you are! It is the sherry. Never forget the sherry. Very carefully pour 3 tablespoons of sherry into the bowl. Sip away at the sherry you have reserved in the measuring cup. Good old Harvey's. Here's to you, Harvey!

Carefully toss the stuffing with two wooden spoons until all ingredients are evenly mixed. Do not bruise the sausage! If mixture is too dry, add warm water.

Voila! It is done. Lightly stuff the bird fore and aft. You'll have dressing left over. Place it in casserole dish, cover with foil, place in oven for the last hour of roasting time.

Drizzle on the giblet gravy.

November 4, 1982

Culinary home run

BASEBALL AND BRISKET.

October is a great month for both. The World Series is upon us and there is enough of an edge to the air to justify whipping up the world's greatest recipe for brisket.

Brisket is an inexpensive cut of beef from the chest of the steer. It doesn't cost very much because it is tough. Really tough.

A couple of years ago, there were instructions in this column on how to fix pot roast while watching the Super Bowl between the Denver Broncos and Dallas Cowboys.

Those who tried it wrote in to say that the pot roast was better than the game. They now fix it regularly without waiting for the Broncos to return to the Super Bowl. That could be some time.

With that in mind, I am going to give you instructions on how to fix brisket while watching a Sunday World Series baseball game. When the game is over, the brisket will be ready to eat.

About an hour before game time, dust a fresh, 4-pound brisket with seasoned flour. Brown in a Dutch oven with two tablespoons of bacon grease. Remove the brisket and pour off the fat.

Chop two cups each of white onion and celery. By all means, use the celery tops. Slice a large green pepper into strips. While you are at it, peel and quarter a couple of pounds of potatoes. Peel and slice an appropriate amount of carrots and parsnips.

Put the spuds, carrots and parsnips in a plastic bag and into the refrigerator. The idea is to have this part done so you won't miss any of the game.

Back to the brisket. Put half the onions, pepper and celery on the bottom of the Dutch oven. Place the brisket on top of the mixture, fat side up.

The next step is to season the top of the meat. Put two cloves of garlic right on the meat. It isn't absolutely necessary, but I prefer to mince the garlic and spread it around.

If you have a pepper mill, use about one-half teaspoon of freshly ground pepper. Store-bought ground pepper works almost as well.

Sprinkle on some paprika. About a teaspoon. Maybe a little more. Add three pinches of dried dill seed, a couple of bay leaves and two smashed up beef bouillon cubes.

Place the rest of the onions, celery and green pepper slices on top of the seasoned brisket. You are almost there.

Do you have a gallon of cheap burgundy jug wine around the house? Good. Take a little nip for yourself. Then measure out a pint of the wine and mix it with two tablespoons of white vinegar.

Pour the mixture around the edge of the brisket. No water. Just wine. Cover the Dutch oven and put it in a pre-heated oven at 325 degrees.

Use the rest of the time before the game starts to make an apple, nut and celery Waldorf salad. Any kind of fruit salad goes well with brisket. Set the table.

Play ball! Sit back and watch the game on TV. It is a matter of your own choice whether you turn down the television sound and listen to the radio.

Howard Cosell will be doing the TV commentary. He does seem to be more knowledgeable about baseball than he is about football.

About the third inning you will become aware of the brisket's exquisite aroma. It reminds some of home and Mother. Others believe it to have an aphrodisiac quality.

Place the carrots, potatoes and parsnips into the Dutch oven at the top half of the eighth inning.

When the game is over, the dinner should be ready. Just be sure cooking time is about four hours and the vegetables are tender. Discard the peppers, celery and onion. Strain the liquid and thicken with flour for gravy. Slice brisket diagonally and serve with vegetables.

Fantastic!

October 4, 1979

Back to the basics

CRICKETS.

You know it is late summer when they begin to rasp away at the nights. The kids get antsy. Mornings become pleasantly cool. A few leaves at the top of the old cottonwood are turning yellow.

It is time to put up chili sauce!

Messy business. Worth it, though. It has been a great year for backyard gardeners and making chili sauce is the best way to make use of surplus tomatoes.

Chili sauce fits right in. It is marvelous slathered over pork loin on a cold Sunday afternoon. It dresses up rump roast and is perfect with pumpernickel meat loaf.

You will need a jug of burgundy wine, a peck of tomatoes, six green peppers, six big white onions and some spices. A peck, by the way, is about a quarter of a bushel.

Wash, peel, core and quarter the tomatoes. You probably know the easy way to peel tomatoes. For the few who do not, just lower each tomato with a slotted spoon into boiling water. Hold it there for about a minute. Take it out and run some cold water over it. The skin will slip right off.

Put the tomatoes in a large stainless steel or procelain-lined kettle. Remove stems, seeds and membranes from the peppers. Either grind or chop the onions and the peppers and add to the tomatoes.

Use a food processor if you have one. Some find it good therapy to do the chopping by hand. Sense of personal accomplishment. Back to the fundamentals.

You'll need about a tablespoon of crushed red pepper pods. For Pete's sake, don't put in the seeds. They would make the sauce hotter than a depot stove. Too hot.

Add two level cups of brown sugar. I like a couple of tablespoons of dry mustard. Some prefer mustard seed. Put in three tablespoons of salt, coarse if you have it. Then comes the fresh ground black pepper. About a tablespoon. Maybe a tad more.

Now the good stuff. You will need a tablespoon of allspice. Put in a teaspoon each of ginger, cinnamon, nutmeg, celery seed and ground cloves.

Don't forget the vinegar. Get cider vinegar, the brown kind. Look on the label. Be sure it has 5 percent to 6 percent acetic acid. Use three cups. That's it.

Some people like their chili sauce more exotic, using crushed garlic, cumin and curry powder. I don't. Chili sauce is good because it is simple, honest, without guile.

Back to the kettle. Stir the ingredients with a long-handled wooden spoon, preferably an old one. Simmer over low heat for at least three hours.

Now don't go running down to the shopping center or go to sleep on the patio. Stay near the kitchen and stir the sauce frequently. Don't scorch the sauce! Keep the heat low.

By the time the sauce cooks down to the right consistency, there should be about a gallon. While this is taking place, your house will be flooded with exquisite aroma.

Crack the window so that it wafts out into the neighborhood.

Lovely children will come to your door. A great peace will descend. That aroma is so American. You'll want to run up Old Glory.

Ladle the chili sauce into small sterilized jars and seal tightly according to the instructions on the box in which the jars came. Be sure the jars are sterilized, otherwise your family could get the trots.

The wine? Don't put it in the chili sauce. It's for you. Take a little nip every now and then while you are doing all that stirring.

August 24, 1980

Absorbing the shock of a bumper crop

ZUCCHINI.

Someone wrote a funny column a couple of years ago about zucchini squash. I think it was Jack Kisling. I wish I could write a funny column about zucchinis like that, but I can't.

I don't remember eating zucchinis as a child. I had heard of them, of course. But I thought they were a family trapeze act with the old Sells-Floto Circus. You know, "The Flying Zucchinis."

I learned about zucchinis as an adult. They are in such abundance because they are so easy to raise. There is no self-respecting bug or worm that will touch them. It is virtually impossible to screw up a zucchini crop. Even so, the zucchini squash is one of the few vegetables I can live without.

But I don't have to. I haven't seen any official figures, but it is clear we are having a bumper zucchini harvest. Every backyard gardner I know has unloaded his zucchini surplus on me.

Anytime someone comes up to me with a benevolent grin and a brown paper bag, I know I am about to be blessed with more zucchini squash. Let me go on record right now as saying we are up to here in zucchinis at our house.

I have sauteed, steamed, boiled french fried, baked and stuffed zucchini. I have made zucchini relish, zucchini brownies, zucchini muffins, zucchini cookies and even zucchini pancakes. We slice zucchinis raw in salads. I have explored every possible zucchini use, and I am sick of all of them.

But the least objectionable zucchini recipe I have is for zucchini nut loaf. It is probably no better than anyone else's recipe, but I am going to lay it on you in case you don't have one of your own and want to get rid of your zucchini overload.

Using a steel blade in your processor, chop two cups of zucchini. If you don't have a processor, you can shred by hand, or better yet throw out the zucchini and forget the whole thing.

Combine the zucchini with two cups of sugar, two eggs and one cup of cooking oil. Mix well by hand until it is a bile-colored glop. In another bowl, mix three cups of flour with one teaspoon of baking soda, one-half teaspoon of baking powder, one teaspoon of nutmeg, two teaspoons of cinnamon, one teaspoon of grated lemon peel.

Gradually mix the dry ingredients with the glop. Then add four to six ounces of chopped walnuts. Pour into two greased and floured loaf pans. Bake for a little more than an hour at 325 degrees. The loaves are done when a toothpick inserted in the center comes out clean.

The most rewarding part of this culinary adventure comes while they are baking. The aroma is not half bad, not because of zucchini, mind you, but because of the nutmeg and cinnamon.

Cool pans on a rack. Remove loaves and wrap with foil and refrigerate for 24 hours. Don't try to slice until the next day, otherwise those suckers will fall apart on you.

The reason you make two loaves is so you can throw one of them away and freeze the other and give it to some unsuspecting soul at Christmas.

Ho, ho!

September 2, 1982

Coq au vin — cool

CHILLED.

That's the way the white wine ought to be when *coq au vin* is prepared. I was reminded of this when I read the recipes in last Wednesday's Food Fare section of the Rocky Mountain News. Food editor Pat Hanna called it "The Cosmopolitan Chicken."

The thrust of her excellent recipes was that chicken needn't be boring. I know some people feel that way about it. Not this kid. I grew up thinking chicken was very special. It didn't matter whether it was my mother's glorious stewed chicken and dumplings, or Grandma's crisp fried chicken. It wasn't Sunday at our house unless there was chicken on the table.

Readers of this column know that when I come up with a recipe, it has to be simple. Not being a surgeon, I don't like to fool around with boning or removing skin. On the other hand, it is fun to serve something that looks special and has a French name.

With that in mind, I offer my recipe for *coq au vin,* a simple way of cooking chicken in wine. I have been experimenting with this for some time, and I don't hesitate to recommend it for your Sunday dinner. It's also nice enough for a small candlelight party for two, you romantic devil, you.

Some of the French recipes for *coq au vin* call for red wine. I don't like it unless only the drumsticks and thighs are used. Red wine discolors the white meat — makes it look gray.

I prefer to cook with a *Chablis.* It doesn't have to be expensive. Any jug stuff will do. Just be sure it is chilled. It doesn't matter to the recipe, but you'll want a nip or so along the way. Warm white wine tastes lousy.

Salt and pepper one cut-up 2½- to 3-pound fryer. Use about a quarter of a cup of oil in an electric fry pan to brown the pieces on both sides. Remove the chicken and set aside. Take a sip of the *Chablis* and return bottle to the refrigerator.

Drain off most of the oil, leaving enough to saute, until transparent, one finely chopped white onion. Add six peeled and diagonally sliced carrots — about a half-inch thick. Continue to stir so the onions don't stick to the skillet. Next comes the celery. Use about six stalks, also diagonally sliced.

Continue to stir until the onions, carrots and celery are well mixed. Add one full can of chicken broth. (This is not a Campbell's recipe, even though it should be.) Fill the empty can with *Chablis* and add to the pan. While you continue to stir, gradually add enough Wondra flour to thicken until it is a light gravy consistency.

Season to taste — about one teaspoon of salt and a generous (three-finger) pinch of pepper. Return chicken to pan, adding 1½ cups of thick-sliced fresh or canned button mushrooms. Carefully mix gravy, vegetables and chicken with wooden spoon. Sprinkle with chopped parsley, cover and simmer for one hour. When the carrots are fork tender, the chicken will be done.

Remove chicken and place on a platter of Kluski egg noodles. Actually, any pasta will do. I like the Kluskies because there is a nice firmness to them if they aren't overcooked. With a slotted spoon, remove carrots, celery and mushrooms and arrange on top of the chicken. Looks nice. The onion will have cooked up into the gravy.

Serve the gravy separately so that guests may drizzle it over the noodles. Save any leftover gravy and use it over biscuits or toasted English muffins for a robust breakfast a couple of mornings later.

Coq au vin is nice with broccoli or asparagus spears, endive and scallion salad and crisp-crust French bread. If you are home alone, it is nice to use the bread to mop up the gravy. We used to call this "sop." The French probably call it bad manners. Whatever you call it, it sure is good. If there is any *Chablis* left, serve it with the chicken.

Voila! Coq au vin.

May 12, 1981

Foul and fowl recipes

KA-POW!

It must have been awful. Two Denver Post readers reported last week their chickens exploded. Don't laugh. There is nothing amusing about a detonated pullet.

Put yourself in their place. There you are in your kitchen. You are carefully following a recipe for "Chicken with Apricots" that appeared in the Feb. 7 edition of Empire magazine. The sauce calls for two cups of apricot brandy.

But shortly after you put the bird in a 350-degree oven, BAM! The oven door blows open, and there is what is left of tonight's dinner. A drumstick here. What's left of the wishbone over there. And look at that pathetic little wing!

Well, you can see why the Post had to publish a "Notice to Readers" Feb. 18 warning the recipe "may be unsafe." May be? It certainly was for the readers who had their dinners go blasto on them.

Now you are thinking I am going to make sport of the Post over this. To the contrary, being a person of sensitivity, I extend my heartfelt sympathy to all who have been touched by this tragic chicken mutilation incident.

And because of my generous nature, I have decided to lend a

helping hand. I am going to donate one of my favorite chicken recipes to The Denver Post to replace the flawed one it printed in Empire. What are friends for?

I call my recipe "Chicken and Dumplings." It is not actually mine. It has been handed down for generations in our family. My Great-grandma Fiedler gave it to my Grandma Amole, who in turn, bequeathed it to my mother.

Like the Post recipe, mine also calls for apricot brandy. We'll get to that later.

Get a nice plump hen at the butcher shop. Second-best is a 5- or 6-pound roasting chicken. The fatter, the better. Cut up the chicken, put it in a pot and cover with water. Add salt, pepper, one onion, one carrot and a celery stalk with leaves. Cover and simmer for at least two hours.

You are thinking that is just stewed chicken, and you are right. Nothing complicated. It is absolutely the simplest way to cook chicken. Nothing to it. The aroma is marvelous. When I was a boy, it wasn't Sunday unless we had stewed chicken.

So what's so special? The dumplings! Yes, those wonderful, light, fluffy dumplings. Your old Uncle Geno is going to reveal Grandma Fiedler's dumpling secret right here and now.

Combine 1½ cups of sifted flour with two teaspoons of baking powder, three-quarters teaspoon of salt, one-half cup of milk and one egg. Mix with old wooden spoon. And the shortening? No shortening. Not one bit. That's the first half of the secret. Grandma used to say, "It's just like making biscuits, except you don't use fat."

Uncover the pot and reduce the pot likker until it is just below the level of the chicken. Leave it as stock for the gravy. Spoon the dumpling dough on top of the chicken. Don't let it get in the liquid that's left in the pot. That's the second half of the secret.

Most recipes say to float the dough right in the soup. Not this one. We don't want soggy dumplings, now do we? We want those dumplings to draw up the steam of that rich pot likker.

Simmer uncovered for exactly 10 minutes. Cover the pot and simmer for another 10 minutes. DO NOT PEEK! Never peek. Don't mess up the dumplings by peeking. Ever. Trust me.

While the dumplings are steaming, make gravy with reserved pot likker. Usual way, milk, flour, salt and pepper. Uncover pot. Lift out those lovely dumplings and serve with chicken and gravy.

The apricot brandy? You drink that. Whatever you do, don't put it in the pot. You don't want to blow up the chicken, do you?

February 21, 1982

Spicy meatballs
are the order of the day

SPICY!

I am trying to see this from your perspective. Would you rather have me write an umpteenth column about John Elway, or would you prefer a dandy little recipe for Uncle Geno's North Side Spicy Meatballs?

Now that we have our priorities straight, let us proceed to the meatballs. Their genesis is on Denver's North Side, where the water is truly colder, and where people still sit on front porches and listen to children play "run sheep run" in the warm summer evenings.

We are talking about the north Denver where old Italian men play *bocce* in the park, where geraniums still bloom in window boxes. It would naturally figure that the most savory of meatballs would come from that part of our town old-timers still call the Highlands.

I became addicted to the meatballs served at Ernie Capillupo's Restaurant and Lounge back in 1946. You remember the place. It's at 2915 W. 44th Ave., just a block east of Federal Boulevard. Lordy, how I loved those meatball sandwiches!

I was never able to get Ernie's recipe, so I have evolved my own. Like Edward Elgar's "Enigma" musical composition, Uncle Geno's North Side Spicy Meatballs recipe is a variation on an original theme.

Certainly you will require three-quarters of a pound of ground beef and one-half pound of ground pork. Do not hesitate to throw in a modest amount of Italian bulk sausage, if available.

Combine two eggs in a large bowl with one-half cup of milk, 1½ teaspoons of salt, three tablespoons of Mexican *picante* sauce, one tablespoon of parsley and a pinch each of black pepper, oregano, marjoram, thyme, basil, rosemary and sage.

Fine chop one medium size onion, either by hand or by using the steel blade in your processor. Add the onion and one minced clove of garlic to the other ingredients and beat them mercilessly.

Put the the meat in the bowl and stir with an old wooden spoon. Take care that the ground beef and pork are properly blended. We don't want a lump of pork here, and another lump of beef there, do we?

Now you are ready to add one cup of seasoned Progresso bread crumbs and one-half cup of Parmesan cheese. The mixture will become thick and difficult to manage, but manage it you will. And after that is done, form meatballs of 1⅜ inches diameter by rolling the meat between your palms. This is sticky work but wonderful stress-reduction therapy.

The meatballs should be fried in oil until brown all over and done clear through. You should be alone during this part of the process, as family members will be drawn to the kitchen by the aroma and will eat the meatballs as rapidly as you cook them.

Simmer them in your favorite tomato sauce for at least 45 minutes. Serve those little beauties on firm-but-yielding homemade pasta. The flavor of egg pasta, by the way, is enhanced by the addition of a bit of Parmesan cheese and a shake or so of cayenne pepper to the dough. That, I suppose, is another story.

Don't forget the Chianti.

August 15, 1983

Cheap cuts of meat aren't always tough

TRADE-OFF.

It's usually true that good meat ain't cheap and cheap meat ain't good. But I have found that when you buy all the stuff to make cheap meat taste good, you might just as well buy good meat in the first place.

But that kind of trade-off doesn't exactly apply in the case of a braised beef brisket recipe you must try one of these frosty January nights. Lordy, it's good snappin', as my pop used to say, and it really isn't too expensive.

I wish I could tell you the recipe was handed down in our family from Aunt Gladys, but it wasn't. I adapted it from one that appeared last year in a Gourmet magazine article on braising, a method of slow-cooking meat with liquid in a tightly covered container.

Brisket, I'm sure you know, is that tough, grainy meat from the lower chest or breast of the animal. It is the cut of beef most frequently used for corned beef. Its current price at King Soopers is $1.79 a pound.

You're going to love this recipe because it is so easy, and it makes one of the incredibly delicious gravies of our time. I mean that.

Chop and brown one-quarter pound of generic bacon (99 cents a pound) in your Dutch oven (heavy flameproof casserole). Remove bacon bits with a slotted spoon and keep for further use. Dredge 3-pound brisket in seasoned flour, shake on generous amount of paprika and brown that baby on both sides in the pot.

While the brisket is sizzling, peel and cut four carrots into 1-inch pieces. Cut up similar amount of celery into 1-inch pieces. Process three onions with steel blade, or chop onions as fine as possible.

Remove browned brisket from the pot and place on a plate. Toss the onions, carrots, celery and bacon bits back into the pot and stir and saute until onions become transparent. Return the brisket to the pot, placing it fat side up on top of the vegetables.

Mix one tablespoon of brown sugar in one pint of dark ale and pour over meat. Actually, that's about a bottle and a half. What do you do with the remaining ale? Throw it out. Whatever you do, don't drink it. Makes you gassy and tastes terrible.

Sprinkle a couple of pinches of dill seed on top of the brisket. Bring it to a simmer on top of the range. Cover and put pot in 300-degree oven for 2½ hours. You'll know it's done when it's fork-tender.

It's a good idea to turn the brisket every half-hour or so. You'll like that part because you liberate more beautiful aroma into the kitchen. This part will drive your family crazy, crazy, crazy.

When the brisket is tender, remove to a cutting board and cover with foil. Scoop out the carrots and celery with a slotted spoon. Strain the remaining liquid and thicken with Wondra flour for gravy. You will not need to add any seasoning at all. It will be perfect.

Thin-slice the brisket across the grain and arrange slices on a platter, surrounding them with carrots and celery. Drizzle a little gravy on top and serve with Kluski noodles.

Good snappin'.

January 18, 1983

Soup's on

ONIONS.

Have you noticed the string bags of small white onions in the supermarkets? They start turning up in early spring. Those little beauties are wonderful in *boeuf bourguignon.*

That's really a fancy term for what we used to call slumgullion. Actually, *boeuf bourguignon* is a French version of beef stew. There is a common misapprehension that all French food is too rich, too spicy, too expensive.

Not so with the recipe old Capt. Sunshine is going to lay on you today. I have been tinkering with this one for several years. I think I have it down so it is ready for you.

Readers of this column know that we leave *cuisine minceur* — that's French for low-cal — to others. There are some of us who believe that there are things in this world more important than hollow cheeks and a skinny rear end.

We'll need a couple of pounds of stew meat — chuck, or round, if you want to be fancy. Cube, trim off the fat and throw the whole works into a Dutch oven. Do not brown. Instead, toss the meat with one tablespoon of Kitchen Bouquet. Next, sprinkle with one-quarter cup of uncooked cream of rice cereal. Mix.

Isn't that slick? No grease. No flour.

You'll need one cup of thinly sliced celery. You can do this with your processor, or as has been pointed out here before, slicing by hand builds character and gives one a sense accomplishment. Add the celery and one minced clove of fresh garlic.

You now are ready for the spices. Use two teaspoons of salt and a generous pinch each of pepper, marjoram and thyme. For Pete's sake, don't forget the wine. That's where the *bourguignon* comes in. Use el cheapo red burgundy. You'll need 2½ cups. One cup for you to nip at, and the rest goes into the stew. *A votre sante.*

Peel four good-sized carrots. Either quarter them or cut them in 1-inch pieces. I like the pieces better. They'll be about the size of the meat cubes. Looks nicer. Add the carrots and mix lightly with the rest of the ingredients.

Cover and put in a pre-heated 325-degree oven. It will take about

2½ hours before it is ready. Figure on stirring with a wooden spoon about every 30 minutes. This will keep the ingredients from sticking and will flood your kitchen with a beautiful aroma.

You are not finished. After you put the pot in the oven, peel 12 of those little onions we talked about in the second paragraph. Next, thick-slice about a half-pound of fresh mushrooms. If the mushrooms are small, no need to slice. The onions and mushrooms are added for the last hour of cooking time.

You will know your *boeuf bourguignon* is ready when the vegetables are tender. Not too tender, mind you. As Lao-tse, the Chinese philosopher, once wrote of bean sprouts, "They should resist, but not too much." Come to think of it, that's true of many of life's pleasures.

This *boeuf bourguignon* should be served on noodles — big flat ones. It can be prepared a day in advance. Matter of fact, it sometimes tastes even better if you do. Just refrigerate and reheat. Needless to say, the leftovers are superb.

You may find you want to Americanize this French classic by eliminating the noodles and putting spuds in with the carrots, and maybe adding a pack of frozen peas the last half hour in the oven. That makes it more like slum.

I kind of like it the French way. You know, tossed green salad, fresh Brussels sprouts, more el cheapo wine, candlelight, maybe a little TV after dinner.

Ooh la-la!

March 10, 1981

Joy of meat loaf

NOUVELLE MEAT LOAF.

I have been looking into the new French cuisine, and it seems to me that what these fancy chefs have done is reinvent the half-cooked carrot. Hot cucumbers are also involved.

I guess that kind of thing is OK now and then, but this kid is still on the side of meat and potatoes. That is why I am going to lay on you an outstanding meat loaf recipe.

Meat loaf is a much maligned entree. People avoid it on restaurant menus because they are not sure what's in it. They suspect the worst about yesterday's leftovers. Wasn't it Erma Bombeck who defined a refrigerator as a place to keep leftovers until they are thrown away?

There are no leftovers in this meat loaf. *Au contraire,* it is made with fresh ingredients and is a fairly routine recipe, but with one exception. I wish I could claim credit for it, but I can't. My wife, Trish, made the discovery.

Now that there is a little chill in the evening air, and there are yellow leaves at the top of the cottonwoods, there is nothing nicer to come home to than meat loaf and oven-browned potatoes.

There are certain rewards to the actual making of meat loaf. I find it relaxing to squish the ingredients by hand. I suppose it is a form of regression, resembling in some ways the making of mud pies. Some kids sucked their thmbs I was more of a mud pie man. You can read into that any kind of psychological meaning you wish.

Get a great big mixing bowl. Begin with one egg and one cup of milk. In no particular order, add 1½ teaspoons of salt, one table-spoon of Worcestershire sauce and a teaspoon of A-1.

You'll need some garlic salt, sage, celery salt, pepper and dry mustard. Add about a quarter-teaspoon each. If you like a peppy meat loaf, drizzle in a teaspoon of Mexican *salsa.* Mix like crazy with an egg beater.

Add one chopped white onion. Do not use yellow onions; they are too stout. Combine with 1 pound of lean ground beef and one-half pound of ground pork. Fairly ordinary so far, huh?

Here's the big difference. Instead of using bread crumbs, tear up three medium slices of Jewish pumpernickel bread and mix with the rest of the ingredients.

Wow, does that ever make it special! The meat loaf has a robust, down-home flavor. The aroma when it is baking is even more enticing.

As I pointed out, it wasn't my idea. Trish was making meat loaf one night and found we were out of bread crumbs. We had nothing but the pumpernickel we keep around for hot corned beef and pastrami sandwiches. So, she improvised.

After you have completely mixed all the ingredients, place into ungreased loaf pan. Be sure to punch it down well to eliminate all air pockets.

Now you would just know to slather the top with a generous layer of chili sauce, wouldn't you? Ketchup is OK, but chili sauce is better. Sprinkle on some chopped parsley. Pop into a preheated 350-degree oven and bake two hours.

The loaf will shrink somewhat, making it easy to remove from the pan with a couple of spatulas. Let it sit a spell on a trencher cutting board before slicing. Gravy made from the drippings is mighty tasty with the spuds.

A good vegetable with this pumpernickel loaf is backyard green beans. They should be simmered with fatback or bacon until all the vitamins are cooked out. Serve with chopped raw onion on top.

Collard or turnip greens are also nice. Steam them with more fatback, chopped green onions and a little Tabasco. This gives the meat loaf a sort of soulful touch.

Voila!

September 6, 1981

9

YULE SPIEL: HOLIDAYS

POSSLQ possibilities

TWO BY TWO.

As Valentine's Day approaches, a couple of Los Angeles clergymen have come up with a plan that offers lovers the best of both worlds. It is a marriage ceremony that isn't a marriage ceremony.

The Rev. Robert D. Johnson and Rabbi Allen Malker announced at a news conference that they have devised a religious ceremony in which couples commit themselves to each other in the eyes of God, "but not in the eyes of the Internal Revenue Service," as Malker put it.

The plan was in response to tax laws that put a heavier burden on legally married couples who filed joint returns than on singles who live together.

"It is not a legal ceremony," as Johnson explained it, "but it is not an illegal ceremony." As one event seems to follow another, would it be possible for the woman to be pregnant and not be pregnant? The IRS will probably figure a way of getting the money anyhow. It always does.

The government, by the way, has it own term for those who live together without legal marriage. It is POSSLQ, an acronym for "persons of opposite sex sharing living quarters." It means roughly the same thing as what another arm of bureaucracy calls "spouse equivalent."

Some POSSLQs get together by chance. They meet in single bars, while jogging and in car pools. Others advertise in the classified sections of snooty literary magazines.

The typical pitch goes something like this. "Single man, 38, attractive, likes Chopin, weekends in the mountains, doesn't smoke, wants to meet cultured, well-groomed woman."

The reader conjures up an image of a guy wearing a tweed jacket with leather elbow patches. He has a Swedish ivy plant hanging in his apartment window. He listens to Chopin records on the hi-fi while authoring sensitive little verses.

The lady who reads the ad is indeed well-groomed. A touch of gray in her auburn hair, but she is lovely in a mature way. Probably is an assistant librarian at a small private college. Has mastered *nouvelle cuisine.*

We never really know if he gets in touch with her. Do they meet and share a quiet but blissful life? Do they stroll through the park in the evening? Does she stay on at the library? Do his poems get published?

Unfortunately, we never know. There's rarely any follow-up to classified ads. Those involved feel no responsibility toward those of us who read them for their literary and romantic values.

That's all right, though. We can end the stories any way we like. We can endow these lovely people with the good things of life. We can imagine them at concerts, plays, and we can visualize them alone by fire in the mountains they both love so much.

That's not the only kind of advertisement to be found in those magazines. There was one in recent issue of the New York Review of Books that may have been a bit short on dignity, but it did have a rare tone of honesty about it: "Nasty, dissatisfied, rapidly decaying WPF (white, Protestant, female), with arthritic knees. Seeks deaf-mute male with stamina. No poets."

She puts it right on the line. One thing about it, though, if some lonely soul does contact her, any surprises can't help but be good ones. Of course, there is the remote possibility that she is the librarian, and he is the guy with the leather elbow patches, and they are both lying.

We all know there can be too much honesty in relationships. What one partner doesn't know about the other's past isn't likely to hurt either of them. It all balances out.

His stamina will probably run out about the time her arthritic knees go.

February 12, 1981

Drummer boy

DECORATION DAY.

Will Fiedler, my great-grandpa, served as grand marshal of Decoration Day parades in Denver during the 1920s. That was before we started calling May 30th Memorial Day.

He had run away from home during the Civil War, joining the Union Army as a drummer boy. He was only 16. After the war, he came back to Iowa and married his childhood sweetheart.

I can remember watching those parades as long as I can remember anything. Grandpa always led the march with his drum and fife corps.

Mom and Pop would get me as close to the marchers along 16th Street as we could. If we were in the front, I could sit on the curb. Sometimes Pop would hold me on his shoulders.

There was always excitement before the parade began. We'd crane our necks to see Grandpa. We could usually hear the drums before we could see him. There were quite a lot of veterans of the Grand Army of the Republic then.

Grandpa and his drum were first. And then came the W.A. Fiedler Drum and Fife Corps. Most of the proud old gentlemen had white hair. Grandpa had a drooping mustache. They marched an easy, swinging cadence and all of them kept their shoulders square, their heads high.

I can still feel goose bumps at the memory of "Hell on the Wabash," "Wrecker's Daughter," "The Belle of the Mohawk Vale," "Sergeant O'Leary" and, of course, "Yankee Doodle."

The GAR vets wore white shirts, black ties and long blue coats with brass buttons. Gold laurel-leaf badges were on the center of their broad-brim hats. Some wore decorations and insignia from past GAR conventions.

They were followed by the blue and khaki-uniformed veterans of the Spanish-American War. Bringing up the rear were still-young World War I veterans in their olive drab uniforms with wrapped puttees.

When the parade was over, we'd go to the house he built on the North Side to eat Grandma's chicken and dumplings. He would let me look at his drum and wear his hat.

I don't recall that he ever said much about the war. Sometimes, though, he would sit back and sing "Tenting Tonight on the Old Campground." I tried to imagine what it must have been like for him as a boy at war. I could almost smell the smoke of those campfires. I wondered what he looked like when he was trying to drum courage into frightened men on a line of skirmishers.

After he and Grandma came to Denver from Fairfield, Iowa, after the war, Grandpa became what he called a "builder," constructing quite a few houses and churches, mostly near his home — the house in which I grew up.

He died in 1931 while taking a nap on the couch in the living room.

Grandma didn't say much after his death. She just sat near the window, waiting for him to step up on the porch.

Grandma died exactly a year later. The drummer boy and his sweetheart were together again.

The war was over.

May 30, 1982

We'd do it again

DEAR OLD DAD.

He may be neither dear nor old, but his existence is about to be recognized again. June 15 is Father's Day and there is little we can do to stop it.

It is an event to compel people to purchase gifts or suffer the consequence of guilt. The theory is that if you give Dad a new golf putter, you'll feel better about yourself.

It isn't that fatherhood is all that easy. As William Butler Yeats put it, "I have certainly known more men destroyed by the desire to have a wife and child and to keep them in comfort than I have seen destroyed by drink and harlots."

No question about that. It is to man's credit, however, that he gives the business of fatherhood his best shot. Failure to be a good father results more from ignorance than lack of effort.

I sometimes think that the children and the mother should get the gifts on Father's Day. It probably isn't true for everyone, but I have been more gratified in life by being a father than I have by doing anything else.

We have become so goal-oriented that we sometimes lose sight of the simple pleasure of just doing things. Gov. Richard Lamm put it rather well in his telegram to this year's graduates from the University of Colorado.

He said, "Reach for the stars. Grab one or two and enjoy the stretch." Something like that. Pleasure comes more from the doing than the getting.

In a materialistic world, so much emphasis is placed on acquisition. Happiness is a new car, a $200,000 house in the suburbs, a seat on the board of directors.

We sometimes look at our kids that way. We are so wrapped in trying to get them where we think they ought to go, that we don't take time to enjoy the growth.

It is sort of like hurrying through the park just to get to the other side without enjoying the grass, the trees and the birds. Lack of awareness.

The major problem of being a father is that you don't realize you are making mistakes until you have made them. I have always thought that it is too bad that you have to learn to be a father on someone as precious to you as your own child.

In the process of begetting, mistakes are passed from one generation to the next. Like father, like son. That's the human condition.

One of the commonest of human errors in the raising of children is the attempt to be popular with them. It begins early when the proud father bends over the crib and manages to coax a tiny smile.

It isn't much more of a step to the point where indulgence becomes a substitute for learning. Where is wisdom when we need it the most?

Some say the pain of being a parent outweighs the pleasure. I don't think so, although the two are often mixed and difficult to separate.

The conflicts are endless. Certainly not the least of these is genuinely wanting children to grow up and be on their own, but down deep inside not wanting them to leave.

The process of letting go can be so difficult. It is one of those things in life that is intellectually easy. It is quite another matter to manage it emotionally.

Maturity comes at long last to the father when he is able to take pleasure at the separation and to be gratified by it. Memory permits him to retain those tenderest of times when both parent and child were growing up together.

Some are better at this than others. And there is always the hope that each generation has learned something from the one before.

From my own point of view, being a father is its own reward. It is a priceless experience. I don't believe I am alone in feeling that way. Given the choice, most of us would probably do it all over again.

June 3, 1980

Visionary, indeed

GROVER CLEVELAND.

Let's hear it for our 22nd president! Forget that he broke the general railroad strike because it interfered with mail service. He said, "If it takes the entire Army and Navy of the United States to deliver a post card in Chicago, that card will be delivered." He is better remembered for Labor Day.

Cleveland signed into law a bill designating the first Monday in September Labor Day, thereby inventing the three-day weekend. That was in 1894.

There are 97 other holidays or observances on the calendar. That leaves 268 or 269 days a year to get things done, depending on whether or not it's leap year. By the time we subtract the 104 weekend days, we are left with 164 or 165 work days. Don't forget vacation time and accumulated sick leave.

The number of working days is shrinking all the time. Legislative bodies at all levels keep moving the holidays around to occur on Mondays, thereby extending the weekends.

If a holiday happens to fall on the weekend, we celebrate it the following Monday, adding yet another day away from work. A few years ago, Christmas fell on Sunday. We all took Monday off because, as everyone knows, it is not proper to celebrate a religious day on a religious day. Something like that.

Most holidays commemorate events or people of historical significance. Presidents' Day is a good example. We shut down the third Monday in February to give people an opportunity to stay home and contemplate the lives of George Washington and Abraham Lincoln.

Most American families do this by having little workshops on the lives of the Father of Our Country and the Great Emancipator.

Same thing with Columbus Day. This pops up on the second Monday in October. Columbus was not born on the second Monday in October, nor did he discover America on that date.

We know he was born in 1451 and died in 1506. We're not sure of the exact dates. Maybe the courthouse burned down. Similarly, we are not sure of the precise date he waded ashore in the New World.

Not having this information, we have arbitrarily decided to honor the plucky Italian navigator on October's second Monday. We have thereby lengthened the weekend, giving us more time to honor the discoverer of this continent.

There is just no way we could cram all that into a single holiday. This way, we can honor the Nina on Saturday, the Pinta on Sunday and the Santa Maria on Monday.

Good Lord, we've left out Queen Isabella! The bureaucracy will no doubt take note of this and declare the Friday before the second Monday in October a holiday.

That's one thing about America. We don't take our holidays lightly. No sitting around the house, drinking beer and watching TV. Not a bit of it.

We are on our knees the whole of the National Day of Prayer.

It's a good thing President Cleveland was enough of a visionary to put Labor Day on Monday. We need the extra time. You just can't do justice to Phillip Murray, John L. Lewis, Samuel Gompers, Herrick Roth, Walter Reuther, Jimmy Hoffa and Mary "Mother Jones" Harris in a single day.

Knowing how involved you must be with activities related to sweat and toil, I am grateful for the small amount of time you are giving to this column. Were it not for all the pageantry and celebration, there would be little to do but pack the family in the car and head for the mountains. Or perhaps sit around the house, drink beer and watch TV.

As for me, I also take holidays seriously, particularly Labor Day. Tomorrow I am going to celebrate it in a very appropriate way.

I am going to work.

August 31, 1980

Ode to joy

MY DAY.

Thanksgiving is mine. My interest in it is not proprietary, however. There's enough for all of us. I consider it mine in much the same way I own those pretty November sunrises.

Christmas has become a gimme-gimme holiday. People go into hock in a pitiful attempt to buy each other's affections. The annual squabble is under way over whether we ought to have a plastic Jesus in front of City Hall.

Thanksgiving is different. It may be one of the last of the simple pleasures. No demands. No confrontations. No conflicts. Unless I haven't been told, Madalyn Murray O'Hair hasn't gone to court over Thanksgiving.

It helps that people have a nice attitude about the day. There's no reason to feel guilty, envious or hostile. About the only anxiety is whether the turkey is done.

It is pleasant to have the family together. No pressure. People can just enjoy each other. It's OK to lie on the floor after dinner and doze during the football game.

There are benefits to the ritual preparation of the food. It is good for the spirit to chop celery, onions and walnuts for the sausage and sage dressing. There is magic in the aroma of giblets simmering with a bouquet of spices.

Children seem to behave better on Thanksgiving. Maybe it has something to do with an unconscious respect they have for tradition and structure in their lives.

Gratitude is such a nice quality to perceive in others. It isn't groveling, but more of a dignified awareness of how fortunate we are to be alive.

In reports on recent space explorations, I have noted how some writers reflect on the awesomeness of it all and how insignificant we are in the emptiness of the universe. I don't see it that way. It is the other way around.

As technology extends our touch into space, it becomes more evident to me how really special our lives are. We have been dazzled by Voyager 1's stunning pictures of Saturn and its rings. Our next space probe will explore Uranus and Neptune.

In all we have learned about Saturn, Mars and Jupiter, we have not detected any life as we know it. The vastness of it all doesn't prove us insignificant. It should assure us of our uniqueness. Because we are unique, we most certainly are significant. That is why I suggest we ought to be thankful to be here.

Just being is not enough, though. To only exist is a terrible waste of the senses. There is so much more to living than just eating, sleeping and breathing.

I think it is also wrong to squander the senses in pursuit of every physical pleasure. One risks being so desensitized by experience that no pleasure is left in anything.

Ever had someone ask what your goals are? I have difficulty in dealing with that kind of question. I suppose it is because I think I am expected to come up with some kind of blueprint for success in my work. I don't have any goals of that kind.

My goal, if you can call it that, is to fully experience each day, one day at a time. I started to feel this way about 10 years ago. It was when I began to slow down to watch the flowers grow. I realized how much I had been missing in trying to get where I thought I wanted to be.

That's the real reason I enjoy Thanksgiving so much. It is a celebration of all the little things in life I have discovered.

You can't put a price tag on any of them. What does it cost for a trusting kitten to crawl into your lap and go to sleep? What is the charge to have a child's small hand tighten around your fingers as you walk through the park?

So I am only a speck in the universe, but look at the miracles I have touched and seen!

I am very grateful.

November 27, 1980

McVittie knew what Thanksgiving really means

THANKSGIVING 1931.

The day never managed to warm. The clouds were low over the city. There was hardly enough sun to make a shadow. It was as though we were in mourning.

The Great Depression was just two years old. We knew it had come to Denver when the railroad yards began to fill with the young men who had old faces. Some of them had hopped a freight out of Nebraska where they had worked as gandy dancers. Others were following rumors of work.

Riding the rods under the rail cars was tricky. The idea was to roll free before the big steam locomotives clanked to a stop. Some of the railroad detectives weren't a bad lot. They'd look away until a half-frozen hobo could scramble between the warehouses.

If the army of the unemployed had a uniform, it was usually a tattered World War I army overcoat. The buttons were gone and a rope around the waist closed it against the November cold.

During the summer months, these hungry wanderers would fan out across the city. They'd look for odd jobs along residential alleys.

Sometimes, they'd find something they could eat from a covered garbage can.

But as the days grew shorter and colder, they would stay closer to the downtown area. The word was out that you could get a bowl of soup at Bishop Frank Rice's Liberal Church on Larimer Street. The men liked his mission. Rice would feed them first and preach to them later. At most of the missions, the hymns and sermons came before the food.

Some of the drifters would shamble up 17th Street where the panhandling was supposed to be better. Little clusters of them would wait outside the Brown Palace and try to get handouts from the Capitol Hill swells who were going inside.

Albert A. McVittie knew what that was like. He had come to Denver in 1907 with only one dime in his pocket. McVittie spent the money on a cup of coffee and a doughnut.

It was the kind of dark moment a man vows never to be hungry, cold or frightened again. So it was with Mack McVittie. He parlayed odd restaurant jobs, ambition and a touch of hokum into Denver's largest chain of restaurants.

McVittie was able to ride out the Depression. He never could get used to seeing down-and-outers in front of his restaurant at 17th Street and Glenarm Place. They'd look through the windows and watch McVittie customers eating pork tenderloin sandwiches and oyster stew. Hard times.

Almost on impulse, Mack decided he was going to do something about those empty faces at the windows. A tradition was born. Anyone who was hungry on Thanksgiving Day would be served a complete turkey dinner absolutely free. No questions. No sermons. No strings. No charge.

One of the biggest of these free holiday dinners was Thursday morning, Nov. 26, 1931. McVittie was going to open his doors at 11 a.m. But by 10 a.m., more than 1,500 men, women and children were waiting in line. Before the day was over, McVittie's downtown restaurant had served more than 3,000 turkey dinners.

It was a monumental task. McVittie employees served 555 turkeys, 2,500 pints of oyster soup, 1,200 pounds of dressing, five kettles of turkey gravy, 400 pounds of cranberry sauce, 53 gallons of olives, 40 bushels of potatoes, 5,000 pieces of pie and 2,500 pints of coffee.

McVittie paid for the whole thing. There was no fund drive or donations sought. As Mayor George Begole would say, "Mack was Denver's biggest man yesterday."

The blocklong lines were still there at 9 p.m. It was really cold then. McVittie and his wife, Bonnie, were outside. They were pouring hot coffee to keep people warm and to assure them that there'd be enough for everyone. Their 11-year-old daughter, June, was just inside the door to shake hands and to smile at everyone who came in.

Finally, it was all over. McVittie was exhausted. The windows of his restaurant were covered with steam. There was the smell of coffee, sweat and cinders in the dining room. Mountains of dirty dishes in the kitchen.

McVittie kept his free dinner holiday tradition until the Depression was over. He sold his restaurants, had a fling at politics and went into real estate. He died in 1948.

Thanksgiving meant something to A.A. McVittie.

November 23, 1978

Assembly lines

AT EASE!

I am Sgt. William Malloy, your CEMTAP instructor for the next three weeks of intensive training. As you all know, CEMTAP is an acronym for Christmas Eve Midnight Toy Assembly Program.

You are all volunteers and have passed the rigid physical requirements. Great demands will be made on you and your time.

As our recruiting posters say, we don't promise you a rose garden, but we do promise that by Christmas Eve, every one of you will be able to assemble a three-story Barbie's Dream House.

I know that sounds impossible, but we are going to do it. The little plastic elevator will slide up and down and the doors will open and close.

As I look out at you, I see some familiar faces. Our people like to come back every year or so for refresher training.

I see Bob Carmody out there. Stand up, Carmody. Ladies and gentlemen, you would all do well to stick close to this man during the tough training ahead. He is one of the veterans. Clever. Resourceful. Knows all the tricks.

Hard as it is to believe, when this same Bob Carmody first came to us, he couldn't so much as open the battery compartment on a toy police car. Now, he holds the record in 10-speed bicycle assembly. A real giant here at CEMTAP.

As you all know, parents are the unpaid employees of the toy manufacturers. You all know what it is like to have to try to put together toys late Christmas Eve.

It's rough out there when the holes don't match on the Tiny Toy Cradle and you have misplaced your Phillips screwdriver. The untrained parents will sometimes shout profanities and will hurl Christmas tree ornaments at the fireplace.

That's not what Christmas is all about! Your training here will help you through these frustrations and will make it possible for you to get to bed a couple of hours before your children awaken.

Sure it's tough. But by the time you complete your CEMTAP training, your attitude will be changed. You will see adversity as an opportunity for personal growth. Anybody who can assemble a Big Indy Slot Car track can handle just about any of life's problems.

This year, CEMTAP is offering a special section on boxes. I would advise all of you to take it because of manufacturers' warranties.

You will note in the instruction manual that the customer is advised to retain the packing carton. If the toy is defective, the customer is told to repack it in the original container and return it to the manufacturer in Kobe, Japan.

You and I know that this is not possible. There is absolutely no way that toy will fit back into the carton. It just won't go in.

I don't want to get into the technicalities at this time, but the best advice we can give you now is to immediately discard the toy and retain the box. Small children enjoy playing in boxes.

Now, before we break for callisthenics, I want you all to carefully check the CEMTAP kit that was issued to you. Never be without it. It is more than equipment. It is a parent's best friend.

Hold up each item as I call it off. Quarter-inch drill. Pliers. Regular and Phillips screwdrivers. Scissors. Duct tape. Contact cement. First aid kit.

And a bottle of Gilbey's gin.

December 6, 1979

Just a card, please

CHRISTMAS CARD.

Just send one with a star on it. Maybe a little wise man. Or a snowflake. Anything. But whatever you do, don't send what we have come to know as The Christmas Newsletter.

There are several types of these. There is the kind sent out by the childless couple. Two single-spaced typewritten pages of the cute things their poodle has done over the year. They usually include a Kodacolor snapshot of Pierre. He is wearing a little Santa Claus cap.

And then there is the one from the family preoccupied with sickness. These people really enjoy their poor health and want to share it with you.

Their newsletter is a richly detailed, month-by-month account of their hysterectomies, heart murmurs, psoriasis and problems associated with shortness of breath. This family doesn't want to send greetings. It wants your pity.

The worst of the lot comes from that terribly bright, terribly attractive, terribly busy family. These people are really terrible. It is their mistaken belief that you are just dying to know about how well they are doing.

"Is it December already? Where does the time go? Please excuse this printed newsletter. It is the best way we have found to reach out and touch all of our dear friends.

"Midge is just home from Vassar. She'll be with us through Christmas. And then dear Midge will spend the rest of the holidays at Hyannis Port. She is doing so well at school. Straight A's. She can't decide whether to go into modeling or accept a scholarship for graduate work at Cal Tech.

"She'll have to go some to get ahead of her little brother, David. He's 18 now. We were all proud as punch last August when Reader's Digest published his first article.

"Don't know where he gets the time. Seems like he's down in the basement most of the time. He just loves to fool around with the dumb old computer he designed and built. The man from IBM who came out to see it was very impressed.

"Fred has been promoted to senior vice president! We sort of expected it since he is the only account executive in the history of the company to sell 400 percent of his quota in a single year.

"He's such a doll. He still loves to work in the yard and putter around with his collection of old harpsichords. Not a gray hair on his head.

"As for me, things are just as hectic as ever. I got a little behind in my volunteer work because of those three weeks I spent in a Biafra rescue mission.

"I really learned a great deal and found it so rewarding working with the orphans. But as I always say, 'Charity begins at home.' (ha-ha-ha) I got back just in time to bake my usual 14 kinds of Christmas cookies with enough time left over to make new draperies for the family room."

Those aren't real people. If they are real, they are not telling the truth. What has happened to honesty? In the words of Howard Cosell, "Tell it like it is."

"Midge is back from school. She brought her roommate home for Christmas. His name is Stan. Actually, neither one of them is in school anymore. She flunked out and he lost his job at the carwash.

"It's beginning to look more and more like they'll be moving in. They'll have to go downstairs with David. Let me tell you something, I wouldn't go down there.

"All David does is play rock music on that stereo and smoke those funny cigarettes of his. About the only time we see him is when he brings up his dirty sweat socks.

"Fred was fired last June. Everybody said it would happen. He finally rose to his level of incompetence. Instead of just pushing him to the side, that big-hearted corporation put the rollers under him.

"He doesn't work at all anymore. When people ask him what he does, he just tell them he's in public relations. Absolutely bald.

"I haven't been doing much. I sit around mostly and watch the soap operas. That's about the only excitement in my life. It's either that or go to PTSA meetings. You know what a drag that can be."

Just send a card.

December 7, 1978

Downing 'horse overs' won't bring you cheer

LIMP CELERY.

Is that a light at the end of the tunnel? Is this really the last day of the cocktail party season? It better be. The spirit may still be willing, but the stomach is gone. All gone.

"Cheers!" the invitation says. "Come join us for holiday nog 'n' munchies. 5 p.m. to ???? See map for directions."

The Xeroxed map has instructions to "turn right at the old Pennzoil sign" and "We're the third house in the second cul-de-sac after you pass Armitage Circle. Do not turn on Armitage Way or Armitage Place. Armitage Circle is across the road from where the old firehouse used to be."

The lucky ones get lost and never have to face the hors d'oeuvres, or "horse overs," as my father used to call them. Whatever you call them, they are no substitute for real food.

That's one of the problems with cocktail parties. They come at dinnertime when people are hungry. Since drinking on an empty stomach has a snockering effect, you have no choice but to eat the hors d'oeuvres.

Eating hors d'oeuvres because you are hungry is as self-destructive as drinking martinis because you are thirsty. What seems to make you feel better at the time can only make you feel worse later.

There is nothing more cruel for a wife to whisper to a husband at a cocktail party than: "Better pig out, guy. This is it. I'm not cooking the big meal tonight."

That's when you have to take one of those little paper plates and stack it with crab puffs, Vienna sausages, water chestnuts wrapped with bacon, little meatballs in gravy, chicken drumettes and limp celery.

The celery is always limp. The radishes are always dry. The ripe olives are always mushy. The shrimp is always gone.

You are expected to eat all that with a toothpick that has a little cellophane ruffle at one end. No forks. If you can manage hors d'oeuvres with a toothpick, you'll be a whiz at eating rice with one chopstick.

The table is beautiful when the party begins. But 20 minutes later, juice from the pickled beets somehow finds its way into the cottage cheese. The guacamole separates, leaving little puddles of cloudy vinegar. Potato chips break off in the clam dip. The deviled eggs turn green.

Don't drink the eggnog! Never, never, never! Eggnog is particularly devastating when consumed with Texas fruit cake, cashew nuts, date balls and those flat little yellow, green and pink mints. Believe it — all that is much worse coming up than it is going down.

You will know it is time to leave when your ears begin to ring and your deodorant breaks down. Lurch out of the house and fall into a snow drift. Remain there until consciousness returns.

Go home. Remove from your coat pocket those toothpicks with the cellophane ruffles, tiny wadded cocktail napkins, chicken drumette bones and the Xeroxed map to Armitage Circle. Take a big swig of Pepto-Bismol and go straight to bed.

You may live.

January 2, 1983

The office party

DEVILED EGGS.

They always turn green at the annual office party. The avocado dip changes to a slate gray and the cherry peppers shrivel.

Not only that, the annual company party is right up there with Monday Night Football as one of the nation's greatest dangers to the domestic tranquillity.

It starts innocently enough. Everybody gets a little Xeroxed note that says, "The office will close at 3 p.m., Friday, Dec. 21, so our employees can share in some holiday cheer! Let Marge know if you can't come."

Marge is the one who also arranges for the hors d'oeuvre trays, the plastic glasses and the paper napkins with the Santa face in the corner.

It usually is the sales manager who gets the booze. This is his job every year because of his contacts. The morning of the party, sure enough, he unloads a case of Old Overcoat blended bourbon and a half dozen bottles of 100 proof Moussorgsky vodka.

The sales manager assures everyone that the Old Overcoat is really a good whiskey. Every drop of it, he says, is at least two weeks old.

When someone says that he is not familiar with Moussorgsky vodka, the sales manager says, "Don't worry. If we can't drink it, we'll use it as lighter fluid." This is his annual joke.

Marge mixes some of the vodka into a punch she has made with sparkling water, Hawaiian Punch concentrate and slices of oranges and limes. When she isn't looking, the sales manager adds two more quarts of the Moussorgsky.

There are the usual pleasantries at 3 o'clock. Some of the women in the office have had their hair fixed and are wearing little holiday corsages.

The noise level begins to rise by 3:30 as the effect of Marge's holiday punch is felt. Some of the younger people take note of a peculiar numbness around the mouth.

Phyllis, who has been in accounting for 18 years, entertains a faint hope that someone will take her home after the party. She notes, however, that almost all of the males are crowded around Marvene, the cute new receptionist.

Marge's punch affects each person differently. It makes some amorous. Others laugh uproariously. On Walter, it works like a truth serum.

His voice frequently is heard above the din, and he makes some rather pointed observations about the management of the company and its wage and retirement policies. He uses the word "chicken" frequently and in various contexts.

The boss is a nervous man in his 60s. He gamely pretends not to hear the increasingly strident Walter. Finally, he slips out the side door and goes home to an angry wife and cold tuna casserole.

As the party begins to wind down, the younger people start talking of going somewhere else. Phyllis hopes they will ask her to come with them.

When they don't, she takes a final swig of Marge's punch, picks up her purse and walks unsteadily to the door. Phyllis has a splitting headache and she vows never again to permit her expectations to be elevated.

While Phyllis goes home alone, Marvene does not. She artfully manages to avoid the sales manager and her other pursuers. Marvene is last seen with that tall muscular lad who works in the stock room.

He has an abundance of black hair and wears tight jeans.

Finally, it is over. Somebody puts the sales manager into a cab. Marge takes home the floral centerpiece and her punch bowl.

Ho! Ho! Ho!

November 27, 1979

Yule spiel

Oh, tannenbaum.

The fun has gone out of the Christmas tree game. It has become too organized, too consumer-oriented. And then there is the business of letting people cut down their own trees. Wrong.

The thing I like the least about buying Christmas trees now is charging the customer so much a foot. It's almost as though there were some kind of federal regulatory agency in charge.

Walk into a Christmas tree lot and it is like doing business in a department store. Wander around and pick out a tree, take it to the man and pay him the tag price. No salesmanship. No haggling. Wham, bam, thank you, ma'am.

That's not the way it was when I used to peddle trees at East Colfax and Downing. I was a high school kid at the time, and I really believe I learned more about economic survival then than at any other time of my life.

I wish I could remember the name of the man I worked for. There was a nice spirit of adventure about him. He had a regular job. The Christmas tree lot was for extra holiday money.

There were no prices on our trees. Old John and I ran the lot. He was a drifter who slept in the tiny trailer we used as an office. Our instructions were simple: "Get as much money as you can, but never let a customer get away."

The owner had a streak of gambler in him. He told us if we got hung up on price, it was all right to flip a coin and "go double the price, or nothing."

I liked that. But the part I really enjoyed was the selling of the tree itself. It didn't matter how cold it was, I'd stand out there for as long as it took to make a deal.

Old John thought I was crazy. He'd stay in the trailer, sip a strange mixture of coffee, milk, sugar and whiskey, and let me do the huckstering. Sometimes he'd come out, blow a little warmth into his hands and maybe hammer a few wooden stands on some trees. That's about all.

After I'd get rid of a scrawny little tree for a good price, Old John would cackle, "Kid, I hope Jesus wasn't lookin' down at you when you took that lady's money."

I didn't gouge everyone. I tried to approach my work with a sense of justice. I fancied myself something of a Robin Hood. It was sort of like taking from the rich and giving to the poor. If I overcharged a fat cat I made up for it by selling a good tree to a mouse for less money.

I really enjoyed the stubborn customer. I'd say to him: "Sir, I'm not sure I want you to have this tree. I don't know that you would decorate it properly."

"What?" he would shout.

"Close your eyes, sir. I want you to see this lovely tree as it ought to appear in your home. How the red and green ornaments shimmer in the lights! There are candy canes, tiny Santa faces, miniature toy soldiers, every icicle carefully hung. And sir, look at the radiant angel at the top!"

"I'll take it," he'd say as he peeled bills from his wallet.

If a customer complained that the tree was flat on one side, I'd beam: "We special order them that way, ma'am. Put the flat side against the wall. Makes more room. Needs fewer ornaments. Let me tie it on top of your car."

If I really liked the customer, I'd sometimes deliver the tree with my old '33 Chevy. And, of course, there was the additional incentive of a possible tip. "A merry yuletide to you, sir. Your generosity will not be forgotten."

I'm sure Old John is gone now. He's probably up there with Jesus. I suspect the two of them are looking down to see what I'm up to at this time of year. If so, I would say to them: "Not to worry. I no longer sell Christmas trees. I am, however, in a similar line of work.

"I write a newspaper column."

December 20, 1981

A GI's Christmas gift

THE CHILD.

It was warm that week before Christmas in 1944. The American soldiers had just occupied Tentelingen, a small farming town in the Saar. The front was quiet, and the GIs were maintaining only light contact patrols with the enemy.

It was good to wake up in the morning and not hear the mortars. The soldiers began to settle in, knowing the offensive could resume at any time, and they would have to load their gear back on the tanks and half-tracks and move out.

It was Sidlo who had the idea of the Christmas tree. There was some argument that the outfit wouldn't be there for Christmas, that planning something like that was bad luck.

There weren't many civilians remaining in town. The men were gone. Just some women and few children. They were frightened of the Americans. There wasn't much food, and from their standpoint, practically no hope.

Sidlo ended the argument by slipping out to the edge of town with an ax from his jeep. He came back a few minutes later with a small, perfectly proportioned spruce.

The others began to come up with ideas of how it could be decorated. There wasn't much to work with. Somebody suggested cutting a star from an empty C-ration can. The men began to scrounge for tin foil, empty brass casings from rifle shells, bits and pieces of anything that glittered.

At first, no one was really sure what they would do with the tree. One of the soldiers — it was probably Sidlo — said the tree could be put out where the children could see it. And then the others began to chip in packets of gum and Life Savers from their PX rations.

Even though the men weren't supposed to talk to German civilians, they thought it would be nice if maybe the children could take the little presents from the tree on Christmas.

Nothing was said to the children, but they seemed to know almost immediately. They watched from a distance as the soldiers decorated the tree. One child, a blonde girl of about 6, was always there. She was very pale and drawn. No one ever saw her smile. There was something wistful about her eyes.

As Christmas drew closer, the men began to sing what they could remember of Christmas carols. There was talk of forming some kind of choir and getting the chaplain to say Mass.

The men, who by now were beginning to shave and try to wash their uniforms, put out of their minds that it could all end at any time. It wasn't a good idea to settle in too much. They should have remembered that.

It must have been two days before Christmas when the word came down. It was just before dawn. "March order!" the first sergeant barked. "We're heading north. The Germans have attacked some place called Bastogne."

The men rolled up their blankets, and softly cursing the darkness, began to buckle on their belts and drape ammunition bandoliers around their necks. The engines whined to a shriek as they were cranked, and there was blue flame splatting from the fish-tail exhausts of the big tanks. The ground shuddered under all the power.

Sidlo ran back into the barn where he had been sleeping. He was carrying the tree when he came out. He seemed confused about what he should do with it. There would be no Christmas morning for the men at Tentelingen. No Christmas carols. Sidlo knew he couldn't take the tree. He stood there for a moment, and then he carefully placed it in the street.

As the armored column churned out of the town to the bitter cold and snow of the north, the men looked back. In the dim, half-light of morning, they could see the face of the little girl. She looked at the tree. Then at the men.

She was crying.

December 24, 1981

About the author

Gene Amole has been a columnist for the Rocky Mountain News since 1977. He has spent most of his life in Denver, where he was born May 24, 1923. He was educated in the public schools and has been active in commercial broadcasting since 1942.

Amole's radio career began with KMYR. Following World War II service in Gen. George Patton's Third Army, and a couple of stints as a foreign correspondent, he and his partner, Ed Koepke, founded radio station KDEN in 1956. Their FM station, KVOD, was licensed to broadcast a year later.

His career in television began in 1952. Amole was involved in TV production from the first week Denver had regular programming. He has since written and produced programs for Channels, 2, 4, 6, 7 and 9. "Panorama," one of the programs he wrote and narrated, won the prestigious George Foster Peabody Award. He pioneered news broadcasting on TV and did one of the industry's first talk programs.

In 1983, Amole was named Journalist of the Year by the Colorado Chapter of the Society of Professional Journalists, Sigma Delta Chi, and Columnist of the Year by the Associated Press in Colorado. His other honors include the Tajiri Award for his contributions to radio and television, and being named Man of the Year by the Colorado Speech Association and Educator of the Year by the Colorado Medical Society.

Amole was one of the founders of Denver Magazine and was part owner of KTUX at Pueblo. He was also a partner in Electronic Music Inc., a company supplying background music for business and industry.

He and his wife, Patricia, have lived in the same southwest Denver home for 18 years. Of the four Amole children, Susan, 15, still lives at home.